French VEGETABLE COOKERY

French VEGETABLE COOKERY

Traditional and regional recipes

Patricia Bourne

Macdonald

For Tony

A **Macdonald** BOOK

© Patricia Bourne 1985

First published in Great Britain in 1985
by Macdonald & Co (Publishers) Ltd
London & Sydney

A member of BPCC plc

British Library Cataloguing in Publication Data

Bourne, Patricia, 1927–
French vegetable cookery.
1. Cookery, French   2. Cookery (Vegetables)
1. Title
641.6'5'0944   TX719

ISBN 0-356-10486-9

Filmset by Flair plan photo-typesetting Ltd.
Printed and bound in Great Britain by
Hazell Watson & Viney Ltd, Aylesbury, Bucks.
A member of BPCC plc.

Editor: Victoria Funk
Designer: Sarah Jackson
Photographer: Paul Webster
Stylist: Dawn Lane
Home economists: Jane Suthering
Val Barrett

Macdonald & Co (Publishers) Ltd
Maxwell House
74 Worship Street
London EC2A 2EN

Special thanks to: David Mellor, Mapin & Webb,
Harrods, Boots, Reject China Shops and Elizabeth
David for the use of cookware, cutlery,
crockery and glass.

CONTENTS

ACKNOWLEDGMENTS

Writing a book seems a lonely business at times but without the aid of other people it would not be possible.

To all my friends who enjoy holidaying in France and to all my chef friends, I must say thank you. They have all endured a barrage of questions and with great patience have given me so much information and confirmed so many details for me.

Suppliers of ingredients are important and I must make special mention of Mr Paul Cockerton of Hyams and Cockerton, Nine Elms, London for his help in obtaining vegetables and for all the information he has given me.

To my family and friends who have tasted so much of the food I have tested, I also say a special thank you. Their comments and discussion have been invaluable and, thankfully, always polite, and have enlivened my dinner parties for months past.

In the midst of writing this book we sold our house and, due to unforeseen circumstances, found ourselves homeless. My good friend Alma Wylie not only gave us a home for a few weeks but let me appropriate her kitchen and her study so that I could cook and type without worry or interruption. Without her help, this book would never have reached the publishers in time and her kindness will never be forgotten.

But my greatest thanks must be for my husband, not only for his constant support and valuable criticism but for all the help he has given me. He has willingly, I hope, tasted everything I have tested, and when he offered his assistance in assembling the manuscript, he little knew how time-consuming it would be. He has spent hours reading recipes and, although no cook, making certain he could understand them. He has filled in accents, corrected typing errors and even stuck thousands of reinforcing rings on the hundreds of sheets of typed paper. These were truly labours of love and only he can know how much I appreciate his help and interest.

Without all this help I would have been unable to enjoy writing this book so much. To everyone who has aided me in any way, I am indeed very grateful.

INTRODUCTION

'French markets are full of beautiful vegetables,' a friend of mine remarked at dinner a few nights ago, 'but what on earth do they do with them? Whenever I go there, all I seem to get is a salad and French fried potatoes.'

I seem to have been more fortunate than my friend but, although I can sympathize with him to a certain extent, as in some hotels *pommes frites* and *salade* are served with unfailing regularity, it is important to realize that the French approach to vegetables is different to many others.

For most people, vegetables are an accompaniment to a dish of meat, fowl or fish, but to the French they are considered worthy of their own place in the menu. They are usually served separately or towards the end of the main course so their full flavour and texture can be appreciated. Potatoes are not always served because bread is eaten instead, and often a single vegetable dish or a salad is all that is necessary to provide the right contrast and balance in the meal.

Because of its size and history, France has always been a strongly regional country, the inhabitants holding fast to local customs and traditions. Soil and climate vary tremendously, enabling a wide range of produce to be grown. The French housewife's ingenuity in making the best of locally grown ingredients is the origin of many of the regional dishes we know today: dishes from the Savoy and Dauphine using ingredients available in the depth of winter; Provence reflecting the heat of the sun in its recipes for aubergines (eggplants), peppers and tomatoes, and Burgundy using its wonderful wine in much of its cooking. Chestnuts from Limousin, asparagus from the Loire and truffles from Perigord have all influenced a wealth of dishes. Villages and districts have created their own variations, each believing their own to be the best. Until comparatively recently, many of them were only known and eaten locally, but they are now to be found all over France. A look on the shelves in any French bookshop confirms the upsurge of interest in regional cookery.

With her great forests France has always had a good supply of fuel and this also has affected the cooking of the country. Long, slow cooking over open fires or in the heat of wood-fired ovens was possible and is reflected in many dishes. *Sou-Fassam*, from the south of France, is a good example of this, or more simply braised vegetables, such as lettuce or celery. The well known *Pommes de Terre Boulangère* was cooked in a baker's oven when bread-baking was finished. In Normandy the local variation is made with leeks.

I have tried to include as many regional and traditional recipes as possible. It may seem at first glance that many names are repeated: *à la crème* is one and *à la Provençale* another, but if you read further you will find there are several methods of producing dishes of the same name.

A few modern ideas for cooking vegetables have been included, however, I have noticed that while an increasing number of hotels serve many dishes strongly influenced by such chefs as Paul Bocuse, Michel Guerard, the Troisgros Brothers and other advocates of *nouvelle cuisine*, most vegetables are still cooked the traditional way.

I have also included a few very old recipes from the earliest French cookery books — it is interesting to see how little recipes have changed.

Never let it be thought that vegetables are only served in France if they are cooked in an elaborate way. Many recipes are very simple. One method I have not included, as it is so generally applicable, is *à l'Anglaise*, which is plain, boiled vegetables, sometimes tossed in butter. Most vegetables, with the exception of aubergines, peppers, tomatoes and a very few others, are frequently cooked in this way.

While I was collecting material for this book, I was interested in the number of sweet dishes using vegetables I discovered. Because this book is about the way the French cook vegetables, I have included some. My guests were always pleasantly surprised, and I hope you enjoy them as well.

For the past few months all my dinner parties have included some of the recipes I have been testing. I have broken the rules for serving vegetables the French way and have served several at one meal, mainly because there were so many to test. The main thing that struck us all is that so many dishes need to be tasted individually to get the best flavour. Served with meat in a sauce and with other vegetables, they lost their character, but eaten alone their full savour was enjoyed. The French, as always when it comes to food, have the right attitude towards serving and eating vegetables. Perhaps you will try them in the same way and make them a feature of your dinner parties. I hope you will gain new ideas and much enjoyment from the following recipes.

WEIGHTS, MEASURES AND GENERAL INFORMATION

Metric, Imperial and American measures are all given in this book. They are not always interchangeable, so use whichever you prefer but take care not to use both in the same recipe. American cup measures are given for all the ingredients you are likely to have in your cupboard and for liquids.

I have tried to apply common sense to the quantities so, for example, 1 kilo is given as the equivalent of 2 pounds, 500 grams equal 1 pound and sometimes 250 grams equal 8 oz. I must admit that when I am on the Continent I never buy 175 grams — I use 200 grams. So if you prefer to do this, please do. None of the vegetable recipes will suffer but you must be more accurate when you are making pastries. In some of the pastry recipes 90 grams is given for 3 ounces instead of 75 grams, as is used elsewhere in the book. This is necessary to ensure the correct proportions of the ingredients.

In the recipes for soups, I have given 2 Imperial pints and 1 American quart for 1 litre. A little more or less liquid rarely makes much difference; you can always adjust the consistency of the soup before you serve it.

All teaspoon and tablespoon measures are level spoonfuls and refer to 5-ml and 15-ml measuring spoons, respectively. Standard spoon sizes have been used for American measures.

All eggs used in this book are size 3 (medium).

All recipes serve 4–6 people unless otherwise noted.

As far as possible, cooking terms have been explained in the recipes. One term that is used constantly and requires explanation is 'refresh'. To refresh vegetables means to pour cold water over them (under the tap, or faucet, is best) until they are completely chilled. This preserves their colour and flavour.

Oven Temperatures

The temperatures of individual ovens may vary slightly and because of this there may be small variations in the cooking times given in the recipes. Dishes should always be placed in the centre of conventional gas and electric ovens. In fan-assisted ovens this is not important. Cooking times are for preheated ovens and grills.

°C	°F	Gas Mark
110	225	$\frac{1}{4}$
120	250	$\frac{1}{2}$
140	275	1
150	300	2
160	325	3
180	350	4
190	375	5
200	400	6
220	425	7
230	450	8

1 VEGETABLES GALORE

LES ARTICHAUTS
Artichokes

Artichokes are widely grown throughout France, and Brittany in particular is famous for the large, plump, round ones grown there. Those from the south are often longer and more oval. Also from the south, particularly Provence, come *poivrades* — artichokes picked when little more than buds while the cluster of hairs in the centre, called the 'choke', are barely formed and still tender. *Poivrades* are often eaten raw.

Look for artichokes with fresh, tight heads. The leaves should be greyish-green with a bloom and the points should be fleshy. Avoid any heads with brown-tipped or dry-looking leaves.

To prepare whole artichokes, make a small cut in the stalk as close to the head as possible and then twist the stalk until it comes away from the head (it may be helpful to hold the stalk in a cloth). By removing the stalk in this way the long fibres in the base of the artichoke are also removed. Next, with a sharp knife cut off the top third of the artichoke and then cut off the tip of each leaf with a pair of scissors. To keep them a good colour, brush the cut surfaces with lemon juice or keep them in a bowl of acidulated water (a bowl of water to which 1–2 tablespoons of lemon juice or vinegar has been added). Cook them in acidulated water or a *blanc*. To make a *blanc* blend 1–2 tablespoons of flour with a little water and add to a pan of acidulated, salted water. Bring to the boil and place the artichokes in the pan. Whole artichokes will take about 20–40 minutes to cook, depending on size and quality.

To test if whole artichokes are cooked, pull off a leaf from the base and taste to see if the fleshy end is tender. Drain the artichokes well. If they are to be served cold, place them under cold running water until they are completely chilled. If they are to be served hot, just run them under cold water until they are cool enough to handle.

Pull out the centre leaves — these usually come out in one piece and can be kept for garnishing. Pull out any other small leaves until you uncover the feathery 'choke' in the centre and carefully scrape these out with a teaspoon. Take great care doing this because the hairs are most unpleasant if eaten. Rinse the artichokes well to remove any loose hairs and drain well. If they are to be served cold, chill until required. If they are to be served hot, place them in a steamer over a pan of hot water. The reserved leaves used for garnishing are replaced upside down in the centre after the artichoke has been filled with the appropriate sauce.

To eat whole artichokes, pull off each leaf with the fingers, dip the fleshy end in the accompanying sauce and eat only this part of the leaf. Eat the succulent base with a knife and fork.

For some hors d'oeuvre, and when used in a vegetable dish, artichokes are often pared down to the base, called the heart or 'fond', the fleshiest part of the artichoke. To prepare, remove the stalk as before and with a sharp knife cut off the top half to two-thirds of the artichoke. Remove any remaining centre leaves and, using a teaspoon or ball-cutter, remove all the feathery 'choke' from the centre. With a small, sharp knife or sharp potato peeler, pare away the leaves until only the succulent ends of the leaves remain attached to the base, forming a deep cup. If necessary trim the top of the cup with a pair of scissors to give a good shape. Rinse well to ensure there are no hairs from the 'choke' left in the centre.

Brush with lemon juice or keep in acidulated water until required. The hearts can be cooked in the same way as whole artichokes and will take about 20–30 minutes to cook, or use as stated in the recipe. To test if they are tender, pierce them carefully with the point of a small, sharp knife.

Poivrades need little preparation except to remove the stalks and possibly trim the tips of the leaves. Brush them with lemon juice or keep in acidulated water and drain well before using.

Purée d'Artichauts

ARTICHOKE PURÉE

Serving vegetables en purée *is typically French. Purées are ideal with roast meats because normally very little sauce is served and a moist purée of vegetables makes an appetizing contrast to the meal. In recent years it has become fashionable in France to serve three purées of contrasting flavours and colours, either in separate dishes or, as in the style of* nouvelle cuisine, *as three neatly moulded portions on each plate. (See also: Purée of Brussels Sprouts, Cabbage, Carrots, Celeriac, Chestnuts, Flageolets, Leeks, Mushroom and Pumpkin.)*

This purée requires an abundance of artichokes, but it is delicious. It is an excellent accompaniment to fish, particularly salmon or trout, or it can be served with chicken or steaks.

Prepare the artichokes and cook in a *blanc* (page 10) for about 20 minutes until tender. Drain well and purée through a vegetable mill or in a food processor. Fold in 4 tablespoons of cream with a spatula and add lemon juice and seasoning to taste. Pile the purée into a hot serving dish and make a well in the centre. Add 2–3 teaspoons of lemon juice to the cream, season to taste and pour into the well just before serving.

1 kg (2lb) fresh/frozen artichoke hearts
150 ml (¼ pt) (⅔ cup) double (heavy) cream
2–3 tbsp lemon juice
salt
white pepper

Artichauts à la Crème

ARTICHOKES IN CREAM SAUCE

This dish goes very well with roasted or braised veal.

4–6 large artichokes
1–2 tbsp lemon juice
50 g (2 oz) (¼ cup) butter
pinch sugar
25 g (1 oz) (¼ cup) flour
150 ml (¼ pt) (⅔ cup) milk
150 ml (¼ pt) (⅔ cup) double (heavy)
  cream
salt
white pepper
1 tbsp chopped parsley

Prepare the artichoke hearts (page 10), brush with lemon juice and leave in acidulated water (page 10) until required. Cook in a *blanc* (page 10) for 10 minutes and then strain. Cut each into quarters. Melt 25 g (1 oz) (2 tbsp) butter in a pan. Add the artichokes with the sugar and a teaspoon of lemon juice. Cover with water and cook until tender. Remove the artichokes from the pan and keep hot. Boil the cooking liquor until 3 tablespoons remain. Melt the remaining butter in another pan, add the flour and cook for 2–3 minutes. Stir in the milk and cream a little at a time. Bring to the boil, season with salt and pepper to taste and cook for 2–3 minutes. Add the cooking liquor to the pan and mix well. Return the artichokes to the pan and heat through. Pile into a hot serving dish and sprinkle with chopped parsley just before serving.

Ragoût d'Artichauts

STEWED ARTICHOKES

This dish comes from Provence. Young, small artichokes (poivrades) that have not yet formed a 'choke' are ideal. It is very tasty with roast meats.

6–8 large artichokes/12–18 young, small
  artichokes
2–3 tbsp lemon juice
175 g (6 oz) lean, streaky bacon slices
2 medium onions
3 large tomatoes
2 tbsp olive oil
25 g (1 oz) (2 tbsp) butter
600 ml (1 pt) (2½ cups) chicken stock
bouquet garni
salt
black pepper

If large artichokes are used trim to the hearts (page 11) and quarter. Young artichokes need only the tips of the leaves and the stalks removed and to be cut in half. Brush each each piece with lemon juice and cook in acidulated water (page 10) until tender. Remove the rinds and cut the bacon into strips. Peel and finely chop the onions. Peel, seed and chop the tomatoes. Heat the butter and oil in a heatproof casserole or heavy-based pan. Add the bacon and onions and cook gently until golden brown. Add the tomatoes and cook for 2–3 minutes, stirring continuously. Drain the artichokes and add them to the pan with the stock and bouquet garni. Season lightly. Partly cover the pan and cook for 30–40 minutes until the artichokes are tender. Remove the bouquet garni from the pan and boil rapidly until nearly all the liquid has evaporated. Check the seasoning and serve in the cooking pot or in a hot serving dish.

LES ASPERGES
Asparagus

Asparagus first became popular in France during the reign of Louis XIV, when his gardener La Quintinie established large beds of it at Versailles to supply the royal kitchens. It became one of the most plentiful vegetables and was more easily available and cheaper than green peas which, at that time, were preferred to asparagus.

Asparagus is available with either green or white stems. Generally, the white-stemmed variety is preferred in France, the thick white Argenteuil asparagus being considered the finest. Choose asparagus with pliable, fleshy stems and tight heads. Use these for hors d'oeuvre and other dishes where whole, tender stems are needed. Very thin stalks can be used for soups and sauces. Make sure they are tender and not woody.

For many dishes asparagus is cut into pieces, and I have found that in the country markets in France it is possible to buy ungraded asparagus which is sold loose. Here, thick and thin stems are mixed and it is obvious that much is grown by the stall-owner in his own garden. It is always very reasonable in price. If you can obtain similar asparagus, it is ideal for such dishes.

To prepare asparagus for cooking, scrape the stems (a potato-peeler is useful for this) and trim the bases of the stems. Wash the asparagus carefully and tie them into bundles of similar-sized pieces. If you have one, use an asparagus pan for cooking. This is a tall, slim pan in which the stems, which need more cooking, are immersed in water while the tender heads cook gently in the steam. Otherwise, cook the asparagus in a large saucepan of boiling salted water. Asparagus will take 15–25 minutes to cook, according to their size and tenderness. If you are cooking bundles of varying thicknesses, remove each one from the water as it is cooked.

Asperges au Four

BAKED ASPARAGUS

Prepare and cook the asparagus (above). Meanwhile, peel the tomatoes, slice and season with salt and pepper. Peel and crush the garlic in a little salt. Heat the butter in a rectangular heatproof dish and remove from the heat. Turn the asparagus in the butter until all are coated. Arrange the asparagus and tomatoes in layers, taking care that the tomatoes do not cover the asparagus heads. Sprinkle the tomatoes on the top layer with crushed garlic, oil and herbs and sprinkle the Parmesan cheese lightly over the whole dish. Place in a preheated oven 200°C (400°F) (Gas Mark 6) for 10–15 minutes until the tomatoes are tender and the cheese golden brown. Serve hot.

Serves 4
500 g (1 lb) small green asparagus
4 tomatoes
1 clove garlic
40 g (1½ oz) (3 tbsp) butter
1 tbsp oil
good pinch powdered oregano
good pinch powdered thyme
salt
black pepper
2–3 tbsp grated Parmesan cheese

Asperges aux Petits Pois

ASPARAGUS WITH PEAS

This dish goes well with roast meats. The meat juices from the roasting pan can be added to the vegetables when they are cooked.

Prepare the asparagus (above), cut into 2.5-cm (1-in) pieces and cook in boiling salted water for 15–20 minutes until almost tender. Drain, reserving some of the cooking liquor. Refresh and drain again. Meanwhile, peel and trim the spring onions (scallions). Heat the butter in a heavy-based pan, add the onions and peas and season lightly. Cover and cook over gentle heat for 10 minutes, stirring occasionally. Add the asparagus and a little of the cooking liquor. Bring to the boil, cover and continue cooking until all the vegetables are tender. If necessary add a little more cooking liquor to prevent them sticking. Season to taste. Pour into a hot serving dish with any liquor left in the pan and sprinkle with chopped parsley just before serving.

500 g (1 lb) small asparagus
350 g (12 oz) shelled/frozen peas
1 bunch spring onions (scallions)
50 g (2 oz) (¼ cup) butter
salt
black pepper
1 tbsp chopped parsley

Asperges à la Crème

ASPARAGUS IN CREAM

If the sauce for this dish gets too hot it is likely to curdle, which can easily happen if it is kept in a hot oven after it has been prepared. I find it is better to finish the sauce just before serving. The asparagus can be cooked in the cream in advance and then reheated.

Serves 4

500 g (1 lb) asparagus
50 g (2 oz) (¼ cup) butter
150 ml (¼ pt) (⅔ cup) milk
200 ml (7 fl oz) (1 cup) double (heavy) cream
2 tsp mixed chopped parsley, tarragon and chervil
2 egg yolks
salt
white pepper

Prepare the asparagus (page 13) and cook in boiling salted water for 10–15 minutes until nearly tender. Cut into 2–3-cm (1–1½-in) pieces. Heat the butter in a pan until it is foaming, add the asparagus and cook for 2–3 minutes. Add the milk, cream and herbs, bring to the boil and simmer for 10 minutes. Just before serving, reheat the asparagus, beat the egg yolks and pour on a little of the hot milk and cream. Mix well, return to the pan and season to taste. Heat through carefully, stirring gently all the time. Take care not to break the asparagus or allow the sauce to boil. Check the seasoning and pour into a warm dish (a hot one could curdle the sauce). Serve immediately.

Asperges à la Tourangelle

TOURAINE-STYLE ASPARAGUS

The country on the southern bank of the Loire abounds with asparagus fields. This is one of the ways in which it is cooked in that region.

Serves 4

1 kg (2 lb) small asparagus
1 small onion
3–4 large lettuce leaves
50 g (2 oz) (¼ cup) butter
1 tbsp flour
450 ml (¾ pt) (2 cups) hot water
salt
white pepper
1 egg yolk

Peel and trim the asparagus and cut into finger lengths. Peel the onion and leave whole. Wash the lettuce leaves and remove any coarse stalks. Melt the butter in a heavy-based pan. Add the asparagus and onion and cook over gentle heat for 3–4 minutes, stirring occasionally. Add the flour and mix well. Pour on the hot water, stirring continuously. Season lightly with salt and pepper and bring to the boil. Cover the mixture with the lettuce leaves, cover the pan and cook gently for 30–45 minutes until the asparagus is tender. Remove the onion. Mix the egg yolk well with 1 tablespoon cold water and pour on a little of the liquor from the pan. Return this mixture to the pan and heat through gently without boiling, stirring all the time. Check the seasoning and pour into a warm dish.

LES AUBERGINES
Aubergines (Eggplant)

Aubergines (eggplant) play an important role in much southern French cookery because they grow abundantly in the heat of this part of the country. They also are cultivated under glass and are available year round, but can be expensive out of season.

Generally, aubergines are purple, but it is possible to get purple-and-white mottled ones. They can be long or round and plump, but whatever their shape or colour look for aubergines that feel firm and have shiny skins. Avoid any with brown patches or wrinkled skins.

To prepare aubergines for cooking, first cut off the stalks. There is no need to peel them. Cut them according to the recipe and then place them on a wire rack and sprinkle them lightly with a little salt. Allow the pieces to drain for about 30 minutes so that some of the moisture is drawn out and the slightly bitter flavour is removed (the cookery term for this is *dégorger*). Rinse in cold water and dry well with kitchen paper towel before proceeding with the recipe.

Beignets d'Aubergines

AUBERGINE FRITTERS

This dish also makes an excellent hors d'oeuvre.

Slice the aubergines and prepare (page 14). Make the *Pâte à Frire* and cut the lemons into wedges. Heat a pan of oil to 190°C (380°F). Dip the slices of aubergine into the *Pâte à Frire* and fry a few at a time until golden and crisp. Drain well on kitchen paper towel and serve garnished with lemon wedges.

2 aubergines, approx. 250 g (8 oz) each
salt
Pâte à Frire (page 220)
2 lemons
oil/fat for deep-frying

Aubergines Frites

FRIED AUBERGINES

Slice the aubergines and prepare (page 14). Heat a pan of oil or fat to 190°C (380°F). Toss the aubergines in the seasoned flour, shake well to remove any surplus and fry a few at a time until golden brown and crisp. (It is important that the aubergines are not coated with flour until immediately before they are put into the pan. If coated too soon the flour becomes wet and does not protect them from the oil.) Drain well on kitchen paper towel and keep hot. Season with salt and pepper and serve immediately.

2 aubergines, approx. 250 g (8 oz) each
3–4 tbsp seasoned flour
oil/fat for deep-frying
salt
black pepper

Panaché d'Aubergines et de Courgettes

MIXED AUBERGINES AND COURGETTES (ZUCCHINI)

A very traditional dish from the southern provinces of France.

Peel the aubergines and cut into 1.5-cm (¾-in) dice and prepare (page 14). Wash the courgettes (zucchini) and cut into 1-cm (½-in) slices. Peel the onion and garlic. Wipe or wash the mushrooms. Finely chop the onion and mushrooms and crush the garlic in a little salt. Heat 2 tablespoons oil in a frying pan and cook the courgettes until soft and golden brown. Remove from the pan and keep hot. Add more oil to the pan and cook the aubergines until soft and golden brown. Mix with the courgettes, season to taste and pile on to a hot serving dish. Keep hot. Meanwhile, melt the butter in a small pan and cook the mushrooms for 5–6 minutes until tender. Remove from the pan and keep hot. Add 2 tablespoons oil to the pan and cook the onion until soft and lightly coloured. Add the garlic, breadcrumbs and parsley. Mix well and cook for 3–4 minutes. Return the mushrooms to the pan and stir into the mixture. Season to taste and heat through. Spread the mixture on top of the aubergines and courgettes and serve hot.

1 aubergine, approx. 350 g (12 oz)
4 medium courgettes (zucchini)
1 large onion
2 cloves garlic
250 g (8 oz) mushrooms
6–8 tbsp oil
25 g (1 oz) (2 tbsp) butter
salt
black pepper
4 tbsp white breadcrumbs
2 tbsp chopped parsley

Bohémienne

BOHEMIAN AUBERGINES

Although the correct name of this dish is Aubergines Bohemiénne, it is frequently abbreviated to Bohemiénne. It is a traditional dish from the south of France. Some recipes mix the anchovies with a Sauce Béchamel and coat the aubergine mixture with this and sprinkle cheese over the top, but my favourite is the one I have given. The crunchy topping, well-flavoured with garlic is, to me, truly Provençale. If preferred, the aubergines can be left unskinned.

500 g (1 lb) aubergines
500 g (1 lb) tomatoes
2 large onions
3 cloves garlic
4 tbsp olive oil
4–5 anchovy fillets
2 tsp flour
4 tbsp milk
3–4 tbsp white breadcrumbs
1 tbsp chopped parsley

Peel and cut the aubergines into 2.5-cm (1-in) dice and prepare (page 15). Peel and quarter the tomatoes and remove the seeds. Peel and chop the onions. Peel the garlic, crush two cloves and leave the other whole.

Heat the oil in a heatproof casserole. Cook the onions until soft but without colour. Add the aubergines, tomatoes and the whole clove of garlic. Season. Cook uncovered over gentle heat until the vegetables are tender. If necessary add 1–2 tablespoons water to prevent sticking, but the mixture needs to be fairly dry when cooked. Stir occasionally, using a fork to avoid crushing the vegetables.

Pound the anchovies in a bowl with some of their oil. Stir in the flour and then the milk. Pour into the aubergine mixture and mix well. Taste and season. Mix the chopped parsley, breadcrumbs and the crushed garlic. Sprinkle over the aubergines and place in a preheated oven 220°C (425°F)(Gas Mark 7) for 10–15 minutes until brown. Serve hot.

Papeton d'Aubergines

POPE'S AUBERGINES

There are many stories, both true and apocryphal, about the origins of different French dishes. This recipe is said to have been invented because of rivalry between papal chefs in Avignon and Rome, a chef in Avignon supposedly producing it for the pope to prove he was better than the chef in Rome. At one time it was made in the shape of a pope's mitre. History does not tell us which pope the dish was made for, or if he approved of it, but it has become a traditional Provençale dish. It can be served hot as an accompaniment to roast meats and grills, or sliced and served cold as an hors d'oeuvre.

6 aubergines approx. 250 g (8 oz) each
3 cloves garlic
6–8 tbsp olive oil
5 eggs
¼ tsp chopped thyme
salt
black pepper
50 g (2 oz) (½ cup) grated Gruyère cheese (optional)
300 ml (½ pt) (1¼ cups) Sauce Tomate (page 218)

Remove the aubergine stalks and peel. Slice thickly and prepare (page 15). Peel and crush the garlic. Heat half the oil in a pan, add the aubergines and stew until soft. Add more oil if necessary. Purée the aubergines through a vegetable mill or in a food processor, or mash them to a pulp (a potato-masher is ideal). Beat the eggs together and mix with the aubergine purée, garlic and thyme. Season to taste with salt and pepper. Pour into a buttered ring-mould and place in a bain-marie or roasting pan of hot water. Bake in a preheated oven 180°C (350°F) (Gas Mark 4) for 35–40 minutes until firm. Turn out on to a hot serving dish and pour the hot tomato sauce over.

Alternatively, pour the mixture into a buttered flan dish. Bake in a preheated oven 200°C (400°F) (Gas Mark 5) for about 10 minutes until the top is set. Sprinkle with the grated cheese, lower the heat to 180°C (350°F) (Gas Mark 4), and cook for 25–30 minutes until set and golden brown. Serve hot or slice and serve cold.

Aubergines Arméniennes

ARMENIAN-STYLE AUBERGINES

Instead of a yogurt sauce, this can be served with Sauce Tomate.

Wash the aubergines, remove the stalks, slice lengthways and prepare (page 15). Peel and crush the garlic. Heat half the oil in a frying pan and cook the aubergine slices a few at a time until tender and golden brown on both sides. Drain well on kitchen paper towel and keep hot. Add more oil to the pan when necessary but make sure it is hot before adding the aubergines. Meanwhile, crush the garlic and mix with the yogurt, parsley and chives. Season with salt and pepper. To serve, arrange the aubergine slices on a hot dish, pour a little of the sauce over and serve the rest separately.

2–3 aubergines, approx. 250 g (8 oz) each
2 cloves garlic
150 ml (¼ pt) (⅔ cup) cooking oil
300 ml (½ pt) (1¼ cups) plain yogurt
1 tbsp chopped parsley
2 tsp chopped chives
salt
black pepper
Sauce Tomate (page 218)

Aubergines en Cocotte

AUBERGINE CASSEROLE

This is another typical Provençale way of cooking aubergines.

Remove the stalks from the aubergines, slice lengthways and prepare (page 15). Peel the tomatoes, cut in half and remove the seeds with a ball-cutter or teaspoon. Chop the flesh coarsely. Peel and finely chop the onions. Remove the rind and cut the bacon into strips. Heat 1–2 tablespoons oil in a pan and fry the bacon until golden brown. Remove from the pan. Add the onions and cook until soft and lightly coloured. Peel and finely chop the garlic. Brush the inside of a heatproof dish with oil and sprinkle the garlic over it. Coat the aubergines with seasoned flour and arrange a layer in the dish. Cover with some of the tomatoes, bacon, onion and herbs. Place a bay leaf in the centre, season, and repeat the layers. Sprinkle the remaining oil over the top and cook in a preheated oven 200°C (400°F) (Gas Mark 6) for 45 minutes, or until tender. Serve hot.

2 aubergines, approx. 350 g (12 oz) each
350 g (12 oz) ripe tomatoes
2 medium onions
175 g (6 oz) streaky bacon
5 tbsp olive oil
2 cloves garlic
2–3 tbsp seasoned flour
2 tbsp chopped parsley
½ tsp chopped thyme
1 bay leaf
black pepper

LES BETTERAVES
Beetroot (Beets)

Beetroot (beets) is frequently used in France as a cooked vegetable as well as for salads. It is usually boiled until tender and then used in a recipe.

When boiling beetroot or cooking in a liquid, always add a little lemon juice or vinegar to help retain its colour (occasionally wine is used in a dish and the acid will have the same effect as the lemon or vinegar). Raw beetroot takes about 15–40 minutes to cook, according to size and age. When the skin can be peeled back with the fingers they are done. Beetroot can also be wrapped in aluminium foil and baked in their skins like potatoes. Freshly cooked beetroot are delicious served just with butter.

500 g (1 lb) cooked beetroot
2 medium onions
2 cloves garlic
50 g (2 oz) (¼ cup) butter
150 ml (¼ pt) (⅔ cup) double/whipping
    (heavy) cream
salt
black pepper
1 tbsp chopped parsley

Betteraves aux Oignons

BEETROOT WITH ONIONS

Peel the beetroot and cut into 1-cm (½-in) dice. Peel the onions and garlic and chop finely. Heat the butter in a pan and cook the onion and garlic until soft and golden brown. Add the beetroot and stir over gentle heat until the beetroot is heated through. Keep hot. Just before serving add the cream and heat through without boiling. Season with salt and black pepper and pour into a hot serving dish. Sprinkle with chopped parsley.

750 g (1½ lb) cooked beetroot
2 medium onions
75 g (3 oz) lean, smoked, streaky bacon
25 g (1 oz) (2 tbsp) butter
25 g (1 oz) (¼ cup) flour
600 ml (1 pt) (2½ cups) stock
2 tsp wine vinegar
salt
pepper
pinch quatre épices (page 199)

Betteraves à l'Auvergnate

AUVERGNE-STYLE BEETROOT

Peel the beetroot and cut into 1-cm (½-in) dice. Peel and chop the onions. Remove the rind from the bacon and cut into thin strips. Melt the butter in a pan and cook the bacon for 4–5 minutes. Add the onion and continue to cook until soft but without colour. Stir occasionally. Add the flour and cook the onion until it starts to brown and then add three-quarters of the stock. Bring to the boil and simmer gently for about 15 minutes. Season to taste. Add the beetroot and vinegar to the sauce with a little more stock if necessary. Simmer for 5–10 minutes. Check the seasoning and add the quatre épices. Turn on to a hot dish and, if you wish, sprinkle with chopped parsley just before serving.

500 g (1 lb) cooked beetroot
1 orange
25 g (1 oz) (2 tbsp) butter
300 ml (½ pt) (1¼ cups) Sauce Béchamel
    (page 214)
2 tbsp cream
1–2 tbsp grated horseradish
salt
black pepper
1 tbsp chopped parsley

Betteraves et Sauce à l'Orange

BEETROOT IN ORANGE SAUCE

This dish is an excellent accompaniment to mackerel or roast veal or chicken.

Peel and cut the beetroot into 1-cm (½-in) dice. Grate the rind of the orange and squeeze out the juice. Melt the butter in a pan, add the beetroot and orange juice and heat through, stirring occasionally. Meanwhile, make the Sauce Béchamel and cook for 3–4 minutes. Add the grated orange rind, cream and horseradish. Mix well and pour on to the beetroot. Season to taste with salt and black pepper. Stir together and pour into a hot serving dish. Sprinkle with chopped parsley just before serving.

LES BETTES
Swiss Chard

This vegetable, which is sometimes called *blettes* in France, is known as Swiss chard or seakale beet in English-speaking countries. It has stalks rather like long, flat sticks of celery, and dark green leaves that resemble spinach. The stalks and leaves can be used together or eaten separately. The leaves are also used in *Tourte de Blea*, a sweet tart from Provence.

To prepare the leaves of Swiss chard, strip them from the stems, remove any coarse veins, roll up like a cigar and cut into shreds (called a *chiffonade*). Cook in boiling salted water for 10–15 minutes until tender. To prepare the stalks, scrape or pare the backs to remove the threads. Cut into pieces and cook in boiling salted water for about 25 minutes.

Bettes au Beurre

SWISS CHARD WITH BUTTER

Wash the leaves well and shred them. Cook in a pan of boiling salted water for 12–15 minutes until tender. Drain well in a colander and press with a saucer to remove as much water as possible. Heat the butter in a pan until golden brown. Add the chard and mix well, loosening the strands with a fork. Season with plenty of black pepper and add the meat juices, if used. Serve hot.

750 g (1½ lb) Swiss chard leaves
25 g (1 oz) (2 tbsp) butter
2–3 tbsp roast meat juices (optional)

Bettes au Gratin

BAKED SWISS CHARD

This dish is also suitable as a vegetarian or light lunch or supper dish. To make it more substantial, slice 75 g (3 oz) of Gruyére cheese and place between each layer of leaves instead of the butter.

Wash the chard well. Remove the green leaves from the stalks, roll the leaves up like a cigar and slice thinly. Cut the stalks into 5-cm (2-in) lengths. Cook the stalks in boiling salted water for 25 minutes. Drain well. Meanwhile, heat 25 g (1 oz) (2 tbsp) butter in a pan. Add the chard, season lightly with salt and pepper and cover and cook over gentle heat for 15 minutes. Peel and crush the garlic. Cut the remaining butter into small pieces. Place a layer of stalks in a well-buttered dish. Dot a little of the butter over the surface and cover with some of the leaves. Repeat, ending with a layer of stalks. Beat the eggs, cream/milk and garlic together. Season lightly with salt, pepper and a pinch of nutmeg and pour over the chard. Cook in a preheated oven 180°C (350°F) (Gas Mark 4) for 30–40 minutes until set.

1 large head Swiss chard
75 g (3 oz) (6 tbsp) butter
3 cloves garlic
4 eggs
300 ml (½ pt) (1¼ cups) single (light) cream/milk
salt
black pepper
pinch grated nutmeg

Côtes de Bettes aux Lardons

SWISS CHARD WITH BACON

This dish goes particularly well with veal.

Clean, trim and scrape the chard stalks and cut into 5-cm (2-in) pieces. Remove the rind and cut the bacon into strips. Melt the butter in a heavy-based pan. Add the bacon and cook, stirring occasionally, until a light golden brown. Add the chard, mix well and season with salt and pepper. Cover the pan, and cook over gentle heat for 20 minutes. Quarter the tomatoes and add to the pan. Cover and cook for 30 minutes. If necessary, add a little stock to keep the mixture moist. When the chard is tender, check the seasoning and pour into a hot serving dish.

500 g (1 lb) Swiss chard stalks
100 g (4 oz) streaky bacon
50 g (2 oz) (¼ cup) butter
salt
black pepper
4 tomatoes
100 ml (3½ fl oz) (⅓ cup) stock (optional)

Côtes de Bettes au Jus

SWISS CHARD IN STOCK

500 g (1 lb) Swiss chard stalks
1 medium onion
40 g (1½ oz) (3 tbsp) butter
600 ml (1 pt) (2½ cups) white stock
salt
black pepper
1–2 tsp arrowroot
2 tbsp Madeira
1 tsp glace de viande/2 tbsp roast meat
    juices
1 tbsp chopped parsley

Glace de viande is meat stock that has been reduced until it sets into a very thick jelly. Although it is used in quite a few French recipes, I doubt it would be found in the average French home. It is probably a hang-over from original recipes created by chefs who used it as a normal ingredient. Glace de viande is very concentrated and a teaspoonful would be sufficient for this recipe, but jelly from the dripping pot or juices from a roasting pan can be used instead. Otherwise, use a little meat concentrate; as much as will stick to the point of a knife will be sufficient. Salsify can be prepared in the same way.

Clean, trim and scrape the chard stalks. Cut into 5-cm (2-in) slices. Peel and slice the onion. Melt the butter in a heavy-based pan. Add the chard and onion and cover and cook over gentle heat for 20 minutes, stirring occasionally. Add the stock, season lightly and simmer gently for 30–35 minutes until the chard is tender. Remove the chard from the pan and keep hot. Boil the cooking liquor rapidly until it is reduced by half. Mix the arrowroot with the Madeira and stir into the pan with the glace de viande/meat juices. Bring to the boil, stirring continuously. Return the chard to the pan, heat through and check the seasoning. Pour into a hot dish and sprinkle with chopped parsley just before serving.

Gâteau de Bettes

SWISS CHARD WITH EGGS AND BACON

500 g (1 lb) Swiss chard leaves
175 g (6 oz) unsmoked streaky bacon
3 shallots/small onions
25 g (1 oz) (2 tbsp) lard
25 g (1 oz) (¼ cup) flour
¼ tsp chopped thyme
2 tsp chopped parsley
1 bay leaf
2 whole eggs
2 egg yolks
300 ml (½ pt) (1¼ cups) milk
salt
black pepper

This can be served warm as a dish on its own or with roast or grilled meats.

Wash the chard leaves well, roll up like a cigar and slice thinly. Cook in boiling salted water for 5 minutes, drain well and press with a saucer in a colander to remove excess water. Remove the rind and chop the bacon into small pieces. Peel and finely chop the shallots/onions. Heat the lard in a pan and cook the shallots/onions over gentle heat until soft but without colour. Add the chard leaves and cook over medium-high heat for 7–8 minutes, stirring continuously. When the leaves are soft, stir in the flour, bacon, thyme and parsley and mix well. Add the bay leaf. Remove from the heat. Beat the eggs, egg yolks and milk together. Pour into the chard and mix well. Season to taste with salt and black pepper. Pour into a buttered heatproof dish and cook in a preheated oven 180°C (350°F) (Gas Mark 4) for 35–40 minutes, or until the centre is firm.

LES BROCOLIS
Broccoli

Broccoli is related to cauliflower. It is possible to buy either tight purple or green heads, or a sprouting variety with small florets at the end of the stalks. Unless specified, either type can be used. Heads can be cooked whole or split into pieces. Trim the stems of sprouting broccoli and remove any coarse leaves. If the stems are thick, cut them lengthwise so they will cook evenly.

Brocolis au Beurre

BROCCOLI WITH BUTTER

Wash and trim the broccoli and split any thick stems. Cook in boiling salted water for 12–15 minutes until just tender. Drain well. Heat the butter in a pan until golden brown. Toss the broccoli in the butter and season to taste. Serve hot.

500 g (1 lb) broccoli
50 g (2 oz) (¼ cup) butter
salt
black pepper

Brocolis au Lard

BROCCOLI WITH BACON

A dish from Vendée, on the western coast of France. If a large piece of bacon is used, it can be eaten as a main meal.

Soak the bacon in cold water for about 2 hours. Drain, place in a pan of cold water, bring to the boil and cook for 30–40 minutes or until tender. Meanwhile, wash and trim the broccoli and slash any thick stems. Peel the potatoes and garlic. Cut the potatoes in half. When the bacon is almost cooked, add the broccoli, potatoes and garlic. Cook for 15–20 minutes. Remove the bacon and potatoes from the pan. Drain the broccoli well (retain the cooking liquor to use as a base for soup) and pile into a hot serving dish. Slice the potatoes and place on top of the broccoli. Keep hot. Slice or dice the bacon, heat the butter in a pan and fry the bacon until crisp and golden brown. Pour over the broccoli together with any butter in the pan. Taste and sprinkle with a little salt, if necessary, and plenty of black pepper. Serve hot.

250 g (8 oz) piece unsmoked bacon
500 g (1 lb) sprouting broccoli
4–6 medium potatoes
2 cloves garlic
40 g (1½ oz) (3 tbsp) butter
salt
black pepper

Brocolis à la Paysanne

COUNTRY-STYLE BROCCOLI

Use firm heads of broccoli for this dish. Either the purple or the greenish-white variety can be used.

Wash and trim the broccoli and divide into florets. Blanch in a pan of boiling water for 4–5 minutes, drain, refresh in cold water and drain well again. Remove the rinds and cut the bacon into strips. Peel the carrots, onions and garlic. Cut the carrots into sticks and halve the onions and leave the garlic whole. Wipe and slice the mushrooms. Melt the butter in a heavy-based pan. Add the bacon and fry for 1–2 minutes. Add the carrots, onions and garlic and cook together for 4–5 minutes, stirring occasionally. Add the mushrooms and broccoli and mix gently together. Pour on the stock, season to taste, cover with greaseproof paper and cover and cook over gentle heat for 30–35 minutes, or until the vegetables are tender and most of the liquid has evaporated. Shake the pan from time to time and, if necessary, add a little stock to prevent the vegetables sticking. When the vegetables are cooked, taste and season and pile into a hot serving dish together with any liquor from the pan. Sprinkle with chopped parsley just before serving.

2 heads broccoli
100 g (4 oz) streaky bacon
100 g (4 oz) carrots
12 small onions
2 cloves garlic
100 g (4 oz) mushrooms
50 g (2 oz) (¼ cup) butter
300 ml (½ pt) (1¼ cups) stock
salt
black pepper
1 tbsp chopped parsley

LES CARDONS
Cardoons

Cardoons are related to the globe artichoke but in this case it is the long, tender stalks that are eaten. Their flavour is a cross between celery and artichokes. The name is derived from the French word *chardon*, which means thistle and, like the artichoke, they have prickly leaves. They were very popular in Roman times and recipes for them have been virtually unchanged for hundreds of years: a recipe for *Cardons à la Moelle* was included in a book published in 1674. Cardoons are grown extensively in the Loire Valley but I always associate them with Provence, for it was there that I first saw the tall plants wrapped in newspaper, which, I later learned, is put round them to blanch the stems.

To prepare cardoons, first discard the tough outside stalks. Remove the strings from the back of the stems in the same way as celery and cut into 5-cm (2-in) pieces. Keep and cook them in acidulated water (page 10). They are sometimes also cooked in a *blanc* (page 10). Boil gently for about 20 minutes and drain well.

Cardoons can also be served cold with a vinaigrette dressing (page 218) as an hors d'oeuvre. The roots can also be cooked: trim them and wash well, pare off any discoloured parts and boil whole until tender. Slice and serve cold with a vinaigrette as an hors d'oeuvre.

Cardons aux Anchois

CARDOONS WITH ANCHOVIES

This traditional dish is served in Provence on Christmas Eve.

Prepare the cardoons and cook in salted water with a *blanc* (page 10). Meanwhile, peel and chop the onion and garlic. Wash the anchovy fillets and crush to a paste. When the cardoons are cooked, melt the butter in a pan and cook the onion until soft but without colour. Add the anchovy paste, garlic and parsley. Stir in the flour and cook for 2–3 minutes. Add the milk a little at a time, stirring constantly. Bring to the boil and season to taste with a little salt, a pinch of nutmeg and plenty of black pepper. Add the cardoons to the sauce and cook over gentle heat for 10 minutes. If necessary add a little more milk to maintain a coating consistency. Pour into a hot serving dish.

500 g (1 lb) cardoons
1 medium onion
1 clove garlic
5–6 anchovy fillets
50 g (2 oz) (¼ cup) butter
2 tsp chopped parsley
25 g (1 oz) (¼ cup) flour
300 ml (½ pt) (1¼ cups) milk
salt
black pepper
pinch nutmeg

Cardons à la Moelle

CARDOONS WITH BEEF MARROW

Cardoons have been prepared in this way for at least 300 years. Celery, salsify and the stalks of Swiss chard can also be cooked in this way. To obtain the marrow, buy a marrow bone and ask your butcher to saw it into short lengths. Simmer it in water with some carrots, onions, a leek and a stick of celery for 3–4 hours. This makes excellent stock for soup-making and the marrow inside the bone will be tender. Remove it with a small, sharp knife and cut into 1-cm (½-in) slices.

Prepare the cardoons and cook in boiling salted water with the lemon juice until tender. Heat the butter in a pan, add the cardoons and cook until lightly coloured. Heat the sliced bone marrow in a little stock/salted water. Pile the cardoons into a hot serving dish. Place the slices of marrow on top and pour any butter left in the pan over this. Sprinkle with chopped parsley or chervil just before serving.

1 bunch cardoons
2 tbsp lemon juice
75 g (3 oz) (6 tbsp) butter
175 g (6 oz) bone marrow
1 tbsp chopped parsley/chervil

LES CAROTTES
Carrots

Carrots are an excellent vegetable, readily available year round. Young ones only need to be washed and scraped; as they get older they will have to be peeled.

Two areas in France have given their names to carrot dishes: *à la Nivernaise* comes from the great market gardening area of that name where many carrots are grown; *à la Crecy* is the subject of some conjecture. Some authorities relate this to the town in the Seine et Marne where carrots are grown, but most prefer the town of Crecy in the Somme where the great battle of 1346 was fought.

Carottes Nouvelles Panachées

NEW CARROTS AND POTATOES

Wash and scrape the carrots and potatoes. If the carrots are small leave them whole, otherwise slice. Slice the potatoes. Cook the carrots in boiling salted water for 8–10 minutes. Add the potatoes and cook until both are tender. Drain well. Melt the butter in a pan and gently toss the carrots and potatoes in it, taking care not to break them. Taste and check the seasoning. Pile into a hot serving dish and, just before serving, sprinkle with chopped chervil.

350 g (¾ lb) small new carrots
350 g (¾ lb) small new potatoes
40 g (1½ oz) (3 tbsp) butter
salt
pepper
1 tbsp chopped chervil

Carottes à la Sauge

CARROTS WITH SAGE

500 g (1 lb) carrots
100 g (4 oz) small onions
2–3 tbsp pork or chicken dripping/butter
250 g (8 oz) shelled/frozen peas
150 ml (¼ pt) (⅔ cup) stock
1 tsp sugar
5–6 small sage leaves
salt
pepper

An excellent accompaniment to roast or grilled pork, this dish also goes well with veal and lamb.

Peel the carrots and onions. Slice the carrots. Melt the dripping/butter in a heavy-based pan and add the carrots, onions and sage. Cook over gentle heat for about 20 minutes, stirring occasionally. Add the fresh peas, stock and sugar and season lightly (if using frozen peas add them about 5 minutes before the end of the cooking time). Simmer for 15–20 minutes until the vegetables are tender.

Carottes en Purée

CARROT PURÉE

1 kg (2 lb) carrots
65 g (2½ oz) (⅓ cup) butter
2 tsp sugar
salt
white pepper
4 tbsp thick double (heavy) cream

This dish can be served with roast meats or grills, either alone or with other vegetable purées.

Peel the carrots and quarter lengthways. If the centre is hard, remove it. Slice the carrots thinly. Heat the butter in a heavy-based pan. Add the carrots and sugar and season lightly with salt and pepper. Cover and cook over gentle heat for 25–30 minutes until tender but without colour. Purée the carrots through a fine vegetable mill or in a food processor. Return to the pan, stir in the cream and heat through. Check the seasoning and pile into a hot serving dish.

Fricassée de Carottes

CARROT FRICASSÉE

500 g (1 lb) carrots
175 g (6 oz) small onions
40 g (1½ oz) (3 tbsp) pork or chicken dripping/butter
bouquet garni
100 g (4 oz) lean, streaky bacon slices
½ tsp sugar
salt
pepper
1 tbsp chopped parsley, chervil/summer savory

In modern French cookery the term fricassée is generally understood to be a creamy meat or poultry stew. The word comes from the verb fricasser — to cut into small pieces — and in years gone by applied to a variety of meat, fish or vegetable stews made with brown as well as white stocks. The name was also used for a dish of vegetables cooked in oil or butter with ham or garlic.

Peel the carrots and onions and slice the carrots thinly. Heat the dripping/butter in a heavy-based pan and add the carrots and onions. Mix well, add the bouquet garni and cover and cook over gentle heat for 20 minutes. Meanwhile, remove the rinds and cut the bacon into thin strips. If it is salty, blanch in boiling water for 2–3 minutes. Add to the vegetables with the sugar. Season lightly and continue cooking for 10 minutes, or until the vegetables and bacon are tender. Shake the pan occasionally. Taste and adjust the seasoning. Pile into a hot serving dish and, if desired, sprinkle with chopped herbs just before serving.

Carottes à l'Oriental

ORIENTAL-STYLE CARROTS

This dish is excellent with grilled or fried veal and lamb cutlets, and roast meats.

Peel the carrots and slice thinly. Soak the sultanas (golden raisins) in hot water for 15 minutes, then drain. Melt the butter in a heavy-based pan, add the carrots and toss until they are all coated in butter. Season with a little salt and sugar. Cover with greaseproof paper and a lid and cook for 45–60 minutes over gentle heat until the carrots are tender. When the carrots have been cooking for 25–30 minutes, add the sultanas, mix carefully, replace the greaseproof paper and lid and continue cooking. Check the seasoning and add a little more salt if necessary and plenty of black pepper. Pile into a hot serving dish and, if desired, sprinkle with chopped parsley just before serving.

500 g (1 lb) carrots
75 g (3 oz) (¾ cup) sultanas (golden raisins)
50 g (2 oz) (¼ cup) butter
salt
½ tsp sugar
black pepper
1 tbsp chopped parsley (optional)

Carottes Provençales

PROVENÇALE CARROTS

Peel the carrots and onions and slice the carrots. Melt the butter in a heavy-based pan, add the carrots and onions and season lightly. Cover with greaseproof paper and a lid and cook over gentle heat for 30–40 minutes until the vegetables are tender. Shake the pan from time to time to prevent sticking. (Resist the temptation to look to see how the vegetables are doing or you will lose the steam, which is vital to the cooking process.) Meanwhile, skin the tomatoes, remove the seeds and chop the flesh coarsely. Peel and crush the garlic. Mix the garlic, breadcrumbs and parsley together. When the carrots and onions are cooked, add the tomatoes and stir together over the heat for a moment or two. Check the seasoning. Pile into a hot serving dish and sprinkle with the breadcrumb mixture.

Some recipes include stoned green olives. Use 15–20, or to taste, and mix them in at the same time as the tomatoes.

500 g (1 lb) carrots
250 g (8 oz) small onions
75 g (3 oz) (6 tbsp) butter
2–3 large tomatoes
2 cloves garlic
3–4 tbsp white breadcrumbs
2 tbsp finely chopped parsley
15–20 stoned green olives (optional)

LE CÉLERI
Celery

The colour of celery can vary from white to green according to type. Look for tight heads that are plump at the base with plenty of straight, smooth stalks and fresh, green leaves. To prepare, cut off the base and scrape or pare the outside of the stalks to remove any coarse threads. Small heads can be cut in half or quartered for boiling and braising. Cut large stalks according to the recipe.

Céleri Braisé à la Paysanne

COUNTRY-STYLE BRAISED CELERY

This recipe for braised celery comes from the Loire Valley.

1 good head celery
4 medium onions
250 g (8 oz) piece smoked, streaky bacon
50 g (2 oz) (¼ cup) butter
300 ml (½ pt) (1¼ cups) stock
salt
pepper

Wash and trim the celery and cut into 8-cm (3-in) pieces. Blanch in a pan of boiling salted water for 5–6 minutes. Drain, refresh under cold water and drain well again. Peel and chop the onions, remove the rind and dice the bacon into 1-cm (½-in) pieces. Heat the butter in a heatproof casserole and add the onions and bacon. Cook until golden brown. Add the celery and stir until coated with butter. Pour on the stock and season lightly with salt and pepper. Cover with greaseproof paper and lid and cook over gentle heat or in a preheated oven 180°C (350°F) (Gas Mark 4), for 45–50 minutes, or until tender. Serve in the dish in which the celery was cooked.

Céleri Bonne Femme

HOUSEWIFE'S CELERY

Try this dish with roast veal or chicken, or with braised beef.

1 good head celery
175 g (6 oz) carrots
2 medium onions
250 g (8 oz) tomatoes
boiled bacon rind/rinds from 100 g (4 oz) bacon slices
2 tbsp oil
25 g (1 oz) (2 tbsp) butter
bouquet garni
450 ml (¾ pt) (2 cups) stock
salt
pepper

Wash and trim the celery. Peel the carrots and onions. Cut the celery and carrots into 1-cm (½-in) pieces and slice the onions thinly. Peel the tomatoes, quarter and remove the seeds. Blanch the celery in a pan of boiling water for 2–4 minutes, drain and refresh well. Cut the piece of bacon rind into squares. Melt the butter and oil in a heavy-based pan. Add the carrots and onions and cook over gentle heat until golden brown. Add the bacon rind, bouquet garni, tomatoes, celery and stock. Season lightly with salt and pepper. Cover with a piece of greaseproof paper and lid. Cook over gentle heat for 50–60 minutes or until all the vegetables are tender and most of the liquid has evaporated. Check the seasoning and pile into a hot serving dish.

Céleri en Branches au Parmesan

CELERY WITH PARMESAN CHEESE

1 good head celery
2 medium carrots
2 medium onions
300 ml (½ pt) (1¼ cups) white stock
salt
pepper
½–1 tsp arrowroot
2–3 tbsp grated Parmesan cheese

Wash and trim the celery. Leave the stalks whole and blanch in boiling salted water for 8–10 minutes. Drain and refresh. Peel and chop the carrots and onions and place in a heatproof dish. Fold the celery stalks neatly in half and place on top of the other vegetables. Season lightly and pour on the stock. Cover with a piece of greaseproof paper and lid and cook in a preheated oven 190°C (375°F) (Gas Mark 5) for 45–50 minutes, or until tender. Remove the celery from the pan, drain well and place in a hot serving dish. Strain the cooking liquor into a clean pan. Mix the arrowroot with a little cold water, pour into the pan and bring to the boil, stirring continuously. Check the seasoning and pour over the celery. Sprinkle with the Parmesan cheese and place under a hot grill to brown.

Céleri à la Ménagère

HOME-STYLE CELERY

These vegetables taste particularly delicious when used as a base for braised veal. Brown the meat in the butter and then proceed with the recipe. Place the veal on top of the vegetables and cover and cook in the oven. A 1.5-kg (3–3½-lb) piece of meat will take about 1½ hours.

Wash and trim the celery and cut into 5-cm (2-in) pieces. Blanch in boiling salted water for 5–6 minutes. Drain and refresh in cold water. Peel and slice the onions and carrots. Peel the tomatoes, quarter and remove the seeds. Heat the butter in a heatproof casserole. Add the carrots and onions and cook until golden brown. Add the tomatoes, celery and stock. Season lightly with salt and pepper, cover and place in a preheated oven 180°C (350°F) (Gas Mark 4) for 50–60 minutes, or until tender. Serve the vegetables around the meat with a little of the cooking liquor. Serve the rest separately.

1 good head celery
2 medium onions
2 medium carrots
250 g (8 oz) tomatoes
50 g (2 oz) (¼ cup) butter
300 ml (½ pt) (1¼ cups) stock
salt
pepper

Céleri à l'Orange et aux Noix

CELERY WITH ORANGE AND NUTS

This dish is very good with roast beef, veal or chicken.

Wash and trim the celery and cut into 5-cm × 5-mm (2-in × ½-in) sticks. Wash the oranges and grate the rinds of 2 oranges, or peel very thinly with a small serrated knife, taking care no pith is left on the peel. Cut into very fine strips. Squeeze the juice from these oranges and thinly slice the other orange. Chop the nuts coarsely. Heat the butter in a heatproof casserole, add the celery and orange peel and mix well. Add the nuts and orange juice and season with salt and pepper. Cover with greaseproof paper and lid and cook in a preheated oven 190°C (375°F) (Gas Mark 5) for 50–60 minutes until all the liquid has evaporated and the celery is tender. Taste and adjust the seasoning and serve in the cooking dish or a hot serving dish. Garnish with orange slices and celery leaves.

1 good head celery
3 large oranges
50 g (2 oz) (½ cup) shelled walnuts
25 g (1 oz) (2 tbsp) butter
salt
black pepper
orange slices and celery leaves (optional)

LE CÉLERI-RAVE
Celeriac

Colloquially and in some French recipes *céleri-rave* is often abbreviated to *céleri*. It resembles a rough, creamy-brown swede (rutabaga) but tastes like celery. When buying celeriac, press the roots hard to make sure they are firm because they can be soft and spongy in the centre. Peel them thickly and keep and cook them in acidulated water (page 10) to prevent discolouration. Celeriac is often cooked in a *blanc* (page 10).

Beignets de Céleri-Rave

CELERIAC FRITTERS

This dish can be served on its own or as an accompaniment to grilled meats.

350 g (¾ lb) celeriac
3 tbsp flour
2 tbsp white breadcrumbs
1 egg
3 tbsp oil
50 g (2 oz) (¼ cup) butter
300 ml (½ pt) (1¼ cups) Sauce Tomate
  (page 218)

Peel the celeriac and cut into 1-cm (½-in) slices. Cook in a *blanc* (page 10) for 10–12 minutes. Drain. Cut into even-sized pieces or sticks. Mix the flour and breadcrumbs together. Beat the egg. Dip the pieces of celeriac into the beaten egg and coat with the flour and breadcrumb mixture. Heat the oil and butter in a frying pan and fry the celeriac until golden brown. Drain on kitchen paper towel and serve with *Sauce Tomate*.

Céleri-Rave en Purée

CELERIAC PURÉE

This purée is a delicious accompaniment to all roast meats, particularly game.

750 g (1½ lb) celeriac
250 g (8 oz) old potatoes
50 g (2 oz) (¼ cup) butter
1–2 tbsp milk
salt
white pepper
pinch nutmeg

Peel the celeriac thickly and cut into medium-sized dice. Peel the potatoes and cut into large pieces. Place the celeriac in a pan of salted water, bring to the boil and cook for 10–15 minutes, then add the potatoes and cook until tender. Drain well. Purée the vegetables through a vegetable mill or in a food processor. Beat in the butter and, if necessary, enough milk to give a soft, but not sloppy, consistency. Taste and season with salt, pepper and a pinch of nutmeg. Heap the purée into a hot serving dish and peak with a fork.

Céleri-Rave en Croquette

CELERIAC CROQUETTES

The flavour of these croquettes contrasts wonderfully with braised meats and game.

500 g (1 lb) celeriac
500 g (1 lb) old potatoes
3 egg yolks
salt
pepper
pinch nutmeg
100 g (4 oz) (1 cup) seasoned flour
1–2 eggs
1 tbsp oil
100 g (4 oz) (2 cups) white breadcrumbs
fat/oil for deep-frying

Peel the celeriac and potatoes and cut into pieces. Place the celeriac in a pan of cold water, bring to the boil and cook for 5–10 minutes. Add the potatoes and cook until tender. Drain well and return to the pan. Shake over gentle heat for 5–10 minutes until the vegetables are dry. Purée through a vegetable mill or in a food processor. Add the egg yolks and season with salt and pepper and a pinch of nutmeg. Beat well together.

Lightly flour a board and with floured hands roll the mixture into a sausage. Cut off even-sized pieces and shape into balls the size of an apricot, or into sausage shapes. Beat the egg with the oil until smooth. Coat the croquettes with the seasoned flour, then with the egg and finally the breadcrumbs. Roll the croquettes on the board to press the breadcrumbs into the surface. If there are bare patches, brush with egg and press on more breadcrumbs. Heat a pan of fat to 190°C (380°F). Place a few croquettes in a frying basket and lower into the fat. Fry for 4–5 minutes or until golden brown. Drain on kitchen paper towel and serve.

Céleri-Rave en Sauce Moutarde

CELERIAC IN MUSTARD SAUCE

Peel the celeriac and cut into 1-cm (½-in) dice. Cook in a pan of boiling salted water for 10–15 minutes until just tender. Drain and keep hot but reserve some of the cooking liquor. Peel and finely chop the onion. Melt the butter in a pan and cook the onion over gentle heat until soft but without colour. Add the flour, mix well and cook for 1–2 minutes. Remove from the heat and stir in the mustard, vinegar and sugar. Add the milk a little at a time and bring to the boil, stirring constantly. Add sufficient cooking liquor to make a creamy consistency. Bring to the boil and cook for 2–3 minutes. Taste and season with salt and white pepper and stir in the cooked celeriac. Pour into a heatproof dish. Mix the breadcrumbs and cheese together and sprinkle over the celeriac. Place under a hot grill for 10–15 minutes to brown. Serve hot.

750 g (1½ lb) celeriac
1 medium onion
25 g (1 oz) (2 tbsp) butter
20 g (¾ oz) (3 tbsp) flour
2 tsp Dijon mustard
1 tbsp white wine vinegar
1 tsp caster (superfine) sugar
100 ml (3½ fl oz) (½ cup) milk
salt
white pepper
2 tbsp white breadcrumbs
25 g (1 oz) (¼ cup) grated Parmesan cheese

Galettes de Céleri-Rave

CELERIAC CAKES

These cakes are particularly delicious with red meats and game.

Prepare the celeriac and cook in a *blanc* (page 10) for 30–35 minutes or until tender. Drain well. Return the celeriac to the pan and mash with a fork or potato-masher. Return to the stove and stir over gentle heat until dry and smooth. Add 25 g (1 oz) (2 tbsp) semolina and mix well, then add the egg, cream, and season with salt and pepper and a pinch of nutmeg. Beat over the heat for 2–3 minutes until the mixture becomes firm. If necessary add a little more semolina. Turn out on to a plate and leave to cool.

Lightly flour a board and roll or press the mixture to flatten it. Cut out 8 or 9 cakes approx. 6 × 1 cm/2½ × ½ in. Be careful not to make them too thin. A wine glass or tumbler can be used if you do not have a pastry cutter of the right size. Place on a greased baking tray. Melt the butter and brush over the top of each cake. Bake in a preheated oven 220°C (425°F) (Gas Mark 7) for 10–15 minutes until golden brown. Serve hot.

750 g (1½ lb) celeriac
25–40 g (1–1½ oz) (3–4 tbsp) fine semolina
1 egg
3 tbsp double (heavy) cream
salt
black pepper
pinch nutmeg
25 g (1 oz) (2 tbsp) butter

LES CHAMPIGNONS
Mushrooms

When I am in France I am always looking at cookery books. Last autumn I was struck by the number of books on mushrooms and what are described as 'other edible fungi' in all the bookshops. They seemed to appear overnight, almost as quickly as the mushrooms themselves.

Many wild mushrooms grow in France, but not all are edible, and some are positively dangerous to eat. This does not, however, prevent them from being gathered and in fact it is a weekend pastime to go out and pick them. French chemists boldly display posters showing the edible varieties, and will identify any brought to them as safe or unsafe to eat.

Cultivated mushrooms (*champignons de couche*) are grown extensively around Paris, and the small, white button ones are known as *champignons de Paris.* The caves near Saumur on the Loire are also well known for their mushrooms, the temperature inside the caves being just right for mushroom production. Cultivated mushrooms rarely need to be peeled, in fact there is a lot of flavour in the skins. Nor should they be washed unless they are very dirty because they discolour easily. Trim the ends of the stalks and wipe the mushrooms with a damp cloth. If you wash them, do so quickly, immediately before you plan to use them. Field mushrooms, however, may need peeling and washing.

Cèpes, known in some countries as *boletus,* are the size of large mushrooms. They have a thick, fleshy cap with a brown, shiny skin and the underside is full of closely packed, spongy tubes. They can be found all over France in the summer and autumn, and grow in sunny woods and forests under chestnut and beech trees. Because *cèpes* are so large and heavy most recipes call for a kilo (2 lb) for four people. The best way to buy them is to judge the number you need and have them weighed afterwards. To prepare *cèpes,* trim the stalks and peel only if necessary. Separate the caps from the stalks. The stalks are sometimes wormy, so soak them in cold water with 1–2 tablespoons of vinegar for about 15 minutes. If the caps need to be washed, rinse them quickly; they have a delicate smell which is lost if they are soaked in water. *Cèpes* can also be bought dried, canned and bottled. Dried ones have a delightful, spicy smell and should be soaked in cold water for 1–2 hours. They can then be used like fresh ones.

Girolles, or *chanterelles,* are small, orangey-yellow mushrooms with upturned, frilly caps and pale yellow stalks. They grow in damp, leafy woods and need to be rinsed carefully to remove the debris of leaves and twigs. But do so quickly, just before using, because they have a delicate but delectable earthy flavour that can soon be lost. *Girolles* do not need peeling — just trim the ends of the stalks and any damaged bits. They usually contain a lot of water, so cook them until they have re-absorbed their moisture before adding other ingredients.

Morilles, or morels, have rounded honeycombed heads that can range from pale brown to nearly black. They are available only for about 5–6 weeks in May and early June. They can be bought dried but are expensive. They grow on the edge of woods and because of the open texture of their heads they retain a lot of grit and must be washed well in several changes of water, but don't soak them. Dried *morilles* have a distinctive but delicate fruity aroma with a hint of apricots. Soak them for 1–2 hours and rinse them very well to remove sand and grit. All other mushrooms can be substituted for *morilles.*

Pleurotes, or oyster mushrooms, are also very good to eat. They have thick, bluish, oyster-coloured cups, which are upturned. They grow in layered clumps at the base of ash or beech trees. They also can be cultivated. The skins are very thin and rarely need to be peeled, just trimmed. Wipe clean, cut into pieces and use for any mushroom recipe.

Champignons en Purée

MUSHROOM PURÉE

This recipe comes from the Ile de France, the area around Paris where mushrooms are grown widely. It goes very well with roast meats.

Trim the mushrooms and wipe or wash them. Chop finely; a food processor is ideal. Heat half the butter in a pan, add the mushrooms and cook until tender and dry. Season to taste with salt and pepper and a pinch of nutmeg. Melt the remaining butter in another pan, add the flour and cook for 1–2 minutes, then add the milk a little at a time, stirring continuously. Boil for 3–4 minutes, then add the cream. Mix in well and stir in the mushroom purée. Taste and adjust the seasoning and pile into a hot serving dish. Serve hot.

500 g (1 lb) white button mushrooms
75 g (3 oz) (6 tbsp) butter
salt
black pepper
pinch nutmeg
40 g (1½ oz) (6 tbsp) flour
300 ml (½ pt) (1¼ cups) milk
4 tbsp cream

Champignons à la Crème

MUSHROOMS IN CREAM

Trim, wash/wipe and slice the mushrooms. Peel and finely chop the shallots/onions and garlic. Cut the ham/bacon into thin strips. Melt the butter in a pan, add the shallots/onions and garlic and cook over gentle heat until soft but colourless. Add the mushrooms and ham/bacon. Season lightly with salt and pepper and cook gently for 10–12 minutes. Add the flour and cook for a further 1–2 minutes, then add the cream, stirring continuously. Bring to the boil and cook for another 3–4 minutes, stirring continuously, until the mixture thickens. Pour into a hot serving dish. Just before serving, sprinkle with parsley.

500 g (1 lb) button mushrooms
2 shallots/small onions
1 clove garlic
100 g (4 oz) raw ham/bacon
50 g (2 oz) (¼ cup) butter
salt
pepper
1 tbsp flour
100 ml (3½ fl oz) (½ cup) double (heavy) cream
1 tbsp chopped parsley

Champignons Montagnards

HIGHLANDER'S MUSHROOMS

A dish from Savoy — the mountainous region near the Swiss-Italian border. It can be served hot, or cold in individual ramekins as an hors d'oeuvre.

Trim, wash or wipe the mushrooms, quarter and sprinkle with lemon juice. Peel and finely chop the onions and garlic. Peel, seed and coarsely chop the tomatoes. Heat 1 tablespoon of oil in a pan and add the mushrooms. Cook until tender and all the liquid in the pan has evaporated. Season lightly. In another pan heat 2 tablespoons of oil. Add the onions and garlic and cook until soft and lightly browned. Add the vinegar, bring to the boil and reduce by half. Add the tomatoes and the bouquet garni. Season lightly with salt and pepper and cook uncovered for 20–25 minutes over gentle heat. Remove the bouquet garni, add the mushrooms and heat through. Pile into a serving dish, sprinkle with parsley. Serve hot or cold.

500 g (1 lb) mushrooms
2 tbsp lemon juice
2 medium onions
1 clove garlic
250 g (8 oz) tomatoes
3 tbsp olive oil
5 tbsp wine vinegar
bouquet garni
salt
black pepper
1 tbsp chopped parsley

Cèpes à la Bordelaise

BORDEAUX-STYLE CÈPES

1 kg (2 lb) cèpes
2 shallots
2 cloves garlic
3–4 tbsp olive oil
1 lemon
salt
black pepper
1 tbsp chopped parsley

Prepare the *cèpes* (page 30). Cut the caps in half or quarter. If the stalks are thick, cut into pieces lengthways. Peel and chop the shallots and garlic and squeeze the lemon. Heat the oil in a frying pan. Add the *cèpes* and cook for 10-15 minutes, stirring occasionally. Season with salt and pepper and cook for 2–3 minutes. Add the chopped shallots, garlic and parsley and mix well. Cook for 6–7 minutes, stirring when necessary to prevent the *cèpes* from sticking. Taste and adjust the seasoning. Pile into a hot serving dish. Heat the lemon juice in the pan with the liquor and pour over the *cèpes*. Serve hot.

Cèpes à la Pergourdine

PERIGORD-STYLE CÈPES

This dish can also be served as an hors d'oeuvre.

1 kg (2 lb) cèpes
2 cloves garlic
2 shallots
2 large ripe tomatoes
4 tbsp oil
salt
black pepper
sprigs of parsley or chervil

Prepare the *cèpes* (page 30). Peel the garlic and shallots. Chop the *cèpe* stalks, garlic and shallots very finely. Peel and seed the tomatoes and chop finely. Heat 3 tablespoons of oil in a large heatproof casserole and cook the heads of the *cèpes* over gentle heat for 10 minutes. Season with salt and pepper, cover and cook in a preheated oven 160°C (325°F) (Gas Mark 3) for 30–40 minutes. Remove from the oven and turn the *cèpes* gill-side up. Meanwhile, heat the remaining oil in another pan, add the shallots and garlic and cook for 3–4 minutes. Add the chopped stalks and cook for 5 minutes. Season lightly. When the *cèpes* are tender, place some of the chopped shallot mixture on top of each. Sprinkle with chopped tomato and return to the pan, uncovered, and cook for 10 minutes. Garnish with parsley or chervil just before serving.

Girolles Sautées à la Forestiére

FRIED GIROLLES — FORESTER'S-STYLE

Morilles can also be cooked in this way.

500 g (1 lb) girolles
150 g (6 oz) firm, waxy new potatoes
100 g (4 oz) smoked, streaky bacon
50 g (2 oz) (¼ cup) butter
salt
black pepper
1 tbsp chopped parsley

Trim and wash the *girolles*. If they are large cut in half or quarter. Scrape the potatoes and cut into 1-cm (½-in) dice. Remove the rind and cut the bacon into thin strips. Cook the potatoes in boiling salted water for 5-7 minutes until tender but firm. Drain well. Heat half the butter in a frying pan and add the *girolles*. Season lightly and cook until the liquid which seeps from them has evaporated. Remove from the pan. Add the remaining butter to the pan and cook the bacon until golden brown. Return the *girolles* to the pan and cook for 10–15 minutes. Add the potatoes and cook together for 5 minutes. Turn the *girolles* and potatoes frequently with a spatula so they are well mixed and the potatoes begin to colour. Check the seasoning and pile into a hot dish. Sprinkle with chopped parsley just before serving.

Girolles au Lard

GIROLLES WITH BACON

Trim and wash the *girolles*. Drain well. Remove the rind and cut the bacon into thin strips. Heat the oil in a pan and cook the bacon until golden brown. Add the garlic and cook for a moment or two, then add the *girolles* and season with salt and pepper. Cook over gentle heat until most of the liquid which seeps from the *girolles* has evaporated. Cover the pan and cook for 10–15 minutes until the *girolles* are tender. Just before serving, add the cream. Bring to the boil and check the seasoning. Pile into a hot dish and sprinkle with chopped parsley.

500 g (1 lb) girolles
250 g (8 oz) smoked, streaky bacon
1 tbsp oil
2 cloves garlic
salt
black pepper
100 ml (3½ fl oz) (½ cup) double (heavy) cream
1 tbsp chopped parsley

Croûtes aux Morilles

MORELS ON TOAST

The Massif Central is the mountainous region that runs through the centre of France. It is a region of great variety, from gently rolling hills to extinct volcanoes and craggy mountains. This recipe is from that part of France. Many types of mushrooms can be found growing there and can be cooked in the same way. The dish can be eaten as a separate vegetable dish, especially after pork or veal. It can also be served as an hors d'oeuvre.

Trim and wash the morels. Melt about 50 g (2 oz) (¼ cup) butter in a pan, add the morels and season lightly. Simmer for 10–15 minutes until tender. Remove from the pan and keep hot. Add the flour, mix well and cook for 2–3 minutes, then stir in the cream/milk a little at a time. Bring to the boil, stirring continuously. Cook for 5–6 minutes. Season to taste. In the meantime, remove the crusts from the bread. Heat the oil with the remaining butter in a frying pan and cook the bread until golden brown on both sides. Keep hot. Beat the egg yolk and pour in some of the sauce. Mix well and return to the pan. Heat through, stirring constantly. Do not allow the sauce to boil. Place the bread on a hot dish and spoon the morels on top of each slice.

500 g (1 lb) morels
75 g (3 oz) (6 tbsp) butter
25 g (1 oz) (¼ cup) flour
300 ml (½ pt) (1¼ cups) single cream/milk
4–6 slices bread
8 tbsp oil
1 egg yolk

Pleurotes à la Tomate

PLEUROTES WITH TOMATOES

Cooked in this way, pleurotes can also be served cold as an hors d'oeuvre.

Trim and wash the *pleurotes* and slice thickly. Peel and finely chop the onions. Peel, seed and finely chop the tomatoes. Heat the oil in a heavy-based pan and cook the onions until soft and lightly coloured. Add the *pleurotes*, tomatoes, stock/wine, bay leaves and lemon juice. Season lightly with salt and pepper. Cover the pan and cook over gentle heat for 20–25 minutes until the *pleurotes* are tender and the sauce has reduced to a coating consistency. If necessary, raise the heat for the last few minutes. Remove the bay leaves, check the seasoning and pile into a hot dish.

500 g (1 lb) pleurotes
4 medium onions
4 large ripe tomatoes
4 tbsp olive oil
100 ml (3½ fl oz) (½ cup) stock/white wine
2 bay leaves
3 tbsp lemon juice
salt
black pepper

500 g (1 lb) pleurotes
4 cloves garlic
75 g (3 oz) (6 tbsp) butter
3 tbsp lemon juice
salt
black pepper
3–4 tbsp Parmesan cheese
1 tbsp chopped parsley

Pleurotes à l'Ail et au Fromage

PLEUROTES WITH GARLIC AND CHEESE

Trim and wash the *pleurotes*. Peel and finely chop the garlic. Heat the butter in a pan, add the *pleurotes* and lemon juice and garlic, season with salt and pepper and cook over moderate heat for 10–12 minutes until tender and golden brown. Check the seasoning. Stir in the Parmesan cheese and sprinkle with chopped parsley just before serving.

LA CHICORÉE
Curly Endive (Chicory)

This curly leafed vegetable, with its blanched centre and dark green outer leaves, is the source of great confusion. In France it is known as *chicorée* or *chicorée frisée*, in the United States as chicory, and in Great Britain it is called endive or curly endive. To complicate matters further, the tight, bleached heads known as endive in France and the United States are known as chicory in Great Britain (page 48). Escarole is similar to *chicorée frisée*, but its leaves are coarser and not so curly.

Chicorée is an excellent salad vegetable. It is crisp with a mild, bitter flavour that adds a slight astringent touch to salads. It can also be cooked (the green outer leaves need to be cooked longer than the white centre). The stumps of curly endive can also be cooked and eaten. They are called *gourilos* or *moelles*. Blanch them for 7–8 minutes in boiling, salted water with a little lemon juice, then use any of the recipes for cardoons, salsify or celery, including *Céleri à la Grecque*.

Chicorée à la Crème

CREAMED ENDIVE

1 kg (2 lb) head curly endive (chicory)
50 g (2 oz) (¼ cup) butter
20 g (¾ oz) (3 tbsp) flour
300 ml (½ pt) (1¼ cups) stock
salt
black pepper
2–3 thin slices white bread
6–8 tbsp oil
4 tbsp double (heavy) cream

Wash the endive and remove any damaged leaves. Break the leaves apart and cook the dark outside leaves in boiling salted water for 5 minutes, then add the pale leaves and cook for another 5–7 minutes. Drain, refresh and drain well again. Chop the endive finely. Melt 25 g (1 oz) (2 tbsp) butter in a pan, add the flour, mix well and cook for 1–2 minutes. Stir in the stock, stirring continuously. Bring to the boil and cook for 2–3 minutes. Add the endive to the sauce and season to taste. Pour into a casserole, cover with a piece of buttered greaseproof paper and lid and cook in a preheated oven 200°C (400°F) (Gas Mark 6) for 50–60 minutes. Meanwhile, remove the crusts from the bread and trim each slice to an 8-cm (3-in) square. Cut into 4 triangles. Heat the oil and remaining butter in a frying pan and fry the bread until golden brown on both sides. Drain on kitchen paper towel. When the endive is cooked, stir in the cream, adjust the seasoning and reheat. Pour into a hot dish and arrange the bread around the dish.

Pain de Chicorée

ENDIVE CREAM MOULD

Trim and wash the endive and chop the leaves and stalks coarsely. Cook in boiling stock for 20–25 minutes until tender. Drain well, reserving the stock. Press the endive with a saucer or in a cloth to remove as much water as possible. Purée the endive in a food processor or liquidizer. (If using a liquidizer it may be necessary to add 1–2 eggs.) Melt the butter in a pan. Add the flour and cook for 1–2 minutes. Stir in a scant 200 ml (7 fl oz) (¾ cup) of the stock and double (heavy) cream. Mix well and bring to the boil, stirring all the time. Cook for 8–10 minutes. Beat the eggs and add to the sauce with the purée. Mix well and season to taste with salt, pepper and nutmeg. Pour into a well-buttered, 15-cm (6-in) charlotte or cake pan and place in a bain-marie or roasting pan of hot water. Cook in a preheated oven 200°C (400°F) (Gas Mark 6) for 50–60 minutes until firm to the touch and shrinking slightly from the sides of the pan. Boil the single (light) cream for 2–3 minutes, season to taste. Turn the mould out on to a hot dish and pour the cream over.

1 kg (2 lb) head curly endive (chicory)
40 g (1½ oz) (3 tbsp) butter
40 g (1½ oz) (6 tbsp) flour
600 ml (1 pt) (2½ cups) stock
100 ml (3½ fl oz) (½ cup) double (heavy) cream
3 eggs
black pepper
pinch nutmeg
150 ml (¼ pt) (⅔ cup) single (light) cream

LE CHOUFLEUR
Cauliflower

Cauliflower originated in the East. It was introduced into Spain in the twelfth century, but was not known in France until the sixteenth. Always look for tight, white heads with fresh, green leaves. The small inside leaves can be cooked with the cauliflower, but if the leaves are young and plentiful, cook them on their own and serve as a separate vegetable. Any recipe for spinach or cabbage can be used. To cook cauliflower the French way, break it into even-sized florets. Wash well and soak for 5–10 minutes in water containing a little vinegar. Rinse and drain. Cook in boiling salted water for 10–12 minutes until just tender. If cauliflower is to be reheated, it is important to refresh in cold water until it is *completely* cold to preserve the freshly cooked flavour.

Choufleur aux Croûtons

CAULIFLOWER WITH CROÛTONS

This recipe can also be used as a supper or vegetarian dish.

Cook the cauliflower until tender. Drain well. Meanwhile, remove the crusts from the bread and cut into even-sized triangles. Heat the oil and butter in a frying pan and fry the bread until golden brown on both sides. Drain well on kitchen paper towel. Hard-boil the eggs and shell and quarter them while still hot. Cover and keep hot. Make the sauce. Pile the cauliflower into a hot serving dish. Arrange the eggs on top, pour the sauce over, and put the croûtons around the edge. Sprinkle with chopped parsley just before serving.

1 cauliflower
2 slices bread
6–8 tbsp oil
25 g (1 oz) (2½ tbsp) butter
2 eggs
300 ml (½ pt) (1¼ cups) Sauce à la Crème (page 215)
1 tbsp chopped parsley

Choufleur au Gratin

CAULIFLOWER IN CHEESE SAUCE

1 cauliflower
300 ml (½ pt) (1¼ cups) Sauce Béchamel
  (page 214)/Sauce à la Crème (page
  215)
75 g (3 oz) (⅔ cup) grated cheese
  (preferably Gruyère)

Gratin is the name given to dishes that are browned on top. This is usually done in a hot oven or under a hot grill, but can also apply when a dish is cooked and browned slowly in the oven, for example Gratin de Pommes de Terre. Au gratin is associated frequently with vegetables in a cheese sauce. Although cheese is often used to assist the browning, breadcrumbs — either sprinkled with butter or mixed with cheese—can also be used to give a crisp topping. In advanced cookery a sabayon (a mixture of eggs and wine cooked as a custard), or a reduction of stock or wine with butter added is sometimes poured over a dish and quickly browned under a hot grill just before serving.

Cook the cauliflower. If it is to be reheated later, refresh well. Drain and arrange in a serving dish. Take the sauce and mix in half the cheese. Pour over the cauliflower and sprinkle the remaining cheese over the top. Brown in a preheated oven 220°C (425°F) (Gas Mark 7) for 12–15 minutes or under a hot grill.

Choufleur à l'Italienne

ITALIAN-STYLE CAULIFLOWER

1 cauliflower
300 ml (½ pt) (1¼ cups) Sauce Tomate
  (page 218)
2–3 tbsp grated Parmesan cheese

Cook the cauliflower and make the Sauce Tomate. When the cauliflower is cooked, drain well and pile into a hot serving dish. Pour the sauce over. Sprinkle with the grated cheese and brown in a preheated oven 220°C (425°F) (Gas Mark 7) for 10–15 minutes, or under a hot grill.

Choufleur à la Polonaise

POLISH-STYLE CAULIFLOWER

The cauliflower in this dish is often re-formed to its original shape after cooking, and looks most attractive for a dinner party. If you prefer, simply arrange the florets in a serving dish.

1 cauliflower
2 eggs
50 g (2 oz) (¼ cup) butter
3 tbsp white breadcrumbs
salt
pepper
2 tbsp chopped parsley

Cook the florets, refresh and drain well. Arrange in a small, well-buttered bowl with the stalks in the centre. Press lightly to keep in shape and stand in a pan of boiling water to reheat then turn out or pile into a hot serving dish. Meanwhile, cook the eggs in boiling water for 10 minutes. Rinse under cold water until completely cold, then shell. Separate the yolks and whites. Sieve the yolk and chop the whites finely. Melt the butter in a frying pan and cook the breadcrumbs, stirring constantly until crisp and golden brown. Sprinkle with the breadcrumbs, then the egg white, yolk and, finally, the chopped parsley.

Fritots de Choufleur

CAULIFLOWER FRITTERS

Serve this dish with lemon wedges, Sauce Tomate or Sauce Piquante. Fritots can also be served as an hors d'oeuvre.

Break the cauliflower into small florets and boil for 5–7 minutes. Take care not to overcook; they must remain firm. Refresh and drain well. Sprinkle with vinegar and leave for 30 minutes. Make the *Pâte à Frire*. Heat the pan of oil/fat to 180°C (360°F). Dip the florets one at a time into the batter and carefully drop into the hot oil/fat. Cook for 4–5 minutes until golden brown. Drain well on kitchen paper towel.

1 medium cauliflower
2 tsp wine vinegar
Pâte à Frire (page 220)
oil/fat for deep frying
1 lemon/300 ml (½ pt) (1 ¼ cups) Sauce Tomate (page 218) or Sauce Piquante (page 217)

Pain de Choufleur

CAULIFLOWER CREAM MOULD

If cheese is included in this recipe, serve the mould with Sauce Tomate. Otherwise, either Sauce Tomate or Sauce Maltaise can be served.

Cook the cauliflower for 10–12 minutes or until just tender. Drain well. Make and cook the mould in the same way as for *Pain de Choux de Bruxelles*, adding the cheese at the same time as the purée. Serve with the sauce of your choice.

1 large cauliflower
40 g (1 ½ oz) (3 tbsp) butter
40 g (1 ½ oz) (6 tbsp) flour
300 ml (½ pt) (1 ¼ cups) milk
3 eggs
50 g (2 oz) (½ cup) grated cheese (optional)
salt and pepper
pinch nutmeg
300 ml (½ pt) (1 ¼ cups) Sauce Tomate (page 218)/Sauce Maltaise (page 217)

LE CHOU ROUGE
Red Cabbage

Each region in France seems to have its own recipe for red cabbage. Choose small, tight heads; young ones will have a bloom on them. To keep cabbage a dark red, add a little vinegar or, occasionally, wine (without some acid, the cabbage fades to pale pink). Very little water should be used; it will simmer gently in its own juices.

Chou Rouge aux Pommes

RED CABBAGE WITH APPLES

Serve this dish with pork or other fat meats, such as duck or goose.

Trim the cabbage, quarter and slice finely. Wash and drain well. Peel the apples, onion and garlic. Core and slice the apples, slice the onion and crush the garlic in a little salt. Heat the oil and butter in a heavy-based pan. Add the onion and cook gently for 5–6 minutes. Stir in the garlic, then add the cabbage, apple, brown sugar, cumin and nutmeg. Pour on the vinegar and water and season lightly with salt and pepper. Cover with greaseproof paper and lid and cook over a very gentle heat for 50–60 minutes until the cabbage is tender and the liquid has evaporated. Stir occasionally to prevent the cabbage from sticking. When the cabbage is cooked, taste and adjust the seasoning and pile into a hot serving dish.

750 g (1 ½ lb) red cabbage
250 g (8 oz) cooking apples
1 large onion
1 clove garlic
2 tbsp oil
25 g (1 oz) (2 tbsp) butter
3 tbsp brown sugar
½ tsp cumin seeds
pinch nutmeg
4 tbsp wine vinegar
4 tbsp water
salt
black pepper

Chou Rouge à l'Alsacienne

RED CABBAGE WITH BACON AND SAUSAGE

This dish from the Alsace uses the cooked sausage of the region (saucisse cuire) but any Continental cooking sausage can be used. If desired, use a larger amount of sausage and serve as a main dish. Some recipes include ½ teaspoon of caraway seeds.

750 g (1½ lb) red cabbage
100 g (4 oz) smoked, streaky bacon
2 medium onions
50 g (2 oz) (¼ cup) lard
salt
black pepper
4 tbsp wine vinegar
250 g (8 oz) Continental cooking sausage

Trim and finely shred the cabbage. Wash and drain well. Remove the rind and cut the bacon into strips. Peel and finely chop the onions. Heat the lard in a heavy-based pan. Add the bacon and cook for 2–3 minutes, then add the cabbage and onion and cook together for about 10 minutes, stirring frequently. Season with salt and pepper and pour in the wine vinegar. Cover with greaseproof paper and lid and cook over gentle heat for 1–1½ hours. Stir or shake the pan occasionally. Meanwhile, cut the sausage into 2.5-cm (1-in) pieces and 20 minutes before the end of the cooking time add to the pan. When the cabbage is tender, taste and adjust the seasoning and pile into a hot serving dish.

Chou Rouge à la Bourguignonne

RED CABBAGE IN RED WINE

This recipe comes from Burgundy and uses the wine and mustard of the region. In fact, any red wine can be used, but use only Dijon mustard.

750 g (1½ lb) red cabbage
100 g (4 oz) smoked, streaky bacon
2 tbsp pork dripping/lard
1 tbsp Dijon mustard
150 ml (¼ pt) (⅔ cup) red wine
    (preferably Burgundy)
salt
black pepper

Trim and slice the cabbage finely. Wash and drain well. Remove the rind and dice the bacon into small pieces. Heat the dripping/lard in a heavy-based pan and cook the bacon for 4–5 minutes. Add the cabbage and cook over gentle heat for 10 minutes, stirring occasionally. Mix the mustard and red wine together and stir into the cabbage. Season lightly with salt and pepper, cover with greaseproof paper and a lid and cook over gentle heat for 1–1½ hours or until the cabbage is tender. Stir or shake the pan from time to time. When the cabbage is cooked, taste and adjust the seasoning, pile into a hot serving dish and serve hot.

Chou Rouge à la Couventine

RED CABBAGE FOR THE CONVENT SCHOOLGIRL

Serve this dish alone or with a salad, or as an accompaniment to stews and sautés.

1 small red cabbage, approx. 500 g (1 lb)
2 tbsp wine vinegar
750 g (1½ lb) old potatoes
3–4 tbsp milk
50 g (2 oz) (¼ cup) butter
350 g (12 oz) streaky bacon slices
175 g (6 oz) (1½ cups) grated Gruyère
    cheese

Trim the cabbage and remove any coarse or damaged leaves. Cut the cabbage in half, cut out the thick stalk and separate the leaves. Blanch the leaves in boiling salted water with the vinegar for 15–20 minutes until nearly tender. Drain well. Meanwhile, peel the potatoes and boil in salted water until tender. Drain well and mash until smooth. Heat the milk. Beat in the butter and enough hot milk to give a firm but creamy texture. Remove the rind from the bacon and place a layer of bacon in the bottom of a large heatproof dish. Cover with a layer of cabbage, a layer of potato and some grated cheese. Repeat, ending with a layer of bacon. Cover and cook in a preheated oven 180°C (350°F) (Gas Mark 4) for 1½ hours.

Chou Rouge à la Limousine

RED CABBAGE WITH CHESTNUTS

This is a regional variation of Chou Rouge aux Pommes. *The use of chestnuts is typical of the cooking in the countryside around Limoges. This dish is very good with pork and other fat meats.*

If using fresh chestnuts, make a slit in the shell of each, place in a pan of cold water, bring to the boil and cook for 3–4 minutes. Drain, refresh and peel. Place in a clean pan with the stock and simmer for 25–30 minutes. Drain, reserving some of the cooking liquor. Cut each chestnut, fresh or canned, into 3–4 pieces. Prepare the cabbage and slice thinly. Heat the dripping in a heavy-based pan. Add the cabbage, mix well and cook for 2–3 minutes. Add the chestnuts, vinegar and 150 ml (¼ pint) (⅔ cup) chestnut liquor/stock. Season lightly. Cover with greaseproof paper and lid and cook over very gentle heat for 45–50 minutes, shaking or stirring the pan occasionally. Meanwhile, peel, core and slice the apples. Add to the pan with the sugar and continue cooking for 15–20 minutes. If necessary add a little more stock to the pan to prevent the cabbage from sticking. When the cabbage, chestnuts and apples are tender, taste and adjust the seasoning and pile into a hot serving dish.

250 g (8 oz) fresh chestnuts and 500 ml (1 pt) (2½ cups) stock
or
200 g (6 oz) canned whole chestnuts and 150 ml (¼ pt) (⅔ cups) stock
750 g (1½ lb) red cabbage
50 g (2 oz) (¼ cup) pork dripping
2 tbsp wine vinegar
salt
black pepper
2 large cooking apples
2 tbsp brown sugar

LE CHOU VERT
Cabbage

Cabbage, available year round, is a great standby for the cook, and French recipes provide a variety of flavours. There are many types of cabbage available. Either green or white can be used, whichever you prefer, but always choose tight heads with unblemished leaves.

Chou Braisé

BRAISED CABBAGE

Trim and quarter the cabbages. Remove most of the thick stalks, leaving just enough to keep the quarters in one piece. Blanch in boiling salted water for 5 minutes. Drain, refresh in cold water and drain well again. Fold each piece in half and press in a dish towel or kitchen paper towel to form a good shape. Peel and slice the carrots and onions and cut the bacon into strips. Place in the bottom of a heatproof dish. Lay the pieces of cabbage on top, pour on the stock and season lightly with salt and pepper. Cover with greaseproof paper and a lid. Bring to the boil and cook in a preheated oven 180°C (350°F) (Gas Mark 4) for about 1 hour or until tender. Remove the pieces of cabbage, drain well and place on a hot serving dish. Strain the cooking liquor into a clean pan. Mix the arrowroot with a little water and add to the pan. Bring to the boil, stirring all the time, for 2–3 minutes. Taste and adjust the seasoning and pour over the cabbage.

2 small cabbages
2 carrots
2 onions
3–4 streaky bacon slices
600 ml (1 pt) (2½ cups) stock
salt
black pepper
1 tsp arrowroot (optional)

Chou Braisé aux Fruits Secs

BRAISED CABBAGE WITH RAISINS

A dish that is excellent with pork or chicken.

750 g (1½ lb) green/white cabbage
250 g (8 oz) onions
40 g (1½ oz) (3 tbsp) seedless raisins
25 g (1 oz) (2 tbsp) butter
pinch nutmeg
salt
black pepper
40 g (1½ oz) (½ cup) salted peanuts

Trim, cut and finely shred the cabbage. Peel and chop the onions. Wash the raisins, cover with hot water and leave to soak. Heat the butter in a heavy-based pan. Add the onions and cook for 4–5 minutes until soft but without colour. Add the cabbage and season lightly with nutmeg, salt and pepper. Cover and cook over gentle heat for 15–20 minutes, stirring occasionally. Drain the raisins, add to the pan and mix well. Cover and cook for 15–20 minutes until the cabbage is tender. Place in a hot serving dish and sprinkle with the peanuts.

Chou Vert en Purée

CABBAGE PURÉE

This dish has a delicate flavour and is an ideal accompaniment to fat meats, such as pork, duck or goose. It also goes well with pheasant and other game.

1.5 kg (3 lb) green cabbage
2 medium onions
bouquet garni
25 g (1 oz) (2 tbsp) butter
25 g (1 oz) (¼ cup) flour
150 ml (¼ pt) (⅔ cup) cream
salt
black pepper
pinch nutmeg

Trim the cabbage, quarter and remove the centre core. Peel and slice the onions. Place the cabbage in a pan of boiling salted water and cook for 5 minutes. Drain. Separate the leaves and return to the pan with the onion and bouquet garni. Cover with water, season lightly with salt and cook until the cabbage and onion are just tender. Drain very well. If necessary return to the pan and stir with a fork over gentle heat until the surplus water has evaporated and the vegetables are dry. Purée through a vegetable mill or in a food processor. Melt the butter in a pan, add the flour and cook for 1–2 minutes. Add the cream a little at a time, stirring constantly. Bring to the boil and cook for 2–3 minutes. Add the cabbage and onion purée. Season to taste with salt, black pepper and a pinch of nutmeg. Heat through thoroughly, stirring continuously. Pile into a hot serving dish and peak the top with a fork. Serve hot.

Chou au Jambon et à la Crème

CABBAGE WITH HAM AND CREAM

750 g (1½ lb) green/white cabbage
100 g (4 oz) cooked ham
1 medium onion
1 tbsp oil
40 g (1½ oz) (3 tbsp) butter
150 ml (¼ pt) (⅔ cup) double (heavy)
   cream
1 tsp paprika
salt
black pepper

Trim and cut the cabbage into 1-cm (½-in) slices. Cut the ham into similar-sized pieces. Peel and chop the onion. Heat the oil in a heatproof casserole. Add the butter and when melted add the cabbage and onion. Cook for 9–10 minutes, stirring frequently, until all the butter has been absorbed. Add the ham with three-quarters of the cream and paprika. Season lightly with salt and black pepper. Mix well, cover with a piece of greaseproof paper and a lid and cook in a preheated oven 190°C (375°F) (Gas Mark 5) for about 40 minutes. When the cabbage is cooked, check the seasoning, put in a hot serving dish and pour the remaining cream in the centre.

Chou à la Lorraine

LORRAINE-STYLE CABBAGE

If you wish, an extra 150 ml (¼ pint) (⅔ cup) of stock can be used instead of wine.

Trim the cabbage, quarter and blanch in boiling salted water for 7–10 minutes. Drain, refresh and drain well again. Press in a clean dish towel or kitchen paper towel to remove excess water. Peel and slice the onions. Skin, pit and chop the tomatoes. Heat the oil in a pan and cook the onions until soft but without colour. Add the flour and mix well. Stir in the tomatoes, wine and stock and season lightly with salt and pepper. Bring to the boil. Place the cabbage in a casserole. Pour the sauce over and add the bouquet garni. Cover with greaseproof paper and lid and cook in a preheated oven 180°C (350°F) (Gas Mark 4) for 1 hour or until tender. Fifteen minutes before the end of the cooking time, pour the soured cream over the top. When the cabbage is cooked, remove the bouquet garni. Taste and adjust the seasoning and either serve in the cooking dish or place the cabbage in a hot serving dish and pour the sauce over. Sprinkle with chopped parsley just before serving.

2 small cabbages
100 g (4 oz) onions
2 large ripe tomatoes
1–2 tbsp oil
2 tsp flour
150 ml (¼ pt) (⅔ cup) white stock
150 ml (¼ pt) (⅔ cup) white wine
bouquet garni
salt
black pepper
75 ml (2½ fl oz) (⅓ cup) soured cream
1 tbsp chopped parsley

LE CHOU-RAVE
Kohl-rabi

Kohl-rabi is a vegetable with a flavour similar to turnips. Although not used widely in France, a little is grown and cooked. Turnips or celeriac can be used as a substitute in any recipe. When young, kohl-rabi can be used raw in salads; the leaves can also be used in the same way as spinach. Peel kohl-rabi thinly. If the roots are small, cook them whole, otherwise cut them into large pieces and cook in boiling salted water with 2 tablespoons of lemon juice or vinegar for 20–30 minutes. Drain and slice or cut into cubes. If preferred, kohl-rabi can be cooked first and the skin removed afterwards.

Chou-Rave à la Vinaigrette

KOHL-RABI WITH VINAIGRETTE

Cooked in this way kohl-rabi is particularly good with veal, turkey or pork escallops, which have been coated with egg and breadcrumbs and fried.

Cook the kohl-rabi as above, drain and mix with the vinaigrette dressing while still hot. Season to taste with salt and black pepper. Serve hot.

750 g (1½ lb) kohl-rabi
2 tbsp lemon juice or vinegar
4–5 tbsp Sauce Vinaigrette (page 218)
salt
black pepper

LES CHOUX DE BRUXELLES
Brussels Sprouts

Brussels sprouts are available from late autumn until early spring. Small ones are best. They should be tight and firm with shiny, pale-green leaves. Yellow leaves are a sign they are stale and should be avoided. To prepare Brussels sprouts, remove any damaged or marked outer leaves and trim the stalk. There is not need to cut the base of the stalk in a cross, as this spoils the shape when they are cooked. Overgrown or large sprouts can be used in purées and soups.

Choux de Bruxelles Sautés

SAUTÉ BRUSSELS SPROUTS

500 g (1 lb) Brussels sprouts
50 g (2 oz) (¼ cup) butter
salt
black pepper
1 tbsp chopped parsley

Trim the sprouts and cook in boiling salted water for 10-12 minutes or until just tender. Drain well. Heat the butter in a frying pan, add the sprouts and cook, turning frequently, until golden brown. Season to taste with salt and pepper. Pile into a hot serving dish and sprinkle with chopped parsley just before serving.

Choux de Bruxelles en Fricassés

BRUSSELS SPROUTS FRICASSÉE

This is a useful way to use leftover vegetables.

500 g (1 lb) Brussels sprouts
250 g (8 oz) carrots
175 g (6 oz) small onions
3 tbsp goose/duck/pork dripping or butter
1 tsp sugar
salt
black pepper
bay leaf
good pinch chopped thyme

Trim, wash and cook the Brussels sprouts in boiling salted water for 5 minutes only. Drain, refresh and drain well again. If the carrots are small, leave whole and scrape, otherwise, peel and slice. Peel the onions. Heat half the dripping in a heavy-based pan. Add the onions. Cover and cook over gentle heat until they become transparent, then add the sugar and cook until golden brown. Remove from the pan. Add the carrots to the pan. When they begin to colour, remove. Heat another tablespoon of dripping in the pan, add the Brussels sprouts and cook for 3–5 minutes. Return the carrots and onions to the pan with the bay leaf, salt, pepper and thyme. Cover and cook over gentle heat for 20–30 minutes so any moisture evaporates very slowly and the vegetables become tender. Stir occasionally, taking care not to crush the sprouts or onions. If necessary add a little more dripping. When the vegetables are tender, taste and adjust the seasoning and pile into a hot serving dish.

Choux de Bruxelles à la Polonaise

POLISH-STYLE BRUSSELS SPROUTS

This garnish is usually served with cauliflower but also provides a very pleasing textural contrast to Brussels sprouts or cabbage.

500 g (1 lb) Brussels sprouts
2 eggs
50 g (2 oz) (¼ cup) butter
3 tbsp white breadcrumbs
2 tbsp chopped parsley
salt
black pepper

Trim the sprouts and cook in boiling salted water for 10–12 minutes or until just tender. Drain well. Prepare the garnish as for *Choufleur à la Polonaise* and finish the dish in the same way.

Purée de Choux de Bruxelles

BRUSSELS SPROUTS PURÉE

Trim and wash the sprouts and cook in boiling salted water for 10–12 minutes until tender. Drain, refresh and drain well again. Peel the potatoes and cut into pieces. Cook in boiling salted water for 15–20 minutes until tender. Drain well and return to the pan and cook over gentle heat, shaking the pan from time to time until the potatoes are quite dry. Purée the sprouts and potatoes through a vegetable mill or in a food processor. Heat the butter in a pan, add the purée and heat through, stirring constantly. Season well with salt and black pepper. Serve hot.

500 g (1 lb) Brussels sprouts
250 g (8 oz) old potatoes
50 g (2 oz) (¼ cup) butter
salt
pepper

Pain de Choux de Bruxelles

BRUSSELS SPROUTS CREAM MOULD

This recipe is an excellent way of using very large or overgrown Brussels sprouts. Cauliflower can also be cooked in this way.

Trim the sprouts, wash and cook in boiling salted water for 15–20 minutes until just tender. Drain and refresh in cold water and drain well again. Meanwhile, heat the butter in a saucepan, add the flour and cook for 1–2 minutes. Add the milk, stirring constantly. Bring to the boil and cook for 2–3 minutes. When the sprouts are cooked and drained, purée through a vegetable mill or in a food processor. Mix the eggs together and stir into the sauce with the purée. Mix well and season with a pinch of nutmeg, salt and pepper. Pour into a buttered 15-cm (6-in) charlotte tin, or deep pudding mould, and place in a bain-marie or roasting pan containing hot water. Bake in a preheated oven 190°C (375°F) (Gas Mark 5) for 45–50 minutes. Turn the mould out on to a hot serving dish, cover with a damp dish towel and leave for 2–3 minutes, then carefully remove the tin. Pour some tomato sauce gently over the back of a spoon to coat the mould (if the sauce is poured directly on to the mould it may split). Pour the rest of the sauce round the mould or serve separately.

750 g (1½ lb) Brussels sprouts
40 g (1½ oz) (3 tbsp) butter
40 g (1½ oz) (6 tbsp) flour
300 ml (½ pt) (1¼ cups) milk
3 whole eggs
pinch nutmeg
salt
white pepper
300 ml (½ pt) (1¼ cups) Sauce Tomate (page 218)

LE CONCOMBRE
Cucumber

In many countries cucumbers are used only as a salad vegetable, but in France they are frequently cooked as well. Many of the cucumbers available in the summer in France are small, short, fat ones with knobbly skins that are often streaked with yellow. The seeds in these are very large and best removed, even for salads. To do this, cut the cucumber in half and run down the centre with a ball-cutter. If the skins are very thick, peel the cucumber first; it is a matter of choice whether the skins and seeds of cultivated ones are removed.

All cucumbers should be firm. Green ones should be long and straight with dark, shiny skins. Flabby cucumbers with pale or yellowish skins can be bitter. For salads in particular excess water should be removed from the sliced or cut cucumber by sprinkling it with a little salt and leaving it to drain for about 30 minutes (don't be too heavy-handed with the salt or the cucumber will absorb it with unpleasant results; a light sprinkling is all that is necessary). Wash and dry the cucumber well on kitchen paper towel before using.

Concombre Glacé

GLAZED CUCUMBER

Serve this dish hot with meat or game.

1 large cucumber
50 g (2 oz) (¼ cup) butter
salt
pepper
1 tbsp chopped herbs (parsley, chervil,
  chives, summer savory)

Peel the cucumber and cut into two or three pieces lengthwise and remove the seeds with a ball-cutter or teaspoon. Thickly slice the cucumber into half-rings. Place in a pan of boiling salted water and cook for 4–5 minutes. Drain well. Heat the butter in a frying pan, add the cucumber and cook over gentle heat, turning occasionally until tender and glazed with butter. Season with salt and pepper and pile into a hot serving dish. Sprinkle with herbs just before serving.

Concombre aux Fines Herbes

CUCUMBER WITH HERBS

This dish is excellent with grilled or baked fish.

1 large cucumber
salt
150 ml (¼ pt) (⅔ cup) plain yogurt
2 tsp chopped fresh sage/1 tsp dried sage
1 tbsp chopped parsley
black pepper

Wash but do not peel the cucumber. Cut into 1-cm (½-in) dice. Sprinkle with a little salt and place in a heavy-based pan with 2–3 tablespoons of water. Cover and cook over gentle heat for 15–20 minutes until the cucumber is just tender and the water has evaporated. Take care not to overcook. Add the yogurt with most of the sage and parsley. Season to taste with salt and pepper and return to the heat. Cook gently, stirring all the time, for 3–4 minutes. Place in a hot serving dish and sprinkle with the remaining herbs just before serving.

Concombres à la Normande

NORMANDY-STYLE CUCUMBERS

1–2 cucumbers
50 g (2 oz) (¼ cup) butter
25 g (1 oz) (¼ cup) flour
200 ml (7 fl oz) (1 cup) milk
200 ml (7 fl oz) (1 cup) double (heavy)
  cream
salt
white pepper
1 tbsp chopped chives

Peel the cucumbers and cut in half lengthways. Remove the seeds with a ball-cutter or teaspoon. Cut into 5-cm × 1-cm (2-in × ½-in) sticks. Cook in a pan of boiling salted water for 5 minutes. Drain, refresh and drain well again. Heat the butter in a heavy-based pan and add the cucumbers. Cook for 5–6 minutes until all the pieces of cucumber are glazed in butter. Shake the pan occasionally. Add the flour and mix well with a wooden spoon. Stir in the milk and cream, taking care not to break the cucumber. Season to taste with salt and pepper. Bring to the boil and continue cooking over gentle heat for 10–12 minutes, stirring occasionally until the cucumbers are cooked. Check the seasoning and pour into a hot serving dish. Sprinkle with chopped chives just before serving.

LA COURGE
Marrow (Summer Squash)

Marrow (summer squash) cooked the French way seems a different vegetable to the pale, boiled marrow so often served elsewhere, but in keeping with the French tendency to pick vegetables while they are young and small, there are not many recipes for marrow because most are picked as courgettes (zucchini). Choose medium-sized marrows of even shape with clear, shiny skins. Very large marrows can be coarse and stringy.

Gratin de Courges et d'Oignons

BAKED MARROW AND ONIONS

Peel the marrow, remove the seeds and cut into large dice. Peel the onions. Soak the sultanas (raisins) in hot water for 15–20 minutes. Heat 4 tablespoons of oil in a frying pan, add the almonds and cook until golden brown, turning them continuously with a spatula so they brown evenly. Drain on kitchen paper towel and sprinkle lightly with salt. Cook the onions in a pan of boiling salted water for 5–6 minutes, add the marrow and cook for 4–5 minutes. Drain well. Heat the butter with 1 tablespoon of oil in a heavy-based pan. Add the onions and marrow and cook over gentle heat for 15–20 minutes until the vegetables are tender and lightly coloured. Strain the sultanas and add to the pan, stirring carefully to avoid breaking the onions. Pile into a hot heatproof dish, sprinkle with the nuts and bake in a preheated oven 200°C (400°F) (Gas Mark 6) for 10–15 minutes.

1 medium marrow
175 g (6 oz) small onions
25 g (1 oz) (2 tbsp) sultanas (golden raisins)
5 tbsp olive oil
50 g (2 oz) (½ cup) blanched almonds
40 g (1½ oz) (3 tbsp) butter
salt
black pepper

Courge à la Provençale

PROVENÇALE MARROW

Peel the marrow, quarter lengthwise, remove the seeds and slice thinly. Peel the onions and garlic. Chop the onions finely and crush the garlic. Peel the fresh tomatoes and remove the seeds. Chop finely. Heat 2 tablespoons of oil in a pan. Add the onions and garlic and cook until tender but without colour. Add the tomatoes. Cook fresh ones for 3–4 minutes. Canned ones must be cooked for 10–15 minutes to reduce the liquid. Brush the inside of a heatproof dish with oil. Place a layer of sliced marrow as the base and season lightly with salt and pepper. Cover with a little of the tomato mixture and a light sprinkling of basil. Repeat the layers, ending with a neatly arranged top layer of marrow. Brush the top with the remaining oil. Cover and cook in a preheated oven 200°C (400°F) (Gas Mark 6) for 40–50 minutes until the marrow is tender. Uncover for the last 10 minutes to brown the marrow slightly.

Alternative method: Dice the marrow and prepare the other vegetables as before. Cook the onions and garlic in the oil until soft, then add the fresh tomatoes and 150 ml (¼ pint) (⅔ cup) water, or the can of tomatoes together with the marrow. Season lightly with salt and pepper. Cover and cook for 15–20 minutes until the marrow is tender.

Pour into a hot serving dish and sprinkle with chopped basil.

1 medium marrow
2 medium onions
2 cloves garlic
500 g (1 lb) ripe tomatoes/ 400 g (14 oz) canned tomatoes
3 tbsp olive oil
salt
black pepper
few basil leaves/1–2 tsp dried basil

Courge au Four

BAKED MARROW

1 medium marrow
3 cloves garlic
3–4 tbsp olive oil
2 tsp flour
1 tbsp chopped parsley
salt
black pepper

Peel the marrow, remove the seeds and cut into 1-cm (½-in) dice. Peel and crush the garlic. Brush the inside of a heatproof dish with oil. Place the marrow in the dish and sprinkle with the flour, garlic and parsley. Season well with salt and black pepper. Pour the oil over. Bake in a preheated oven 200°C (400°F) (Gas Mark 6) for about 50 minutes until the marrow is tender and crisp and brown. Serve hot.

LES COURGETTES
Courgettes (Zucchini)

Courgettes (zucchini) are now available year round. They need little preparation — just trim off the ends and use as required. The flowers from courgettes are a great delicacy and usually made into *Beignets*. They can also be stuffed.

Courgettes à la Meunière

FRIED COURGETTES

500 g (1 lb) courgettes
2 tbsp oil
50 g (2 oz) (¼ cup) butter
2–3 tbsp seasoned flour
1 tbsp chopped parsley

Trim the courgettes and cut into 1-cm (½-in) slices. Heat the oil and butter in a frying pan, coat the courgette slices in seasoned flour and cook until golden brown on both sides. Pile into a hot serving dish and sprinkle with chopped parsley just before serving.

Courgettes aux Amandes

COURGETTES WITH ALMONDS

This is a variation of *Courgettes à la Meunière*. Use the same ingredients with the addition of 40 g (1½ oz) blanched almonds. Prepare and cook the courgettes in the same way. Remove from the pan and add the almonds and cook until golden brown. Sprinkle with almonds.

Courgettes aux Yaourts

COURGETTES WITH YOGURT

500 g (1 lb) courgettes
1 clove garlic
salt
200 ml (7 fl oz) (1 cup) plain yogurt
1 tbsp chopped chives
black pepper
50 g (2 oz) (½ cup) grated Gruyère cheese

Serve with cold meats or on its own for a vegetarian or light meal.

Cut the courgettes into finger-sized sticks and blanch in boiling salted water for 3–4 minutes. Drain, refresh and drain well again. Crush the clove of garlic in a little salt. Mix the yogurt, stir in the garlic and chives and season with salt and pepper. Place the courgettes in a buttered heatproof dish. Pour on the yogurt mixture and sprinkle with grated cheese. Bake in a preheated oven 200°C (400°F) (Gas Mark 6) for 40–45 minutes until the courgettes are tender.

Courgettes à la Vauclusienne

BAKED COURGETTES WITH TOMATOES

This dish comes from Vaucluse, on the eastern side of the Rhône Valley, where I have stayed many times. It is typical hard-baked Provence countryside, but the fields are full of courgettes, tomatoes and aubergines.

Trim and slice the courgettes. Blanch in boiling salted water for 2–3 minutes. Drain, refresh and drain well again. Peel and seed the tomatoes and chop coarsely. Peel and crush the garlic. Heat 2 tablespoons of oil in a pan, add the tomatoes and garlic, mix well and cook for 2–3 minutes. Add the parsley and season with salt and pepper. Brush the inside of a heatproof dish with oil. Place the courgettes in the dish and pour the tomato mixture over. Sprinkle breadcrumbs over the top and drip oil evenly over the breadcrumbs. Bake in a preheated oven 200°C (400°F) (Gas Mark 6) for 30–40 minutes until the courgettes are tender and the top crisp and golden brown.

500 g (1 lb) courgettes
500 g (1 lb) tomatoes
2 cloves garlic
3–4 tbsp oil
1 tbsp chopped parsley
salt
black pepper
2–3 tbsp fresh white breadcrumbs

Ragoût de Courgettes

STEWED COURGETTES

Serve this as an accompaniment to meats or poultry, or as a vegetarian dish.

Trim the courgettes and cut into 1-cm (½-in) slices. Peel and finely chop the onion. Heat the oil in a heavy-based pan. Add the courgettes and onions and cook over gentle heat for 5–7 minutes. Meanwhile, peel and seed the tomatoes and chop coarsely. Stone the olives, slice the mushrooms and peel and crush the garlic. Add them all to the pan with 1 tablespoon chopped parsley. Season to taste with salt and pepper. Cover and cook over gentle heat for 20–25 minutes until the vegetables are tender. Taste and adjust the seasoning. Pour into a hot serving dish and sprinkle with the remaining parsley just before serving.

To make the dish more substantial, when the ragoût is in the dish make 4 hollows with a wooden spoon. Break an egg into each hollow and bake in a preheated oven 180°C (350°F) (Gas Mark 4) for 10–15 minutes.

500 g (1 lb) courgettes
1 medium onion
2 tbsp olive oil
4 large tomatoes
50 g (2 oz) black olives
100 g (4 oz) mushrooms
2 cloves garlic
2 tbsp chopped parsley
salt
black pepper

LES CROSNES
Chinese Artichokes

In 1882 a Monsieur Pailleuz, who lived in the small village of Crosnes near Paris, received a present of small tubers from the French Doctor to the Russian Ambassador in Peking. He cultivated them and it was the first time that *crosnes*, as they came to be called, were grown in France. In other parts of the world they are known as Chinese artichokes, Japanese artichokes or stachys. They are easy to grow and produce an abundance of small, creamy tubers with a delicate flavour similar to Jerusalem artichokes.

Crosnes are best when newly gathered. Use only those with creamy-white skins — yellow skins are hard to remove. Raw *crosnes* can be peeled, thinly sliced and added to salads. To prepare, wash well and place in a bowl or pan. Cover with boiling water and leave for a few moments— the skins should then peel off quite easily. If any skin remains, dry them well and rub in a tea towel with a little coarse salt. Wash well. Boil in salted water for 7–10 minutes, drain, refresh in cold water and drain well again, then proceed with the recipe. Recipes for Jerusalem artichokes can also be used.

Crosnes Sautés

SAUTÉ CHINESE ARTICHOKES

Serve with roast or grilled meats.

500 g (1 lb) Chinese artichokes
50 g (2 oz) (¼ cup) butter
1 clove garlic
1 tbsp chopped parsley
salt
black pepper

Prepare and cook the artichokes (page 47). Heat the butter in a frying pan and cook the artichokes for 5–7 minutes until golden brown and tender. Finely chop the garlic and mix with the parsley. Pile the artichokes into a hot dish and season to taste with salt and pepper. Just before serving sprinkle with the parsley and garlic mixture.

Crosnes à la Crème

CHINESE ARTICHOKES IN CREAM SAUCE

500 g (1 lb) Chinese artichokes
40 g (1½ oz) (3½ tbsp) butter
6 tbsp double (heavy) cream
1 egg yolk
salt
pepper
1 tbsp chopped chervil

Prepare and cook the artichokes (page 47). Heat the butter in a pan, add the artichokes and cook for about 10 minutes over gentle heat until tender. Beat the double (heavy) cream and egg yolk together. Season with salt and pepper. Add this mixture to the pan and heat through gently without boiling. Pour into a hot serving dish and sprinkle with chopped chervil.

LES ENDIVES
Belgian Chicory

I have already explained the difference between endive and chicory (page 34). Chicory was first marketed on a large scale in Belgium in the mid-nineteenth century, and now it exports nearly half its production to France. Nonetheless, a lot of chicory is still grown in France, some of it in caves, which provide just the conditions it needs, as it must be blanched either in the dark or under the earth to make it less bitter. When preparing chicory trim the base and remove any soiled leaves. Either leave it whole or break the leaves apart, but take care not to soak the chicory in water when you wash it because it will become very bitter.

Endives Gratinées

BAKED CHICORY

Wash, trim and slice the chicory. Peel and finely slice the onions. Melt 20 g (¾ oz) (1½ tbsp) butter in a heavy-based pan. Add the chicory and lemon juice. Season lightly. Cover with greaseproof paper and a lid and cook over gentle heat for 20 minutes. Melt another 20 g (¾ oz) (1½ tbsp) butter in another pan and cook the onions until soft and lightly coloured. Season to taste. Wash the potatoes well. Place in a pan of cold salted water and bring to the boil and cook for 5 minutes. Drain, refresh and peel. Slice thickly. Butter the inside of a heatproof dish and arrange the potatoes, chicory and onion in layers. Pour on the stock and cover with the breadcrumbs. Melt the remaining butter and pour over the top. Bake in a preheated oven 200°C (400°F) (Gas Mark 6) for 40–45 minutes until the potatoes are cooked and the top is golden brown.

500 g (1 lb) Belgian chicory
2 medium onions
75 g (3 oz) (6 tbsp) butter
2 tbsp lemon juice
500 g (1 lb) small potatoes
300 ml (½ pt) (1 ¼ cups) white stock
3–4 tbsp fresh white breadcrumbs
salt
black pepper

Chiffonade d'Endives à la Crème

SHREDDED CHICORY IN CREAM

Trim and wash the chicory and slice thinly. Melt the butter in a heavy-based pan and add the chicory, lemon juice and sugar. Cover with greaseproof paper and a lid and cook over gentle heat for 40 minutes or until tender. Keep hot until required. Just before serving, add the cream and season with salt and pepper to taste. Bring to the boil and cook for 2–3 minutes, then pour into a hot dish. If you wish, slice a lemon thinly and place half-slices round the edge of the dish as a garnish.

750 g (1 ½ lb) Belgian chicory
65 g (2 ½ oz) (⅓ cup) butter
2 tbsp lemon juice
¼ tsp sugar
100 ml (3½ fl oz) (½ cup) double (heavy) cream
salt
white pepper
1 lemon (optional)

Endives à la Flamande

FLEMISH-STYLE CHICORY

Some recipes for Endive à la Flamande *suggest using nut-brown butter to coat the chicory instead of Sauce Demi-glace. It may be easier, but the rich sauce goes so well with the chicory I much prefer it. To save time and trouble, do as I do: whenever you make Sauce Demi-glace, make 2–3 times the recipe. It takes no longer to make a larger quantity and the extra can be frozen, ready for dishes such as this.*

Trim and wash the chicory. Place in a casserole with the butter, season with salt and pepper and pour in the lemon juice and water. Cover with a piece of greaseproof paper and lid and cook in a preheated oven 200°C (400°F) (Gas Mark 6) for 50–60 minutes or until tender. In the meantime, make the *Sauce Demi-glace*. When the chicory is cooked, place in a hot dish and pour the sauce over. If you prefer to use nut-brown butter, simply melt 75 g (3 oz) (6 tbsp) of butter in a pan and cook to a golden chestnut colour.

8 small heads Belgian chicory
40 g (1½ oz) (3 tbsp) butter
salt
black pepper
3 tbsp lemon juice
4–5 tbsp water
300 ml (¼ pt) (1 ¼ cups) Sauce Demi-glace (page 215)

Endives à la Flamande (page 49).

8 small heads Belgian chicory
40 g (1½ oz) (3 tbsp) butter
3 tbsp lemon juice
4–5 tbsp water
4 slices ham
75 g (3 oz) (¾ cup) grated Gruyère cheese

Endives au Jambon

CHICORY WITH HAM

Prepare and cook the chicory as for *Endives à la Flamande*. When the chicory is cooked, wrap each head in half a slice of ham and place in a buttered dish. Pour over any butter left in the cooking dish and sprinkle with the Gruyère cheese. Cook in a preheated oven 200°C (400°F) (Gas Mark 6) for 10–12 minutes until golden brown.

LES ÉPINARDS
Spinach

*Petits Pains d'Épinards
à la Crème* (page 52).

Spinach has always been a popular vegetable in France. In the Middle Ages small balls of cooked spinach were sold in the street, and it was prescribed as a cure for intestinal disorders. La Varenne, the great chef of the seventeenth century, included a recipe for *Épinards à la Crème* in his book, published in 1651.

Spinach must be washed well because the leaves retain grit very easily. Rinse them several times. (I remember my grandmother — a wonderful cook right up to her death at nearly 103 — always insisting that I wash it exactly *six* times.) Drain well and remove any coarse stalks. It is possible to cook spinach without any water other than that clinging to the leaves, but French recipes generally cook it in boiling salted water. It needs little cooking — 8–10 minutes is usually enough. Drain the spinach well and press it in a colander with a saucer or potato masher to remove the excess water. Then tease the spinach into strands with two forks. Frozen spinach can be used in any of the recipes; use half the given amount.

Petits Pains d'Épinards à la Crème

SMALL SPINACH CREAM MOULDS

1 kg (2 lb) spinach
40 g (1½ oz) (3 tbsp) butter
40 g (1½ oz) (6 tbsp) flour
450 ml (¾ pt) (2 cups) milk
4 eggs
salt
white and black pepper
pinch of nutmeg
4 tbsp double (heavy) cream
small spinach leaves
sliced tomato (optional)

Butter the inside of 4 large ramekins or individual pudding moulds, or 8 smaller ones. Wash and trim the spinach and reserve a few small leaves for garnish. Cook in a pan of boiling water for 6–7 minutes. Drain well and press with a saucer to remove as much water as possible. If necessary return the spinach to the pan and stir over gentle heat until quite dry. Purée the spinach in a food processor or liquidizer, adding some egg if necessary. Meanwhile, melt the butter in a pan and add the flour. Mix well and cook for 2–3 minutes, then add 300 ml (½ pint) (1¼ cups) of milk, stirring all the time. Bring to the boil and cook for a further 2–3 minutes. Season to taste with salt and white pepper.

Mix 2 tablespoons of the sauce with the purée, together with the beaten eggs. Season again with salt and black pepper and a pinch of nutmeg. Pour into the moulds and place in a bain-marie or roasting pan of hot water and cook in a preheated oven 200°C (400°F) (Gas Mark 6) for 25–30 minutes until firm to the touch. If small moulds are not available, cook in a 15-cm (6-in) charlotte or cake pan for 50–60 minutes. Add the remaining milk to the sauce and leave until the moulds are cooked. Reheat the sauce, beating well until smooth. Add the cream and season to taste. Turn the moulds out on to a hot dish. Carefully spoon a little sauce over each and garnish with spinach leaves and sliced tomatoes. Serve the remaining sauce separately.

Épinards à la Crème

SPINACH IN CREAM

1 kg (2 lb) spinach
40 g (1½ oz) (3 tbsp) butter
200 ml (7 fl oz) (1 cup) double (heavy) cream
salt
black pepper
pinch nutmeg
fried croûtons (page 221)

Trim and wash the spinach and cook in a pan of boiling salted water for 5 minutes. Drain in a colander and press with a saucer to remove as much water as possible. Melt the butter in a pan and add the spinach. Pour on the cream, bring to the boil and simmer for 5 minutes, stirring occasionally. Season to taste with salt, pepper and nutmeg. Pour into a hot dish. If desired, garnish with fried croûtons.

Épinards et Navets au Gratin

BAKED SPINACH AND TURNIPS

500 g (1 lb) spinach
250 g (8 oz) turnips
300 ml (½ pt) (1¼ cups) milk
2 eggs
salt
black pepper
pinch nutmeg
20 g (¾ oz) (¼ cup) grated Parmesan cheese

This is an excellent accompaniment to roast or braised white meats and poultry, or serve it on its own as a separate course.

Trim and wash the spinach. Cook in a pan of boiling salted water for 5 minutes. Drain well and press with a saucer to remove as much moisture as possible. Peel and grate the turnips and mix with the spinach. Beat the eggs with the milk and stir into the vegetable mixture. Season with salt, pepper and a pinch of nutmeg. Pour into a well-buttered gratin dish, smooth the top with a spatula and sprinkle with Parmesan cheese. Bake in a preheated oven 180°C (350°F) (Gas Mark 4) for 45–50 minutes until the mixture has set and the top is brown.

Strudel d'Épinards

SPINACH STRUDEL

Serve this as an accompaniment to roast or fried meat.

Peel the potatoes and boil for 15–20 minutes until soft. Meanwhile, trim and wash the spinach and cook in boiling salted water for 5 minutes. Drain, refresh and drain well again. Chop coarsely. Melt 25 g (1 oz) (2½ tbsp) butter in a pan, add the spinach and cook for 5 minutes, stirring occasionally until all the moisture has evaporated. Remove from the heat, season to taste with salt, pepper and nutmeg. Beat in 1 egg and the cheese. When the potatoes are cooked, drain well. Purée through a vegetable mill or in a food processor. Add the flour and the remaining egg and beat well.

Sprinkle a clean cloth lavishly with flour. Roll out the potato mixture on the cloth to 1-cm (½-in) thick. Spread the spinach over the potato mixture and roll up with the cloth. Tie the cloth with string at both ends. Place in a large pan of boiling salted water and cook for 25 minutes. Make certain the strudel is completely covered with water and that the water boils throughout the cooking time. When the strudel is cooked, melt the remaining butter and pour it into a sauce boat. Remove the strudel from the pan and take off the cloth. Cut the strudel into 1-cm (½-in) slices and place on a hot dish. Serve with the melted butter.

500 g (1 lb) floury potatoes
1 kg (2 lb) spinach
100 g (4 oz) (½ cup) butter
salt
black pepper
pinch grated nutmeg
2 eggs
50 g (2 oz) (½ cup) grated Parmesan cheese
90 g (3½ oz) (scant cup) flour

Subrics d'Épinards

SPINACH CAKES

Subrics were originally small, flat spinach cakes. It has been suggested they acquired their name because they were cooked on bricks in the oven. They were later fried in butter — Careme and Escoffier used this method, which is given in the following recipe.

Today, however, lighter preparation is preferred and subrics often are made from a spinach purée mixed with egg yolks and poached in individual moulds, in a way similar to Petits Pains d'Épinards or Subrics de Potiron. They can be served simply as they are or coated with Sauce à la Crème or Sauce Tomate.

Trim and wash the spinach well and cook in boiling salted water for 10–12 minutes. Drain and refresh under cold water and drain well again. Press the spinach with a saucer in a colander or in a cloth to remove as much moisture as possible. Chop finely. Melt the butter in a pan, add the flour and cook for 2–3 minutes. Stir in the milk, bring to the boil and cook for 2–3 minutes, stirring continuously. Beat the egg yolks and cream together and add to the sauce with the spinach. Season well to taste. Heat half the unsalted butter in a frying pan. Drop small tablespoonfuls of the mixture into the hot butter and cook over a moderate heat until set golden brown. Turn the cakes over and cook for a further 1–2 minutes. Repeat until all the mixture has been used. Add more butter as necessary, allowing it to heat thoroughly before adding any more of the mixture, but take care not to overheat the pan or the butter will burn and spoil the appearance of the *subrics*.

500 g (1 lb) spinach
25 g (1 oz) (2 tbsp) butter
25 g (1 oz) (¼ cup) flour
100 ml (3½ fl oz) (½ cup) milk
2 tbsp double (heavy) cream
2 egg yolks
salt
black pepper
75 g (3 oz) (6 tbsp) unsalted butter
300 ml (½ pt) (1¼ cups) Sauce à la Crème (page 215)/Sauce Tomate (page 218)

1 kg (2 lb) spinach
50 g (2 oz) (¼ cup) butter
salt
black pepper

Left: Bohémienne (page 16).
Right: Betteraves aux Oignons (page 18).

Épinards en Branches au Beurre

BUTTERED SPINACH

Trim and wash the spinach and cook in a pan of boiling salted water for 7–8 minutes. Drain well in a colander and press with a saucer to remove the excess water. Heat the butter in a pan and when it is foaming add the spinach. Mix lightly with a fork to separate the leaves and incorporate the butter. Season to taste with salt and plenty of black pepper.

LE FENOUIL
Fennel

Fennel is a bulbous-stemmed plant with a texture similar to celery and a distinct aniseed flavour. It is sometimes known as Florence fennel. Although related to the herb fennel, it is a different plant.

Fennel takes a surprisingly long time to cook — you will find in most recipes that it is generally parboiled before other ingredients are added. Cooked fennel dishes can also all be served as hors d'oeuvre. Allow one-half to one head per person, depending on size. Raw fennel can be sliced as part of a mixed hors d'oeuvre with a vinaigrette dressing.

Fenouil à la Provençale

Fenouil à la Provençale.

PROVENÇALE FENNEL

Trim and wash the fennel and cook in boiling salted water for 20 minutes. Drain, refresh and quarter each head. Meanwhile, peel and finely chop the onion, carrot and garlic. Heat the oil in a pan, add the onion, carrot and garlic and cook over gentle heat until soft and lightly coloured. Add the flour and cook slowly, stirring all the time, until the flour is golden brown. Do not scorch the flour or the sauce will taste bitter. Stir in the stock a little at a time and then mix in the tomato purée. Season to taste, bring to the boil and simmer gently for 15–20 minutes. Strain through a chinois or sieve. Check and adjust the seasoning. Remove the rind and cut the bacon into thin strips. Heat the butter in a heatproof casserole and fry the bacon until golden brown. Place the fennel on top of the bacon and strain/pour the sauce over. Cover and cook in a preheated oven 225° (425°F) (Gas Mark 7) for 40–45 minutes until tender. Serve in the cooking dish.

4 small heads fennel
1 large onion
1 large carrot
1–2 cloves garlic
4 tbsp olive oil
25 g (1 oz) (¼ cup) flour
600 ml (1 pt) (2½ cups) stock
2 tbsp tomato purée
1 slice smoked streaky bacon
50 g (2 oz) (¼ cup) butter
salt
black pepper

Fenouil à l'Étuve

BRAISED FENNEL

Serves 4
4 medium heads fennel
50 g (2 oz) (¼ cup) butter
1 tsp chopped chives
2 tsp chopped parsley
1 tsp chopped tarragon
salt
black pepper

This is an excellent garnish for roast pork and veal.

Trim and wash the fennel and cook in a pan of boiling salted water for 20–25 minutes. Drain, refresh and drain well again. Cut each head in half. Heat the butter in a heavy-based pan. Add the fennel and cook over gentle heat for 40–45 minutes until tender. Carefully turn each piece of fennel once or twice while cooking so it colours evenly. If necessary add 1–2 tablespoons of water or stock to prevent the fennel sticking. When the fennel is tender and lightly coloured, arrange on a hot dish, sprinkle with the herbs and season with a little salt and plenty of black pepper.

Fenouil à la Tomate

FENNEL WITH TOMATOES

4 small heads fennel
2 large onions
500 g (1 lb) fresh tomatoes/400 g (14 oz)
  can
4 tbsp oil
150 ml (¼ pt) (⅔ cup) stock
¼ tsp chopped thyme
1 small bay leaf
salt
black pepper
50 g (2 oz) (¼ cup) grated Gruyère cheese

Trim and wash the fennel and cook in boiling salted water for 15–20 minutes. Drain, refresh and cut each head in half or quarters. Peel and finely slice the onions. Peel the fresh tomatoes, quarter and remove the seeds. Chop canned tomatoes coarsely. Heat the oil in a heavy-based pan and cook the onions until soft and lightly coloured. Place the fennel in the pan with the tomatoes and add half the stock. If canned tomatoes are used add the juice from the can instead of the stock. Add the thyme and bay leaf and season to taste with salt and pepper. Cover and cook very slowly for about 50 minutes or until tender. If necessary moisten the pan with 2–3 tablespoons of stock occasionally to prevent the fennel sticking. When the fennel is tender, remove the bay leaf and arrange on a hot dish. Reduce the sauce, if necessary, to a coating consistency and pour over the fennel. Sprinkle with the grated cheese just before serving.

LES FÈVES
Broad (Lima) Beans

In France broad (lima) beans are always picked when they are very young, so they are small and tender. The skins are usually removed from the beans either before or after cooking. If you prefer you can leave them on, but it is essential to remove them from beans eaten with salt (*Fèves au Croque au Sel*) which otherwise can cause violent indigestion. Beans with brown-mottled pods will be tough. Savory has a flavour which complements broad beans and is frequently used with them.

Fèves à la Française

FRENCH-STYLE BROAD BEANS

Shell the beans and remove the skins. Wash the lettuce, roll the leaves up like a cigar and slice thinly. Peel and trim the onions. Heat the butter in a heavy-based pan and cook the onions until golden brown. Add the beans, lettuce, savory, water and sugar. Season lightly with salt and pepper. Cover and cook gently for 25–30 minutes until the beans are tender and most of the liquid has evaporated. Check the seasoning. Pour the vegetables and cooking liquor into a hot dish and sprinkle with savory just before serving.

1.5 kg (3 lb) young broad beans
½ head lettuce
175 g (6 oz) small onions
50 g (2 oz) (¼ cup) butter
1 small bunch savory
200 ml (7 fl oz) (1 cup) water
pinch sugar
salt
black pepper
1 tbsp chopped savory

Fèves à la Crème

BROAD BEANS WITH CREAM

Shell the beans and cook in boiling salted water for 5 minutes. Drain, refresh and remove the skins. Return the beans to the pan and pour on the milk. Bring to the boil, partly cover the pan and simmer gently for 15–20 minutes until the beans are tender. Beat the egg yolks and cream together. Pour on the milk from the pan. Mix well and strain back into the pan with the beans. Season to taste and heat through thoroughly, stirring continuously and taking care that the sauce does not boil. Pour into a warm — not hot — serving dish and keep in a bain-marie or roasting pan of hot water in a low oven until needed so the sauce does not curdle. Sprinkle with chopped savory just before serving.

1.5 kg (3 lb) broad beans
300 ml (½ pt) (1¼ cups) milk
2 egg yolks
5 tbsp double (heavy) cream
salt
white pepper
1 tbsp chopped savory

Ragoût de Fèves Fraîches

BROAD BEAN STEW

This dish comes from Bayonne, a town on the edge of the Pyrenees in the southwest corner of France. It uses the local salted ham. If this is not available, use gammon steak or Parma ham.

Shell the beans and cook in boiling salted water for 5 minutes. Drain, refresh and remove the skins. Peel and trim the spring onions (scallions), leaving about 4 cm (1½ in) of stalk. Cut each in half. Peel the carrots and cut in half lengthwise. Wash the lettuce, roll up the leaves like a cigar and cut into 1-cm (½-in) slices. Cut the ham into 1-cm (½-in) dice. Heat the oil in a heavy pan and add the onions, carrots, lettuce and ham. Mix well with a wooden spoon, cover and cook over gentle heat for 15 minutes. Add the broad beans and water. Mix well with the other ingredients in the pan and cover and cook for 15 minutes. Check the pan occasionally; if necessary add a little more water to prevent the vegetables and bacon from sticking. When the vegetables are tender and the liquid has evaporated, taste and season with black pepper and a little salt if needed (if the ham is salty this may not be necessary). Pile into a hot dish.

1.5 kg (3 lb) young broad beans
8 spring onions (scallions)
8 new carrots
½ cos (Romaine) lettuce
175 g (6 oz) slice Bayonne (Parma) ham
100 ml (3½ fl oz) (½ cup) water
3 tbsp olive oil
black pepper
salt

Top: Choux de Bruxelles à la Polonaise (page 42). Bottom: Brocolis à la Paysanne (page 21).

Fèves à la Tourangelle

TOURAINE-STYLE BROAD BEANS

1.5 kg (3 lb) young broad beans
150 g (5 oz) piece smoked streaky bacon
25 g (1 oz) (2 tbsp) butter
1 small bunch savory
200 ml (7 fl oz) (1 cup) dry white wine
1 tbsp lemon juice
salt
pepper
3 tbsp double (heavy) cream
1 tbsp chopped chives and savory

This recipe comes from the Loire Valley. If possible use one of the local wines, otherwise any dry white wine will do.

Shell the beans and remove the skins. Remove the rind and cut the bacon into 1-cm (½-in) dice. Heat the butter in a heavy-based pan and add the bacon. Cook the bacon until a light golden brown, then add the beans and savory. Cover and cook over gentle heat for 10–15 minutes, shaking the pan occasionally. Pour on the wine and lemon juice. Season lightly with salt and pepper. Cover and cook gently for another 45–50 minutes. Just before serving stir in the cream, heat through and pour into a hot dish. Sprinkle with chives and savory.

Fèves Printanières

Left: Gombos Sautés (page 60).
Right: Fèves Printanières.

BROAD BEANS WITH HAM AND ONIONS

This dish is delicious with young spring lamb and fresh spring beans. In France it is often served with kid.

Shell the beans and cook in boiling salted water for 5 minutes. Drain, refresh and drain again. Remove the skins. Meanwhile, peel the onions and slice the ham. Heat half the butter in a heavy-based pan, add the onions, ham and savory and cook gently for 20 minutes. Add the beans and 100 ml (3½ fl oz) (½ cup) boiling water. Season lightly with salt and pepper and add the sugar. Cover and cook gently for another 15–20 minutes until the beans and onions are tender. If necessary increase the heat during the last few minutes of cooking to reduce the liquor until it just coats the beans and onions. Just before serving, stir in the remaining butter and check the seasoning.

1.5 kg (3 lb) young broad beans
20 small onions
175 g (6 oz) ham
50 g (2 oz) (¼ cup) butter
few sprigs summer/winter savory
100 ml (3½ oz) (½ cup) water
salt
pepper
¼ tsp sugar

Fèves aux Poivrades

BROAD BEANS WITH YOUNG ARTICHOKES

1.5 kg (3 lb) young broad beans
6–8 small, young artichokes (poivrades, page 10)
1–2 tbsp lemon juice
24 large spring onions (scallions)
175 g (6 oz) ham
50 g (2 oz) (¼ cup) butter
100 ml (3½ fl oz) (½ cup) water
salt
black pepper

Shell the beans and cook in boiling salted water for 5 minutes. Drain, refresh and remove the skins. Trim the artichokes (page 10), brush with lemon juice and keep in acidulated water (page 10) until required. Peel and trim the onions, leaving about 4 cm (1½ in) of the stalk. Cut the ham into 1-cm (½-in) dice. Melt the butter in a heavy-based pan, add the onions and ham and cook for 4–5 minutes. Add the artichokes and water. Season lightly and cover. Cook over gentle heat for 30 minutes. Add the broad beans, mix well with the other ingredients and add a little more water if necessary. Cover and continue cooking for a further 20 minutes, or until the vegetables are tender and the liquid has evaporated. Taste, adjust the seasoning and pile into a hot dish.

LES GOMBOS
Okra

Okra, or ladies' fingers, is described in France as a *légume exotique*. It originally came from South America and features a great deal in the cooking of that continent, and in India. It is becoming increasingly popular in France. To prepare okra, simply remove the stalks. The pods can be left whole or cut into pieces.

Gombos Sautés

FRIED OKRA

Serve this dish with rice and curried meats. It is also excellent with grilled meats.

500 g (1 lb) okra
1 medium onion
2 tbsp oil
1 tsp powdered coriander
scant ½ tsp chilli powder
1 tsp curry powder
1 tbsp lemon juice
salt

Trim the ends from the okra and cut each into 2–3 pieces. Peel and chop the onion. Heat the oil in a frying pan or heavy-based pan with a lid. Cook the onions until lightly coloured, then add the okra and mix in the coriander and chilli powder. Season lightly with salt and cover and cook over gentle heat for 15–20 minutes until the okra is tender. Shake the pan from time to time. When the okra is cooked, add the curry powder and lemon juice. Check the seasoning and add more salt and chilli powder if necessary. Mix well and pile into a hot dish.

Gombos à la Crème

OKRA IN CREAM SAUCE

500 g (1 lb) okra
25 g (1 oz) (2 tbsp) butter
100 ml (3½ fl oz) (½ cup) white stock
300 ml (½ pt) (1¼ cups) Sauce Béchamel (page 214)
4 tbsp double (heavy) cream
pinch nutmeg
pinch cayenne pepper
salt

Trim the okra and cut each into 2–3 pieces. Cook in boiling salted water for 5 minutes. Drain and refresh. Heat the butter in a pan. Add the okra and stock and cook over gentle heat for 15–20 minutes, or until tender. Then increase the heat to evaporate any liquid left in the pan. Meanwhile, make the *Sauce Béchamel*. Stir in the cream and season with nutmeg, cayenne and salt. When the okra is cooked, place in a hot serving dish and pour the sauce over.

LES HARICOTS FRAIS
Fresh Haricot (Navy) Beans

In France it is sometimes possible to buy haricot (navy) beans already shelled. If you buy them in their shells, allow twice the amount given in the recipe. Although fresh beans do not need soaking, they still take a long time to cook. The times given in the recipes are for guidance only; the only way to be sure they are tender is to taste them. Dried beans (page 113) can be used for any of these recipes, but soak them overnight and omit the salt until they are almost cooked.

Haricots Frais à la Lyonnaise

FRESH HARICOT BEANS WITH ONIONS

Peel the onions and stick the cloves into one. Thinly slice the remaining three. Peel the carrots and slice thickly. Place the whole onion, carrots, bouquet garni and beans in a pan of boiling salted water. Simmer gently for 40–50 minutes, or until tender. Drain. Remove the onion, carrots and bouquet garni. Meanwhile, heat the butter in a pan and cook the sliced onions until golden brown. Season lightly. When the beans are cooked, mix with the onions. Pile into a hot dish and sprinkle with chopped parsley just before serving.

500 g (1 lb) shelled fresh haricot beans
4 medium onions
2 cloves
2 small carrots
bouquet garni
50 g (2 oz) (¼ cup) butter
1 tbsp chopped parsley

Haricots Frais à la Poitevinne

POITOU-STYLE HARICOT BEANS

Poitou is the region around Poitiers. It extends roughly from the Loire to a few miles south of Niort, and from the River Creuse in the east to the Atlantic in the west. It is a beautiful agricultural region of gently rolling hills running down to the salt marches (now mostly drained) on the coast. The land is very fertile and is famous for its cabbages from the Vendée and cauliflowers from Niorte, as well as onions, peas, artichokes and white haricot beans (called mojettes in some regions), which are all grown in great profusion. The cooking from this part of France is comparatively simple and makes full use of local ingredients. In this recipe the other vegetables are cooked first, which gives the beans an excellent flavour.

Peel the carrots and onion. Cut the carrots in half and stick the clove into the onion. Trim the celery and leek and wash well. Discard the green part of the leek (save for soup) and cut the celery and leek into large pieces. Peel and chop the garlic. Place the prepared vegetables in a large pan with the bouquet garni and 2 litres (4 pints) (2 quarts) salted water. Cook for 20–25 minutes then add the beans and cover and cook for 40–50 minutes until the beans are tender. If necessary add more water to keep the beans completely covered throughout the cooking time. When the beans are cooked, drain well (if you wish, reserve the cooking liquid for soup). Remove the other vegetables and bouquet garni. Melt the butter in a pan and add the flour. Cook for 1–2 minutes, then stir in the cream a little at a time. Bring to the boil, stirring all the time. Add the beans, mix well, bring to the boil and simmer for 2–3 minutes, stirring occasionally. Season to taste with salt and pepper. Pour into a hot dish and, just before serving, sprinkle with the herbs.

500 g (1 lb) shelled fresh haricot beans
2 medium carrots
1 medium onion
1 clove
2 sticks celery
1 medium leek
2 cloves garlic
1 bouquet garni
2 litres (4 pt) (2 quarts) water
40 g (1½ oz) (3 tbsp) butter
1 tbsp flour
150 ml (¼ pt) (⅔ cup) single (light) cream
salt
white pepper
1 tbsp chopped mixed herbs

Left: Céléri à l'Orange et aux Noix (page 27). Right: Céléri-Rave en Croquette (page 28).

500 g (1 lb) shelled fresh haricot beans
3 medium onions
2 cloves
2 cloves garlic
500 g (1 lb) tomatoes
1 large carrot
3 tbsp oil
bouquet garni
1 sprig basil
Pistou:
    3 cloves garlic
    6–8 leaves basil
    75 ml (2½ fl oz) (⅓ cup) olive oil

Haricots Frais au Pistou

FRESH HARICOT BEANS WITH GARLIC AND BASIL

Peel the onions. Slice two and stick the cloves into the third. Peel and crush the garlic. Peel and seed the tomatoes and chop finely. Peel and slice the carrot. Heat the oil in a heavy-based pan and cook the sliced onions until light golden brown. Add the beans and cover and cook for 5–6 minutes. Pour in sufficient water to just cover the beans. Add the onion with cloves, tomatoes, garlic, carrot, bouquet garni and basil. Cover and cook over a gentle heat for 1¼–1½ hours until tender.

To prepare the *pistou*, peel the garlic and roughly chop the basil. Pound together with a mortar and pestle, adding the oil a little at a time. Alternatively, use the end of a rolling pin in a basin, or put the garlic and basil into a liquidizer, switch on to full speed for a moment or two and then slowly add the oil.

When the beans are tender, remove the onion with cloves and bouquet garni. If necessary raise the heat to reduce the sauce until it just coats the beans. Pour into a hot dish. Just before serving, stir in the *pistou*.

Top: Carottes Nouvelles Panachées (page 23). Bottom: Carottes à l'Oriental (page 25).

Haricots Frais à la Tomate

FRESH HARICOT BEANS WITH TOMATOES

Peel and quarter the onions. Place in a pan of boiling salted water with the beans, cloves and bouquet garni. Simmer for 40–50 minutes until tender, then remove the cloves and bouquet garni. Meanwhile, peel and seed the tomatoes and chop coarsely. Heat the oil in a pan and gently cook the tomatoes for 10 minutes. Season lightly. When the beans are cooked add to the sauce and cook for 10 minutes. Taste and adjust the seasoning. Just before serving add the cream, heat through and check the seasoning again. Pile into a hot dish and sprinkle with a little paprika.

500 g (1 lb) shelled white haricot beans
2 medium onions
2 cloves
bouquet garni
500 g (1 lb) tomatoes
3 tbsp oil
salt
black pepper
100 ml (3½ fl oz) (½ cup) double
* (heavy) cream*
a little paprika

LES HARICOTS ROUGES
Red (Kidney) Beans

Like white haricots, red (kidney) beans can sometimes be bought already shelled. Some varieties are mottled red and white. If you buy them in their shells, allow at least twice the quantity given in the recipes. Dried red beans can be used in place of fresh ones but first *must* be soaked for 18 hours and then boiled for 15 minutes (see page 113).

Haricots Rouges Frais aux Fines Herbes

FRESH RED BEANS WITH MIXED HERBS

See also Haricots Rouges Sec.

500 g (1 lb) shelled red beans
1 clove garlic
50 g (2 oz) (¼ cup) butter
2 tbsp chopped mixed fresh herbs (parsley, chervil, savory, etc.)

Cook the beans in boiling salted water for 50–60 minutes until tender. Drain well. Peel and crush the garlic. Melt the butter in a pan, add the garlic and cook for a moment or two, then add the beans and half the herbs. Mix well. Check the seasoning and pile into a hot dish. Sprinkle with the remaining herbs just before serving.

Haricots Rouges Frais à la Bourguignonne

BURGUNDY-STYLE RED BEANS

500 g (1 lb) shelled fresh red beans
3 medium onions
2 small carrots
bouquet garni
50 g (2 oz) (¼ cup) butter
25 g (1 oz) (¼ cup) flour
200 ml (7 fl oz) (1 cup) red wine
250 g (8 oz) piece lean smoked bacon
salt
blck pepper
1 tbsp chopped parsley

Peel the onions and carrots. Chop 2 onions and leave 1 whole. Place the beans in a pan of water with the whole onion, carrots, bacon and bouquet garni. Bring to the boil, cover and cook for 50–60 minutes until the beans are tender. Drain and keep the cooking liquor. Discard the bouquet garni. Heat the butter in another pan, cook the chopped onion until golden brown, then add the flour and mix well. Pour in the wine and 150 ml (¼ pint) (⅔ cup) cooking liquor. Bring to the boil, stirring continuously. Remove the rind and dice the bacon. Add the bacon and all the vegetables. Season to taste and boil for 10 minutes. Stir occasionally and, if necessary, add a little more of the cooking liquor. Taste again, adjust the seasoning and pour into a hot dish. Sprinkle with chopped parsley just before serving.

LES HARICOTS VERTS
French (Snap) Beans

Very small, thin, dark-green beans are called *mange-touts*, as well as the peas by the same name. Other varieties are larger and paler. Choose small, green beans which are crisp and snap when broken. Avoid any which show the shape of the bean inside. *Mange-touts* only need to be topped and tailed. Larger ones may need the strings on each side removed. If you wish, you can break or cut them into 2–3 pieces. Cook French beans until they are only just tender; they are nicer with a hint of crispness.

Haricots Verts à l'Ail

FRENCH BEANS WITH GARLIC

This is a very simple but extremely delicious way to prepare French beans. For best results, heat the butter just before serving so it is still sizzling when it reaches the table.

Trim the beans and break into 2 or 3 pieces. Cook in boiling salted water for 10–15 minutes until tender. Drain well and keep hot. Meanwhile, peel the garlic and crush with a little salt. Just before serving, heat the butter until it foams, add the garlic and beans and season to taste with salt and plenty of black pepper. Mix well and pile into a hot dish. Sprinkle with chopped parsley.

500 g (1 lb) French beans
2–3 cloves garlic
50 g (2 oz) (¼ cup) butter
salt
black pepper
1 tbsp chopped parsley

Haricots en Allumettes

DEEP-FRIED FRENCH BEANS

In 1739 François Marin wrote 'Le Dons de Comus, ou les delices de la table' ('The Gifts of Comus, or The Delights of the Table'), which contained not only his own recipes but plenty of practical information as well. Subsequently it was enlarged to three volumes and became an extremely popular cooking encyclopedia. It is now regarded as one of the finest cookery books of that era.

This is Marin's recipe for deep-fried French beans. The beans are cooked in stock with onion and bacon to give them extra flavour, but they are still quite delicious if boiled in the normal way. Serve with roast meats, poultry and game.

Make the *Pâte à Frire* and allow to stand for 30 minutes. Trim the beans, peel the onion and stick the cloves into it. Place the onion and bacon fat/rind in a pan with the stock. Bring to the boil, add the beans and season. Cook the beans for 6–8 minutes until almost tender. Drain well and spread the beans on kitchen paper towel until completely dry. Heat a pan of oil to 190°C (380°F) or until a square of bread browns in 20 seconds. Dip each bean in the batter and carefully drop into the oil. Cook the beans a few at a time for 4–5 minutes until crisp and golden brown. If necessary turn the beans while they are cooking so they colour evenly. Remove from the pan and drain well on kitchen paper towel.

350 g (12 oz) small, young, thin beans
Pâte à Frire (page 220)
1 medium onion
2 cloves
1 slice bacon fat/rind
600 ml (1 pt) (2½ cups) white stock
oil/fat for deep-frying

Haricots Mange-Touts aux Champignons

FRENCH BEANS WITH MUSHROOMS

Haricots mange-touts are the very small, thin beans known as bobby beans in Great Britain. They just need topping and tailing. Serve this dish hot, or cold as an hors d'oeuvre.

Trim the beans and cook in boiling salted water for 12–15 minutes until tender. Meanwhile, peel the onions and chop finely. Trim and clean the mushrooms and slice finely. Heat the butter in a pan and cook the onion until soft and lightly coloured. Add the mushrooms and continue to cook for 7–8 minutes. Season to taste. Drain the beans, add to the pan and stir in the cream. Bring to the boil and cook for a moment or two. Check the seasoning. Pour into a dish and sprinkle with a little paprika.

500 g (1 lb) small, thin French beans
2 medium onions
250 g (8 oz) white button mushrooms
50 g (2 oz) (¼ cup) butter
100 ml (3½ fl oz) (½ cup) double (heavy) cream
salt
black pepper
a little paprika

*Left: Haricots Verts à l'Ail et Crème
(page 67). Right: Gratin de
Haricots Verts.*

Gratin de Haricots Verts

FRENCH BEANS WITH CRISPY TOPPING

This is excellent with roast meats, particularly pork.

500 g (1 lb) French beans
100 ml (3½ fl oz) (½ cup) double (heavy)
   cream
salt
black pepper
250 g (8 oz) mushrooms
50 g (2 oz) (¼ cup) butter
3 tbsp white breadcrumbs

Trim the beans and cut into 2 or 3 pieces, or leave whole. Cook in boiling salted water for 5–8 minutes until almost tender. Drain and refresh. Return to the pan with the cream and season lightly with salt and pepper. Simmer over gentle heat for another 5–6 minutes, stirring occasionally. Meanwhile, trim and chop the mushrooms. Heat half the butter in a pan and add the mushrooms. Cook for 4–5 minutes. Season to taste. Stir in the breadcrumbs. Pour the beans into a buttered heatproof dish. Cover with the mushroom and breadcrumb mixture. Melt the remaining butter and pour over the top. Place in a preheated oven 200°C (400°F) (Gas Mark 6) for 10–15 minutes until golden brown.

Haricots Verts à l'Ail et Crème

FRENCH BEANS IN GARLIC AND CREAM SAUCE

Left: Courge à la Provençale (page 45).
Right: Concombre Glacé (page 44).

The flavour of garlic goes so well with French beans that I have included another recipe with plenty of garlic, particularly because it is a great favourite of mine. Broad (lima) beans can be prepared in the same way.

Trim the beans and break into pieces. Cook in boiling salted water for 10–12 minutes until almost tender. Drain and refresh. Peel and crush the garlic with a little salt. Meanwhile, melt the butter in a pan, add the flour and cook for 1–2 minutes. Add the milk and cream, stirring all the time, and bring to the boil. Season lightly and add the garlic. Add the beans to the sauce and cook for a further 4–5 minutes. Pour into a hot dish and sprinkle with chopped chervil just before serving.

500 g (1 lb) French beans
2–3 cloves garlic
25 g (1 oz) (2 tbsp) butter
25 g (1 oz) (¼ cup) flour
150 ml (¼ pt) (⅔ cup) milk
150 ml (¼ pt) (⅔ cup) single (light) cream
salt
black pepper
1 tbsp chopped chervil

Haricots Verts à la Landaise

FRENCH BEANS WITH TOMATOES AND GARLIC

Landes is a département in Gascony in the southwest corner of France. Because it is near Spain, the cooking from this region often has a Basque flavour, using tomatoes and lots of garlic. Choose very fresh beans; it is essential that they are young and stringless.

500 g (1 lb) French beans
500 g (1 lb) ripe tomatoes
1 large onion
3–4 cloves garlic
4 tbsp olive oil
100 g (4 oz) smoked, streaky bacon
bouquet garni
150 ml (¼ pt) (⅔ cup) water
salt
black pepper

Trim the beans and cut/break into 2 or 3 pieces. Cook in boiling salted water for 5 minutes then drain well. Peel and seed the tomatoes and chop the flesh coarsely. Peel the onion and garlic. Chop the onion finely and crush the garlic with a little salt. Remove the rind and cut the bacon into small dice. Heat the oil in a heavy-based pan. Cook the bacon until it begins to colour, then add the onion and cook until both are golden brown. Add the tomatoes, garlic, bouquet garni, beans and water. Season lightly with salt and pepper. Cover with a piece of greaseproof paper and lid and cook over gentle heat for 45–50 minutes, or until the beans are tender. When the beans are cooked, remove the bouquet garni, check the seasoning and pour into a hot dish.

Haricots Verts à l'Angevine

ANGERS-STYLE FRENCH BEANS

This is a recipe from Angers, the capital town of the Maine and Loire départements in the Loire Valley. Like the rest of the Loire, it has a great reputation for good food.

500 g (1 lb) French beans
8 small new carrots
8 small onions
100 g (4 oz) streaky bacon
65 g (2½ oz) (⅓ cup) butter
1 tbsp icing (confectioner's) sugar
150 ml (¼ pt) (⅔ cup) water
3 tbsp double (heavy) cream
salt
black pepper
1 tbsp chopped chervil and parsley

Trim the beans and cut/break into 2–3 pieces. Cook in a pan of boiling salted water for 10–12 minutes. Peel/scrape the carrots. Quarter each lengthways. Peel the onions. Remove the rind and cut the bacon into strips. Heat 40 g (1½ oz) (3 tbsp) butter in a pan. Cook the bacon until golden brown, then remove from the pan. Add the carrots and onions together with the sugar and water. Season lightly. Cook over gentle heat until the vegetables are almost tender. If necessary, raise the heat so the liquid evaporates and the carrots and onions caramelize to a golden brown. Heat the remaining butter in another pan. Add the beans and mix until coated with butter. Add the carrots and onions together with any caramelized butter or liquid in the pan. Pour on the cream, bring to the boil and cook for 2–3 minutes. Taste and adjust the seasoning. Pour into a hot serving dish and sprinkle with chopped herbs just before serving.

Haricots Verts à la Jardinière

GARDENER'S-STYLE FRENCH BEANS

Jardinière is a term usually applied to a selection of vegetables used to garnish a dish. I ate French beans cooked in the same way as this recipe in a small hotel in a village on the edge of the Ardennes Forest. I enjoyed it so much, I asked what it was called. I have tried to reproduce it here just as I ate it.

Trim the French beans and cut/break into 2 or 3 pieces. Trim the celery, peel the turnips and cut both into 1-cm (½-in) dice. Peel and quarter the tomatoes and remove the seeds. Cook the vegetables separately in boiling salted water. If you wish, season them lightly and wrap each one in aluminium foil. Cook in one pan and remove the turnips after 12–15 minutes. The peas and beans will take an additional 4–5 minutes and the celery another 10–12 minutes. The vegetables need to be only partly cooked. Melt the butter in a pan and when the vegetables are cooked toss in the butter and adjust the seasoning. Place in a casserole with the tomatoes and cover and cook in a preheated oven 190°C (375°F) (Gas Mark 5) for 20–30 minutes until tender.

250 g (8 oz) French beans
100 g (4 oz) celery
175 g (6 oz) turnips
3 large, ripe tomatoes
100 g (4 oz) shelled peas
40 g (1½ oz) (3½ tbsp) butter
salt
black pepper

Haricots Verts `a la Portugaise

FRENCH BEANS IN PORTUGAISE SAUCE

Sauce Portugaise is a classic made with tomatoes, onions and garlic. Poulet à la Portugaise is a popular dish in France, and in this recipe the beans are cooked in a similar way.

Trim the beans and cook in boiling salted water for 7–8 minutes. Drain and refresh. To make the *Sauce Portugaise*, peel and finely chop the onion and garlic. Peel, seed and chop the tomatoes. Heat the oil in a heatproof casserole. Add the onion and garlic and cook until soft and golden brown. Stir in the tomatoes and stock. Bring to the boil. When the beans are cooked, mix them into the sauce. Add the bouquet garni and season to taste. Cover with greaseproof paper and a lid and place in a preheated oven 200°C (400°F) (Gas Mark 6) for 30–40 minutes until the beans are tender. When the beans are cooked, remove the bouquet garni and check the seasoning. If necessary, boil the sauce to reduce it to a coating consistency. Serve in the cooking dish or pour into a clean, hot dish. Sprinkle with chopped parsley just before serving.

500 g (1 lb) French beans
1 medium onion
1 clove garlic
250 g (8 oz) tomatoes
2 tbsp oil
200 ml (7 fl oz) (1 cup) white stock
bouquet garni
1 tbsp chopped parsley

LES JETS DES HOUBLONS
Hop Shoots

In the hop-growing parts of France, hop shoots are often eaten as a vegetable. Only the very young shoots are used.

*Top: Girolles au Lard (page 33).
Bottom: Cèpes à la Pergourdine
(page 32).*

Jets des Houblons en Sauce

HOP SHOOTS IN SAUCE

Wash the hop shoots well and trim the ends of the stalks. Cook in boiling acidulated water (page 10) for 10–15 minutes or until tender. Drain well and coat with *Sauce Hollandaise* (page 216) or *Sauce à la Crème* (page 215).

LES LAITUES
Lettuce

*Opposite, top: Chou Rouge à l'Alsacienne
(page 38). Bottom: Chou Braisé aux
Fruits Secs (page 40).*

Lettuce is another salad vegetable that is often cooked in France. I find these recipes invaluable when there is a glut of summer lettuce in the garden. Although round lettuce is given in the recipes, small cos (Romaine) can be used as well.

Laitues au Roquefort

LETTUCE WITH ROQUEFORT CHEESE

Remove any damaged outer leaves but leave the lettuces whole. Wash carefully. Cook in a pan of boiling salted water for 15–20 minutes until tender. Drain well and press with the hands or a cloth to extract as much water as possible. Cut the lettuces in half. Form each piece into a neat shape and place on a hot dish. Cover and keep hot. Heat the butter in a pan, break the cheese into small pieces and whisk into the butter. Season to taste with plenty of pepper and pour over the lettuce.

6 small lettuces
75 g (3 oz) (6 tbsp) unsalted butter
25 g (1 oz) Roquefort/other blue cheese
salt
black pepper

Laitues Braisées

BRAISED LETTUCE

2 large/4 small round, firm lettuces
2 carrots
1 large onion
75 g (3 oz) streaky bacon/bacon trimmings
25 g (1 oz) (2 tbsp) butter
bouquet garni
600 ml (1 pt) (2½ cups) white stock
salt
pepper
1–2 tsp arrowroot

Remove the coarse, outer leaves and wash the lettuces carefully. Place in a pan of boiling, salted water and cook for 5 minutes. Drain and refresh in cold water. Cut the large lettuces into quarters or the smaller ones in half. Meanwhile, peel and slice the carrots and onion and cut the bacon into thin strips. Melt the butter in a heatproof casserole and cook the bacon until golden brown. Remove from the pan and add the carrots and onions. Cook slowly until lightly coloured. Return the bacon to the pan and arrange the pieces of lettuce on top. Pour on the stock and add the bouquet garni. Season lightly and bring to the boil. Cover with greaseproof paper and a lid and cook in a preheated oven 190°C (375°F) (Gas Mark 5) for 30–40 minutes. Remove the lettuce with a slotted spoon. Allow each piece to drain well. *Arrange on a hot dish, cover with greaseproof paper and keep hot in a low oven. Boil the stock and allow it to reduce by one-third. Mix the arrowroot with a little water, add to the stock and bring to the boil again, stirring continuously. Check and adjust the seasoning and strain over the lettuce.

Chevalière de Laitues

LETTUCE WITH HAM

ingredients as above
300 ml (½ pt) (1¾ cups)
    Sauce Demi-glace

Prepare and cook the lettuce as for Laitues Braisées as far as the asterisk. Make the sauce. Cut each slice of ham in half. Heat the remaining butter in a frying pan and cook the ham on both sides. Place the ham and lettuce in a circle on a hot serving dish. Coat with the sauce.

Laitues à l'Italienne

ITALIAN-STYLE LETTUCE

2 large/4 small round lettuces
750 ml (1¼ pt) (3 cups) white stock
1 large onion
150 g (6 oz) white button mushrooms
2 tbsp olive oil
1 scant tbsp flour
150 ml (¼ pt) (⅔ cup) white wine
1 tbsp tomato purée
bouquet garni
salt
black pepper
50 g (2 oz) (½ cup) grated Parmesan
    cheese

Remove the coarse outer leaves from the lettuces. Wash carefully, then cook in a pan of boiling water for 5 minutes. Drain and refresh under cold water. Cut large lettuces into quarters and small ones in half, taking care that all the leaves are left joined to the centre stalk. Fold the edges of the leaves under to form a neat shape. If necessary, tie with thin string. Place in a pan and pour on 600 ml (1 pint) (2½ cups) stock. Bring to the boil, cover with a piece of buttered, greaseproof paper and a lid and simmer gently for 20–25 minutes until tender.

Meanwhile, peel and chop the onion. Trim and clean the mushrooms and slice finely. Heat 1 tsp oil in a pan and cook the mushrooms until golden brown. Remove from the pan and add the onion and a little more oil. Cook gently until soft and golden brown. Stir in the flour and mix well, add the remaining stock and white wine, tomato purée and bouquet garni. Season lightly with salt and pepper and bring to the boil, stirring all the time. Lower the heat and simmer for 20 minutes.

When the lettuce is cooked, drain well. Spread the mushrooms in the base of a buttered, heatproof dish and arrange the lettuce on top, having first removed any string. Remove the bouquet garni from the sauce, taste and adjust the seasoning and pour over the lettuce. Sprinkle the Parmesan cheese over and then the remaining oil. Place in a preheated oven 190°C (375°F) (Gas Mark 5) for 15–20 minutes until golden brown.

LES MAÏS
Sweetcorn (Corn)

Maize is grown extensively for animal and chicken feed and now sweetcorn (corn) is becoming increasingly popular as a vegetable. It is at its best when freshly picked. Look for bright green leaves and dark-brown, silky heads — if they are too light the corn will not be fully developed. Turn back the sheath of leaves to check that the corn is full of milk.

To prepare sweetcorn, peel off the leaves and the silky tassel and trim back the stalk. If the tip of the corn is not developed, cut it off. Cook quickly in boiling unsalted water for 10–12 minutes. Add salt and cook for another 1–2 minutes.

Sweetcorn can be eaten as a separate vegetable dish or served as a garnish for veal or turkey escallopes (scallopini). It can also be served as an hors d'oeuvre. None of the French recipes I read advised using holders or cocktail sticks but, of course, sweetcorn is much easier to eat this way.

Épis de Maïs Bouilli

BOILED SWEETCORN

Trim the sweetcorn and cook in unsalted boiling water for 10–15 minutes until tender. Take care not to overcook or the grains will harden. Meanwhile, melt the butter. Drain the sweetcorn well and place in a hot dish, season with salt and black pepper and serve the melted butter in a sauceboat.

4–6 cobs sweetcorn
100 g (4 oz) (½ cup) butter
salt
black pepper

Épis de Maïs à l'Estragon

SWEETCORN WITH TARRAGON

Try this with grilled steaks and chops. The flavour of the tarragon goes as well with the meat as it does with the sweetcorn.

Prepare and cook the sweetcorn but instead of melting butter, to serve with them, cream the butter with 1 tablespoon chopped tarragon and some black pepper. Just before serving place a knob of butter on each cob and let your guests help themselves to more as desired.

4–6 cobs sweetcorn
100 g (4 oz) (½ cup) butter
salt
black pepper
1 tbsp tarragon

Épis de Maïs Grillé.

Épis de Maïs Grillé

GRILLED SWEETCORN

4–6 cobs sweetcorn
100 g (4 oz) (½ cup) butter
salt
black pepper
tarragon (optional)

Prepare the sweetcorn and cook in unsalted boiling water for 5 minutes. Drain, brush with butter and cook under a moderately hot grill for 15–20 minutes until golden brown. Keep the tray in its lowest position so the cobs cook and brown slowly. Turn the cobs occasionally so they colour evenly. Brush with butter as necessary. Serve with melted or tarragon butter.

Sweetcorn can also be grilled on a barbecue. Prepare as above and grill over a hot fire for 7–10 minutes. Turn and brush with butter occasionally.

LES MARRONS
Chestnuts

Left: *Châtaignes au Lard* (page 76).
Right: *Laitues à l'Italienne* (page 72).

Although chestnuts are not strictly a vegetable, they are used as such in many parts of France and so I thought it appropriate to include them.

Canned chestnuts can be used, but I prefer the flavour and texture of fresh ones. To prepare them for cooking, make a slit in the shell of each and place in a pan of cold water. Bring to the boil and simmer for 4–5 minutes. Drain and cool under cold water. Remove the shell and furry skin with the point of a sharp knife. (Allow plenty of time for this — it is not a job to be done when you are in a hurry.) Simmer the chestnuts in boiling salted water, or milk, until tender, and continue with the recipe.

Marrons Braisés

BRAISED CHESTNUTS

Braised chestnuts are especially good with game or poultry.

1 kg (2 lb) chestnuts
2 sticks celery
1 tsp sugar
50 g (2 oz) (¼ cup) butter
salt
black pepper

Prepare, blanch and skin the chestnuts (page 75). Wash and trim the celery and cut the stalks in half. Place the chestnuts in a heavy-based pan with the celery, sugar and butter. Pour on sufficient water to just cover them and season lightly with salt and pepper. Bring to the boil and simmer for 30–35 minutes until the chestnuts are tender. If necessary raise the heat for the last few minutes so the water evaporates completely and the chestnuts are coated with butter. Check the seasoning, remove the celery and pile the chestnuts into a hot dish.

Châtaignes au Lard

CHESTNUTS WITH BACON

Châtaigne is the name of the chestnut tree and marrons are the nuts. In many country recipes for chestnuts they are called châtaignes. This recipe is from the Nivernaise, the region covering the upper Loire and Morvan Forest.

1 kg (2 lb) chestnuts
175 g (6 oz) lean bacon
25 g (1 oz) (2 tbsp) butter
bouquet garni
600 ml (1 pt) (2½ cups) white stock
salt
pepper
pinch nutmeg
1 tsp sugar

Prepare, blanch and skin the chestnuts (page 75). Remove the rind and cut the bacon into strips. Heat the butter in a pan and cook the bacon until golden brown. Add the chestnuts and bouquet garni. Pour on the stock and season lightly with salt and pepper and a pinch of nutmeg. Bring to the boil, cover and simmer for about 30 minutes or until the chestnuts are tender and most of the liquid has evaporated. Remove the bouquet garni and check the seasoning. Sprinkle the sugar over the chestnuts and pour into a hot dish with any liquid left in the pan.

Purée de Marrons

CHESTNUT PURÉE

Serve this dish with pork, poultry and game.

1 kg (2 lb) chestnuts
600 ml (1 pt) (2½ cups) milk
75 ml (2½ fl oz) (⅓ cup) double (heavy) cream
40 g (1½ oz) (3 tbsp) butter
salt
pepper

Prepare, blanch and skin the chestnuts (page 75). Place them in a heavy-based pan with the milk. Cover and cook over gentle heat for 40–50 minutes. Check that the chestnuts are soft enough to crush easily and if necessary continue cooking for a little longer. Drain and keep the milk. Purée the chestnuts in a vegetable mill or food processor and add 2 tablespoons of the milk in which they were cooked. Return to the pan and beat in the cream and butter. Season to taste. Heat through, adding more milk if necessary to obtain a soft but firm purée. Check the seasoning and pile onto a hot dish.

Variation: Peel a small head of celeriac and cut into large pieces. Cook and purée with the chestnuts.

Croquettes de Marrons

CHESTNUT CROQUETTES

Prepare the chestnut purée as for *Purée de Marrons* but keep it very firm. Place the mixture on a floured board and form into small sausage shapes of about 3 × 2 cm (1½ in × ¾ in). Coat with egg and breadcrumbs as in *Croquettes de Panais* and fry in deep fat heated to 180°C (390°F) for 3–4 minutes until golden brown. Drain well on kitchen paper towel.

1 kg (2 lb) chestnuts
600 ml (1 pt) (2½ cups) milk
75 ml (2½ fl oz) (⅓ cup) double (heavy) cream
40 g (1½ oz) (3 tbsp) butter
salt
pepper

LES NAVETS
Turnips

As well as round turnips, in France a long, tapering variety of turnip is very popular. Small, young ones are best. Make certain they are firm as they tend to go spongy with age. Always peel turnips thickly because the layer under the skin can be bitter.

Navets à la Crème

TURNIPS IN CREAM SAUCE

Turnips cooked in this way are very good with grilled or fried veal cutlets, or fried escallopes (scallopini).

Peel the turnips and slice thickly. Place in a pan of cold salted water, bring to the boil and cook for 15–20 minutes until almost tender. Meanwhile, make the sauce. When the turnips are cooked, drain and add to the sauce. Continue cooking for 7–10 minutes until the turnips are quite tender. Season to taste. Pour into a hot dish.

750 g (1½ lb) turnips
300 ml (½ pint) (1¼ cups) Sauce à la Crème (page 215)
salt
white pepper

Navets aux Fines Herbes

TURNIPS WITH MIXED HERBS

This recipe for turnips comes from the Loire Valley.

Peel the turnips and cut into 1-cm (½-in) slices. Place in a heavy-based pan and just cover with water. Season lightly with salt and add 15 g (½ oz) (1 tbsp) butter and a pinch of sugar. Cook over moderate heat for 10–15 minutes until the turnips are almost tender and all the water has evaporated. Heat the butter in a frying pan and when it begins to froth add the turnips. Cook until golden brown, turning frequently. Sprinkle in the mixed herbs and season to taste. Mix well and pile into a hot serving dish.

500 g (1 lb) turnips
65 g (2½ oz) (⅓ cup) butter
1 pinch sugar
1 tbsp mixed chopped herbs (tarragon, parsley, chives, etc.)
salt
black pepper

Top: Ratatouille de Navets (page 79).
Bottom: Navets a l'Ail.

Navets à l'Ail

TURNIPS WITH GARLIC

Serve this as a separate vegetable dish or with roast meats, especially beef.

750 g (1½ lb) turnips
pinch sugar
1 sprig rosemary
2 cloves garlic
50 g (2 oz) (¼ cup) butter
75 g (3 oz) (1½ cups) breadcrumbs
2 tbsp double (heavy) cream

Peel the turnips and cut into 1-cm (½-in) dice. Cook in boiling salted water with a pinch of sugar and rosemary for 10–15 minutes, or until tender. Meanwhile, peel and crush the garlic. Heat the butter in a frying pan and cook the garlic for a moment or two. Add the breadcrumbs and cook, turning continuously with a spatula, until golden brown. Keep hot. When the turnips are tender, drain well and remove the rosemary. Return to the pan and add the cream. Mix well and heat through. Season to taste. Place in a hot serving dish and sprinkle with the breadcrumbs.

Ratatouille de Navets

Pain de Chicorée (page 35).

TURNIP STEW

This is a recipe from the Dauphine and Savoy regions of France.

Peel the turnips and onions and slice thinly. Skin, seed and chop the tomatoes and chop coarsely. Peel and crush the garlic. Heat the oil in a heavy-based pan and cook the onions until soft and lightly coloured. Add the turnips and mix well. Stir in the tomatoes and garlic and season with salt and black pepper. Cover with a piece of greaseproof paper and lid and cook over gentle heat for 20–25 minutes or until tender. If fresh tomatoes are used it may be necessary to add 1–2 tablespoons of water while cooking to prevent the mixture sticking. If canned tomatoes are used, remove the lid and paper for the last few minutes so most of the moisture can evaporate. When the turnips are cooked, taste and adjust the seasoning. Pour into a hot dish and sprinkle with cheese just before serving.

500 g (1 lb) small turnips
250 g (8 oz) onions
500 g (1 lb) tomatoes/400 g (14 oz) can
2–3 cloves garlic
3–4 tbsp olive oil
salt
black pepper
2 tbsp grated Gruyère cheese

Navets Glacés

GLAZED TURNIPS

1 kg (2 lbs) small, young turnips
40 g (1½ oz) (3 tbsp) butter
150 ml (¼ pt) (⅔ cup) white stock
1 tbsp icing (confectioner's) sugar
salt
pepper

Peel the turnips and cut in half. Place in a pan of cold salted water, bring to the boil and cook for 15 minutes. Drain well. Melt the butter in a heavy-based pan, add the stock, sugar and turnips. Cover and cook for 10–15 minutes until the turnips are tender and the liquid has evaporated. If necessary remove the lid for the last few minutes so the liquid evaporates. Shake the pan to completely coat the turnips in butter. Taste and adjust the seasoning and pile into a hot dish.

LES OIGNONS
Onions

What a cook would do without onions I find hard to imagine, they are such an important ingredient of so many dishes. There are so many to choose from: spring onions (scallions) for salads and sometimes for cooking, small onions for garnishing, to large Spanish ones with a mild flavour. They come in all sizes and colours from white to deep golden- and reddish-brown. Any stall in a French market will display a wide variety. Regardless of type, buy firm onions with bright, dry skins. Wet or soft ones will soon rot, as will any that are sprouting.

One of the best-known French classic sauces is *Sauce Soubise*, named after the eighteenth-century Prince of Soubise, who was very fond of onions. Beauvilliers, who invented this sauce, was chef to the Count of Provence and presumably cooked for the Prince at some time as well. He later opened a restaurant in Paris and eventually included this sauce in a book published in 1814.

To avoid tears when peeling onions (it is a substance in the juice which is volatile and irritates the eyes), try to avoid cutting into the onions as you remove the skin and leave as much stalk and root as possible. Chop or slice them just before you use them. If you have many small onions to peel, put them in a bowl and pour boiling water over them. Leave for a few minutes and the skins will come off easily.

Shallots are frequently called for in French recipes. They are similar to small onions, but grow in clumps and are usually longer in shape. Some have dark-red skins. All have a purplish, veined flesh and a sweeter, milder flavour than onions.

Oignons Marinés

MARINATED ONIONS

500 g (1 lb) large onions
2 small lemons
3 tbsp olive oil
4 tbsp wine vinegar
salt
black pepper
1 small bay leaf

This dish requires 24 hours for marinating. Serve it chilled with cold meats.

Peel the onions, cut into slices and separate the rings. Slice the lemons thinly and mix with the onion rings. Beat the oil and vinegar and season with salt and plenty of black pepper. Place the onions and lemons in a bowl, pour the oil and vinegar over and tuck the bay leaf into the centre of the mixture. Cover and leave for 24 hours or longer. Stir lightly with a fork from time to time.

Beignets d'Oignons

ONION FRITTERS

Onions fried in this way can be served as an accompaniment or as an hors d'oeuvre, garnished with lemon wedges.

Make the *Pâte à Frire* and let stand. Peel the onions, cut into thin rings and separate the layers. Heat a pan of fat to 180°C (390°F) or until a square of bread browns in 20 seconds. Coat the onion rings with the batter and fry a few at a time for 4–5 minutes until crisp and golden brown. Drain on kitchen paper towel and keep hot until all the onions are cooked. Pile into a hot dish and, just before serving, season with salt and black pepper. Garnish with lemon wedges if desired.

Pâte à Frire (page 220)
4 large onions
oil/fat for deep frying
salt
black pepper
1–2 lemons (optional)

Ragoût d'Oignons

STEWED ONIONS

In France, where wine is so inexpensive, it is reasonable to use the given amount of wine for cooking onions, but you may prefer to be more economic. I find cider — a dry one, of course — is satisfactory, or you might use half the amount of wine or cider and make up the rest with stock.

Peel the onions (page 80), leaving as much as the stalk ends as possible to prevent the insides bursting out while cooking. Peel and quarter the tomatoes. Heat the oil in a heavy-based pan and cook the onions until they start to colour. Add the tomatoes, white wine, parsley, bay leaves, thyme and coriander seeds. Season with salt and pepper. Cover and cook over gentle heat for 40–50 minutes until the onions are tender. Shake or stir the pan occasionally. Remove the bay leaves and thyme, check the seasoning and pour into a hot dish.

1 kg (2 lb) small onins
3 tomatoes
2 tbsp oil
300 ml (½ pt) (1¼ cups) dry, white wine
2 tsp chopped parsley
2 bay leaves
1 sprig of thyme
12 coriander seeds
salt
black pepper

Petits Oignons au Caramel

CARAMELIZED SMALL ONIONS

Onions glazed in this way are the perfect accompaniment to roast or grilled meats.

Wash the onions and cook them unpeeled in boiling salted water for 15–20 minutes until tender. Drain, rinse under cold water and remove the skins. Melt the sugar in a pan with 3–4 tablespoons water. When it has dissolved, bring to the boil and cook over a good heat until light chestnut-brown. (Take care when making caramel: if too light it will taste sweet and if too dark it will become bitter.) When the caramel is almost the right colour, remove from the heat and watch the colour change. When it is ready, quickly add the butter and onions and shake the pan to mix them well. When the onions are all coated in caramel, pour into a hot dish. If necessary, season with a little salt.

Hint: To clean the pan easily after making caramel, fill with water, cover and bring to the boil. You will find the residue dissolves quickly.

750 g (1½ lb) small onions
40 g (1½ oz) (3 tbsp) sugar
40 g (1½ oz) (3 tbsp) butter
salt

*Left: Poireaux en Blanquette
(page 90). Right: Petits Oignons
au Caramel (page 81).*

L'OSEILLE
Sorrel

Sorrel grows wild, is easy to grow in the garden and is also produced commercially in France. It has a slightly acidic taste and tends to go a khaki-colour if kept hot for too long. It is not often cooked as a separate vegetable and is more likely to be used in soups and sauces or with spinach in vegetable tarts. To prepare, remove the coarse stalks and veins and wash well. Roll the leaves up like a cigar and shred. Sorrel cooks very quickly, and if stewed in butter the leaves will 'melt' into a purée.

Oseille Fondue

MELTED SORREL

This is a very simple but delicious way of cooking sorrel. It is best to use young plants for this dish because sorrel can become bitter with age. Sorrel can also be prepared in the same way as Chicorée à la Crème, *but needs to be blanched for only 2–3 minutes.*

Wash and trim the sorrel and shred finely. Melt the butter in a pan and add the sorrel. Season lightly with salt and pepper and cook over gentle heat for 10–15 minutes, stirring occasionally until the sorrel 'melts'. Check the seasoning and pour into a hot dish. If you wish, garnish with fried croûtons.

Top: Oseille Fondue
Bottom: Foie de Volaille à l'Oseille
(page 199).

1 kg (2 lb) sorrel
50 g (2 oz) (¼ cup) butter
salt
black pepper
fried croûtons (page 221) (optional)

Oseille à la Crème

SORREL IN CREAM

This recipe comes from the Loire Valley. The cream softens the slightly acidic flavour of the sorrel, however, do be careful to add the cream just before serving — if it is left standing too long there is a chance the acid will curdle the cream.

1 kg (2 lb) sorrel
40 g (1½ oz) (3 tbsp) butter
100 ml (3½ fl oz) (½ cup) double (heavy) cream
salt
black pepper

Wash the sorrel well and cook in boiling salted water for 4–5 minutes. Drain well and chop coarsely. Heat the butter in a pan, add the sorrel and cook for another few minutes until just tender. Remove from the heat. Just before serving, add the cream and heat through without boiling. Season to taste with salt and black pepper and pour into a hot dish.

LES PANAIS
Parsnips

Look for clean, creamy-white roots; avoid any that are marked or blotched with rusty brown. If possible, prepare parsnips just before they are needed because they discolour if kept too long after being cut. Keeping them in acidulated water (page 10) helps.

Croquettes de Panais

PARSNIP CROQUETTES

Serve with braised or roast meat.

500 g (1 lb) parsnips
20 g (¾ oz) (1½ tbsp) butter
salt
black pepper
pinch nutmeg
4 tbsp seasoned flour
4–5 tbsp fresh, white breadcrumbs
1–2 eggs
1–2 tbsp oil
oil/fat for deep-frying

Peel the parsnips and cut into even-sized pieces. Cook in boiling salted water for 15–20 minutes until tender. Drain and return to the pan. Shake the pan over gentle heat until the parsnips are quite dry. Purée through a vegetable mill or in a food processor. Beat in the butter and season with a little salt, plenty of black pepper and a pinch of nutmeg. Turn out on to a plate or lightly floured board and leave to cool.

Divide the mixture into 12 pieces. Roll each one on a board lightly covered with seasoned flour to form a thick croquette about 5 cm (2 in) long. Roll each croquette in breadcrumbs. Beat the eggs and oil together. Coat the croquettes with the egg and breadcrumbs again. Roll lightly on a board to compress the breadcrumbs and, if possible, refrigerate for 1–2 hours. Heat the pan of fat to 190°C (380°F) or until a small cube of bread browns in 20 seconds. Fry the croquettes a few at a time until crisp and golden brown. Drain well on kitchen paper towel and serve.

Beignets de Panais

PARSNIP FRITTERS

Serve this dish as an accompaniment to roast or grilled meats or poultry, or as a separate vegetable course with Sauce Tomate.

Make the *Pâte à Frire* and let stand. Peel the parsnips and cut into even-sized slices. Cook in boiling salted water for 10–12 minutes until just tender. Drain well and toss in the vinaigrette while still hot. Heat the pan of fat/oil to 180°C (390°F) or until a small cube of bread browns in 20 seconds. Coat the parsnips with the batter and cook a few at a time until crisp and golden brown. Drain well on kitchen paper towel.

Pâte à Frire (page 220)
500 g (1 lb) parsnips
2 tbsp Sauce Vinaigrette (page 218)
fat/oil for deep-frying
300 ml (½ pt) (1¼ cups) Sauce Tomate (page 218) (optional)

Galette de Panais

PARSNIP CAKE

This dish can be served in several ways: with roast or braised meats, alone, or as a separate vegetable course with Sauce Tomate *or* Sauce Demi-glace. *It can also be served for a light lunch or supper dish. In this case, slice 75 g (3 oz) of Gruyère cheese and layer it with the parsnips and onions and serve with* Sauce Tomate.

Peel the parsnips and cook whole in boiling salted water for 20–25 minutes until almost tender. Drain and slice thinly. Meanwhile, peel and chop the onions. Heat 25 g (1 oz) (2 tbsp) butter in a pan and cook the onions until soft and lightly coloured. Coat the inside of an 18-cm (7-in) tart ring, deep sandwich tin or small cake pan with a thick layer of butter and sprinkle with the sugar. Arrange a neat layer of sliced parsnips on the bottom and round the sides of the tin. Season lightly with salt and pepper and a little lemon juice. Fill the centre with the rest of the parsnips and the onions in layers, seasoning each layer as before. With a piece of kitchen paper towel or a clean cloth press the layers to compact them. Cover with buttered, greaseproof paper and cook in a preheated oven 200°C (400°F) (Gas Mark 6) for 30–40 minutes. Turn out on to a hot dish.

750 g (1½ lb) medium parsnips
2 medium onions
75 g (3 oz) (6 tbsp) butter
2 tsp caster (superfine) sugar
1–2 tbsp lemon juice
salt
pepper
300 ml (½ pt) (1¼ cups) Sauce Tomate (page 218)/Sauce Demi-glace (page 215) (optional)

LES PETITS POIS
Peas

Peas always seem to taste better in France than anywhere else, possibly because they are picked when young and sweet. When young, pea pods are bright green and fleshy; they dry as they get older or if they are stale. When buying, the pods should be full but the shape of the peas should not be visible.

Mange-touts, or sugar (snow) peas, are flat pods with barely formed peas inside them. They are sweet and tender and take a very short time to cook. They are now available year-round but are expensive out of season. To prepare, the pods are topped and tailed and any strings removed. Cook whole.

Galette de Panais (page 85).

1.5 kg (3 lb) unshelled peas
12–15 small onions
½ lettuce
50 g (2 oz) (¼ cup) butter
1 tbsp flour
small bunch chervil and parsley
1 tsp sugar
1 tbsp chopped parsley and chervil

Petits Pois à la Française

FRENCH-STYLE PEAS

Shell the peas. Peel and trim the onions. Wash and shred the lettuce. Melt the butter in a heavy-based pan, add the peas and onions and cook for a moment or two, then stir in the flour and mix well. Pour on sufficient water to barely cover the peas and add the lettuce, sugar, chervil and parsley. Cook over gentle heat for 20–30 minutes until the peas are cooked and the liquid has reduced to a thin coating consistency. Remove the parsley and chervil and pour into a hot dish. Sprinkle with chopped parsley and chervil just before serving.

Top: Petits Pois à la Bonne Femme. Bottom: Pois Mange-Touts aux Poivrons (page 89).

Petits Pois à la Bonne Femme

HOUSEWIFE'S GREEN PEAS

Remove the rind and chop the bacon. Peel the small onions and finely chop the medium onion. Heat the butter in a pan and cook the chopped onion until almost soft. Add the bacon and cook until both are lightly coloured. Add the peas, onions, flour and sugar. Mix well and pour in sufficient water to just cover the peas. Season lightly and cook over gentle heat for 20–25 minutes until the vegetables are tender and the liquid has reduced and thickened.

100 g (4 oz) lean bacon
12 small onions
1 medium onion
40 g (1½ oz) (3 tbsp) butter
350 g (12 oz) shelled peas
1 tbsp flour
½ tsp sugar
salt and pepper

Petits Pois à la Demi-bourgeoise

GREEN PEAS WITH LETTUCE

Menon was the most prolific cookery writer of the eighteenth century. His first book was published in 1739 and altogether fifteen books are attributed to him. Little is known of him as a person, but he is renowned as one of the best writers on French cookery. This recipe comes from a book published in 1746.

Choose nice young, plump peas. They should be cooked only with the liquid which exudes from the peas and lettuce as they are cooking. Originally they were cooked in a pot with a concave lid which was filled with water to prevent the liquid evaporating. However, a heavy-based pan with a soup plate that fits snugly on top will do just as well, or, if you prefer, add 2–3 tablespoons of water, place a piece of greaseproof paper on top of the peas and cover with a tight-fitting lid.

1.5 kg (3 lb) unshelled peas
1 lettuce
65 g (2½ oz) (⅓ cup) butter
bouquet garni
1–2 spring onions (scallions)
1 tsp sugar
2 egg yolks
2 tbsp double (heavy) cream
salt
pepper

Shell the peas. Trim, wash and quarter the lettuce. Melt the butter in a heavy-based pan and add the peas, lettuce, bouquet garni and onions. Season lightly. Cover with a soup plate or piece of greaseproof paper and a tight-fitting lid and simmer gently for about 30 minutes until the peas are tender. Take the pan from the stove, carefully remove the lettuce and keep hot. Discard the bouquet garni and onions. Stir the sugar into the peas. Beat the egg yolks with the cream and stir into the peas. Return to the stove and heat through carefully, stirring all the time and making certain that the mixture does not boil. Check the seasoning and pour into a hot dish. Arrange the lettuce on top.

Petits Pois à la Paysanne

COUNTRY-STYLE PEAS

This is a great favourite of mine because the amount of vegetables used can be adjusted quickly to cater for the number of people to be served. The quantities given here are approximate; just try to keep them equal. But if you wish to use more potatoes to save cooking extra, then go ahead — I do.

250 g (8 oz) shelled peas
8 small onions
8 small carrots
8 very small, new potatoes
1 small lettuce
50 g (2 oz) (¼ cup) butter
1 tsp flour
½ tsp sugar

Peel the onions and scrape the carrots and potatoes. If necessary, cut the carrots in half. Wash, trim and quarter the lettuce. Melt the butter in a pan. Add the vegetables (if frozen peas are used add 10 minutes before the end of the cooking time) and stir in the flour and sugar. Add sufficient water to just cover the vegetables and season lightly with salt and pepper. Cover the pan and simmer gently for about 30 minutes until the vegetables are tender and the liquid has reduced and thickened slightly. If necessary raise the heat for the last few minutes and remove the lid so that the liquid evaporates more quickly. Taste and adjust the seasoning and pour into a hot serving dish.

Pois Mange-Touts aux Poivrons

MANGE-TOUTS (SNOW PEAS) WITH PEPPERS

This dish is particularly good with grilled pork chops.

Trim the *mange-touts* and remove the strings. Remove the stalk, core and seeds from the pepper and cut into thin strips. Heat the oil in a heavy-based pan and add the peas and pepper. Cook over gentle heat for 10–12 minutes, stirring frequently, until the peas and peppers are just tender. Season with salt and pepper and cook for a further 2–3 minutes. Serve hot.

500 g (1 lb) mange-touts
1 large red pepper
2–3 tbsp oil
salt
black pepper

LES POIREAUX
Leeks

Some years ago, on a very wet summer's evening, we were driving around the countryside east of Mâcon trying to find a particular restaurant. On the way we passed fields and fields of leeks, all well earthed-up to blanch them so there would be plenty of the tender white part. I have never before, or since, seen leeks growing in such profusion — even the gardens had several rows — although, of course, they are grown in many other parts of France as well.

The best leeks to buy are long, thin ones with plenty of white. The green leaves are coarser and on large leeks are very coarse indeed. To trim leeks economically, cut the green leaves to a point, because the inner layers are paler and more tender. Trim off the root end, remove any damaged or coarse layers and slit it down about half way. Wash them under cold water with the pointed ends held down so any grit isn't forced back inside. If they need soaking, place them in a container of water, again with their points down. Take great care when washing leeks: even the tiniest piece of grit can feel like a mouthful of sand. To keep them a good shape and prevent them falling apart when they are boiled, tie them into small bundles at each end.

Mousse de Poireaux

LEEK PURÉE

This recipe is from Île de France, the region surrounding Paris that abounds with excellent restaurants. It is very good with roast meats and chicken.

Trim and clean the leeks and slice finely. Heat half the butter in a heavy-based pan, add the leeks and season lightly. Cover and cook over gentle heat for 30–40 minutes until the leeks are tender but without colour. Purée the leeks through a fine vegetable mill or in a food processor. Heat the rest of the butter until golden brown and stir into the leeks with the cream. Heat through and season to taste. Pile into a hot dish and decorate the top with a fork.

1.5 kg (3 lb) small leeks
75 g (3 oz) (6 tbsp) butter
100 ml (3½ fl oz) (½ cup) double (heavy)
  cream
salt
pepper

Top: Purée de Marrons (page 76). Right: Carottes en Purée (page 24). Bottom: Purée de Choux de Bruxelles (page 43). Left: Purée de Potiron et Céleri (page 104).

Poireaux en Blanquette

LEEKS AND MUSHROOMS IN CREAM SAUCE

8–12 small leeks
250 g (8 oz) small button mushrooms
65 g (2½ oz) (⅓ cup) butter
2 tbsp lemon juice
25 g (1 oz) (¼ cup) flour
300 ml (½ pt) (1¼ cups) dry white wine/cider
150 ml (¼ pt) (⅔ cup) single (light) cream
salt
pepper
1 egg yolk
pinch nutmeg
1 tbsp chopped parsley

Trim and clean the leeks. Cook in a pan of boiling water for 10 minutes. Drain, reserving the cooking liquor. Clean and trim the mushrooms. Heat 25 g (1 oz) (2 tbsp) of butter in a pan. Add the mushrooms and 2 teaspoons of lemon juice. Season lightly, cover and cook for 5–7 minutes.

Heat the remaining butter in another pan, add the flour and mix well. Cook for 1–2 minutes, then add the wine a little at a time together with 150 ml (¼ pint) (⅔ cup) of the liquid the leeks were cooked in, and finally the cream. Bring to the boil and season to taste. Add the mushrooms and leeks to the sauce, cover and cook over gentle heat for 20–25 minutes until the leeks are tender. Remove the leeks and mushrooms and place on a hot dish. Beat the egg yolk and cream together. Pour in a little of the sauce. Mix well and return to the pan with the remaining lemon juice. Heat through without boiling, adding nutmeg to taste. Pour the sauce over the leeks and mushrooms and sprinkle with chopped parsley just before serving.

Poireaux a l'Arbois Rosé

LEEKS IN ROSÉ WINE

Top: Courgettes à la Vauclusienne (page 47). Bottom: Courgettes aux Amandes (page 46).

This recipe from the Jura uses the rosé wine of Arbois — a town famous as the birthplace of Louis Pasteur. If this wine is not available, use any other dry rosé.

Trim and clean the leeks and slice thinly. Heat 25 g (1 oz) (2 tbsp) butter in a heavy-based pan, add the leeks and cook over gentle heat until lightly coloured. Add the flour and mix in well. Stir in the wine and season lightly with salt and pepper. Cover and continue to cook gently for 30–40 minutes until tender. Check the pan occasionally and, if necessary, add 1–2 tablespoons of water to prevent the leeks sticking. Check the seasoning and just before serving stir in the remaining butter.

8–12 small leeks
40 g (1½ oz) (3 tbsp) butter
1 scant tbsp flour
300 ml (½ pt) (1¼ cups) Arbois rosé wine
salt
pepper

Poireaux Gratinés à la Savoyarde

SAVOY-STYLE LEEKS

750 g (1½ lb) small leeks
50 g (2 oz) (¼ cup) butter
1 clove garlic
3–4 tbsp breadcrumbs
150 g (5 oz) (1¼ cups) grated Gruyère
   cheese
salt
black pepper
nutmeg

Trim and clean the leeks and cook in boiling salted water for 20–30 minutes until tender. Drain well. Butter the inside of a heatproof dish and rub well with a cut clove of garlic. Sprinkle a few breadcrumbs on the bottom, place a layer of leeks on top, cover with more breadcrumbs and some of the grated cheese. Season lightly with salt and pepper and a small pinch of nutmeg. Continue the layers, finishing with the cheese. Melt the remaining butter and pour over the top. Place in a preheated oven 200°C (400°F) (Gas Mark 6) for 10–15 minutes until golden brown.

Poireaux à la Paysanne

COUNTRY-STYLE LEEKS

This dish is excellent with sausages.

8–12 small leeks
150 g (5 oz) lean bacon
50 g (2 oz) (¼ cup) butter
salt
black pepper

Trim and clean the leeks. Remove the green part and keep for soup. Slice the white part thinly. Remove the rinds and cut the bacon into thin strips. Heat the butter in a heavy-based pan. Add the bacon and cook until golden brown, then add the sliced leeks. Cover and cook for 30–35 minutes until tender. Season to taste and serve hot.

LES POIVRONS
Peppers

It was Christopher Columbus who discovered what are known generally as peppers in South America and brought them back to Europe. In fact they are not peppers at all but *capsicums* (*piments doux*) and are related to the potato and tomato. It is only the small, pointed varieties that are hot and peppery; the large ones are mild and sweet. Peppers are green when young and turn red as they ripen; there is also a yellow variety. They can all be used in cooking.

The easiest way to prepare peppers is to cut a small slice off the stalk and bottom ends and with a sharp knife run round the inside and cut out the core, seeds and ribs of white pith. Rings are easy to cut or, if you want strips or dice, slit the pepper down and cut into pieces. It is always easier to cut it through the fleshy side — knives tend to slip off the shiny skins. To stuff peppers, simply cut off the stalk end and remove the insides. If peppers are to be eaten raw in salads, they can be blanched first in boiling salted water for a minute or two and then refreshed in cold water to bring back their colour. Some people think they are more digestable this way, although I prefer them when they are crunchy.

Poivrons et Oignons au Four

BAKED PEPPERS AND ONIONS

This dish is excellent with grilled fish or roast meats.

Remove the stalks, core and seeds from the peppers and slice into thin rings. Peel the onions, slice into thin rings and separate the layers. Heat the oil in a heatproof dish. Add the peppers and onions and mix well. Season with salt and pepper and tuck the sprigs of thyme into the mixture. Cover the greaseproof paper and lid and cook in a preheated oven 190°C (375°F) (Gas Mark 5) for 40–45 minutes until tender. Remove the paper and thyme. Check the seasoning and serve in the cooking dish.

1 large red pepper
1 large green pepper
250 g (8 oz) medium onions
2 tbsp olive oil
4 sprigs thyme
salt
black pepper

Poivrons au Beurre d'Anchois

PEPPERS WITH ANCHOVY BUTTER

The savoury flavour of these peppers goes extremely well with grilled meats.

Place the peppers under a hot grill and cook on all sides (this will take about 10–15 minutes). Allow to cool and place them in a plastic bag or box. Seal well and refrigerate for at least 30 minutes. This will enable you to remove the skins easily. Peel the peppers and remove the stalks, cores and seeds. Cut into thin strips. If the anchovy fillets are very salty soak them in a little milk for 30 minutes. Chop them finely and crush to a paste (this can be done with a knife on a board, a pestle and mortar or liquidizer). Blend the anchovies with the butter and mix well. Season with pepper. Place the peppers and anchovy butter in a pan and cook over gentle heat for 10–12 minutes. Serve hot.

6 red peppers
50–75 g (2–3 oz) anchovy fillets
3–4 tbsp milk (optional)
100 g (4 oz) (½ cup) butter
pepper

LES POMMES DE TERRE
Potatoes

Potatoes were first introduced into France in about 1540, but for nearly 200 years they were unpopular and thought unfit to eat. It was Parmentier, an eighteenth-century economist who wrote many books on food, who suggested that it was a good vegetable to eat when food was scarce. He did much to encourage the growth of potatoes and even presented Louis XIV with a bunch of potato flowers. This gave the potato royal approval, but it was not until some years later, during the Revolution when food became very scarce, that it gained general popularity. Parmentier is still remembered: his name has been given to many potato dishes, such as *Potage Parmentier* (potato soup), *Pommes de Terre Parmentier* (fried, diced potatoes), *Oeufs Poche Parmentier*, and *Omelettes Parmentier*.

When I came to look for recipes for potatoes it was not so much a matter of what to put in as what to leave out. There are hundreds of recipes to choose from. I have tried to include as many regional recipes as possible, and some which I had not seen in cookery books for a long time.

I love the waxy, yellow-fleshed potatoes I buy in France. Whether they

Poivrons et Oignons au Four
(page 93).

are new or old they keep their shape when cooked. They are ideal for potato salads and *Pommes à l'Anchois*. Floury ones are best for baking in their skins and for *Aligot.*

Old potatoes can be bought in bulk and stored but always keep them in a dark, airy place, away from frost.

New potatoes are best bought in small quantities as needed. If they are really fresh the skin can be rubbed off with the fingers. Small, even-sized ones are the nicest. They will loose their delicate, earthy flavour if kept too long and will turn green if exposed to light.

New potatoes and small, old ones are usually boiled in their skins. This not only saves time — they are much easier to peel when they have been cooked — but they taste better, too. If you wish you can leave the skins on; they have a slightly nutty taste.

Scrub potatoes well before boiling them. If you want to cool them off to make them easier to hold when peeling, just put them under cold water for a moment or two. Otherwise, you can hold them in a dish towel or piece of kitchen paper towel, but I find this messy. Then toss them in hot butter to reheat.

New and old potatoes are also quite frequently steamed (*Pommes de Terre Vapeur*). They take one-and-a-half times as long to cook as boiled ones.

Pommes de Terre Duchesse

DUCHESS POTATOES

Peel the potatoes, cut into even-sized pieces and place in a pan of cold salted water. Bring to the boil and cook for approximately 20 minutes until tender. Drain well. Return to the pan and toss over gentle heat to dry. Purée the potatoes through a vegetable mill or in a food processor. Turn out into a hot bowl and beat in the butter, egg yolks and seasoning. If the mixture is too soft to pipe, return it to the pan and stir over gentle heat until some of the moisture has evaporated. Place the potato mixture in a piping bag with a large star nozzle and pipe out small cone shapes on to a greased baking sheet. Bake in a preheated oven 200°C (400°F) (Gas Mark 6) for 10 minutes. Beat the egg well, brush over the potatoes and return to the oven for 10–12 minutes or until golden brown.

Left: Gâteau de Bettes (page 20).
Right: Côtes de Bettes aux Lardons (page 19).

Serves 4
500 g (1 lb) old potatoes
25 g (1 oz) (2 tbsp) butter
2 egg yolks
salt
pepper
pinch nutmeg
1 whole egg

Pommes de Terre au Citron

POTATOES WITH LEMON

These potatoes are excellent with ham, pork and veal.

750 g (1½ lb) firm old/new potatoes
1 small lemon
1 large onion
50 g (2 oz) (¼ cup) butter
salt
pepper
1 tbsp chopped chives

Peel the potatoes and cut into 1-cm (½-in) dice. Cook in boiling salted water for 5 minutes. Drain well. Grate the rind of the lemon and squeeze out the juice. Peel and finely chop the onion. Heat the butter in a frying pan or heavy-based heatproof dish. Cook the onion for 3–4 minutes until soft but uncoloured. Add the grated lemon rind and the juice. Boil until the mixture has almost all evaporated, then add the potatoes and mix well. Season to taste. If using a frying pan transfer the mixture to a heatproof dish. Cook in a preheated oven 200°C (400°F) (Gas Mark 6) for 30–40 minutes until the potatoes are tender and golden brown on top. Serve in the cooking dish and sprinkle with chopped chives.

Pommes de Terre des Cendrillon

BAKED POTATOES WITH CHEESE

As well as being the French name for Cinderella, cendrillon is also the name for a household drudge or skivvy. When cooked, these potatoes are meant to look like sabots — the wooden shoes worn by peasants.

Serves 4
4 good-sized old potatoes
50 g (2 oz) (¼ cup) butter
5 tbsp double (heavy) cream
2 egg yolks
1 tbsp chopped parsley
1 tbsp chopped chives
75 g (3 oz) (¾ cup) grated Gruyère cheese
salt
black pepper
pinch nutmeg

Scrub the potatoes well. With the point of a sharp knife make a long, oval-shaped cut through the skin on the top of each potato. Place in a preheated oven 200°C (400°F) (Gas Mark 6) for 50–60 minutes until soft. To check, test with a skewer or pointed knife or press gently. When the potatoes are cooked, remove them from the oven but leave it at the same temperature. With the point of a sharp knife or a pair of kitchen scissors, open the oval incision made in the top and remove the cooked potato with a teaspoon. Place the potato pulp in a bowl and beat in the butter, cream and egg yolks. Mix in the herbs and three-quarters of the cheese. Season to taste with salt, pepper and a pinch of nutmeg. Pile the mixture back into the skins and sprinkle the remaining cheese over the top of each potato. Return to the oven for 10–15 minutes until golden brown.

Variation: (*Pommes de Terre Ardenaises*) Prepare and cook the potatoes as above. Add 100 g (4 oz) (½ cup) chopped mushrooms cooked in a little butter, and use 2 tablespoons of Parmesan cheese instead of Gruyère.

Crêpes aux Pommes de Terre

POTATO PANCAKES

If desired, the garlic, parsley and pepper can be omitted and, after the pancakes have been cooked, they can be sprinkled with sugar and served for dessert.

500 g (1 lb) old potatoes
1 clove garlic
40 g (1½ oz) (6 tbsp) flour
1 egg
1 tbsp chopped parsley
75 g (3 oz) (6 tbsp) unsalted butter/3–4 tbsp oil

Peel the potatoes finely and squeeze out the moisture in a dish towel or kitchen paper towel. Peel and crush the garlic. Mix together the potatoes, flour, garlic, egg and parsley. Season well with salt and pepper. Heat the butter/oil in a frying pan. When it is hot carefully drop spoonfuls of the mixture in to form small pancakes about 5 cm (2 in) in diameter. Fry for 3–4 minutes on each side until tender and golden brown. Serve very hot.

Crique de Pommes de Terre

POTATO CAKE

Serve this with roast, grilled or stewed meats, or separately with a salad.

Peel the potatoes and grate on a moderately fine grater. Wash well and dry on a dish towel or kitchen paper towel. Season with salt and pepper. Heat half the butter/oil in a frying pan. Add the potatoes and flatten into a cake with a spatula. Cover and cook over gentle heat for 25–30 minutes. Turn out on to a plate. Heat the remaining butter/oil in the pan and slide the potato cake back into the pan with the aid of a spatula. Cover and cook for 15–20 minutes until the underside is golden brown and the potatoes are tender. Slide the completed dish on to a hot plate.

750 g (1½ lb) old potatoes
75 g (3 oz) (6 tbsp) butter/3 tbsp oil
salt
pepper

Farcement

POTATOES WITH PRUNES

This dish of potatoes and prunes from the Savoy is also called Farcon. *It is particularly good with stewed or sauté rabbit, or it can be eaten on its own or with a salad.*

Soak the prunes in warm water for 1 hour, then remove the stones. Peel and grate the potatoes. Place them in a bowl and add the eggs, egg yolk and flour. Melt the butter and stir into the mixture with the milk and prunes. Season with salt and pepper and mix well. Butter a deep earthenware dish and pour in the mixture. Cover with a lid or aluminium foil and place in a bain-marie or roasting tin of hot water and bake in a preheated oven 190°C (375°F) (Gas Mark 5) for about 1½ hours. Serve in the dish in which it is cooked, or if you prefer, turn out on to a hot plate.

250 g (8 oz) prunes
1 kg (2 lb) old potatoes
3 eggs
1 egg yolk
50 g (2 oz) (½ cup) flour
50 g (2 oz) (¼ cup) butter
300 ml (½ pt) (1¼ cups) milk
salt
black pepper

Galette au Fromage

CHEESE AND POTATO CAKE

Because potato cakes feature so greatly in French country cooking, I have included a selection of them. This one comes from Franche-Comté and the local cheese is used. Gruyère or Emmenthal will do just as well. Serve it as an accompaniment to roast or grilled meats, or on its own with a salad. Curly endive (chicory) or escarole with a garlic vinaigrette dressing go particularly well with it.

Peel the potatoes and slice very thinly, preferably on a mandolin or the slicing attachment on a food processor or mixer. Wash the slices well and dry them on a dish towel or kitchen paper towel. Heat 50 g (2 oz) (¼ cup) butter in a heavy-based frying pan. Place a layer of potatoes on the bottom, cover with a layer of cheese and season with salt, pepper and a small pinch of nutmeg. Repeat the layers and seasoning, ending with a layer of potatoes. Cut the rest of the butter into small pieces and dot over the top. Cover and cook over gentle heat for 40–45 minutes. When one side is done, turn the cake out on to a plate and then slide it back into the pan with the aid of a spatula so the other side can brown. Cook for 15–20 minutes until the potatoes are tender. Slide out on to a hot dish.

750 g (1½ lb) medium-sized, old potatoes
75 g (3 oz) (6 tbsp) butter
125 g (5 oz) (1¼ cup) grated Comté
  cheese
salt
black pepper
nutmeg

Ratatouille de Pommes de Terre.

Ratatouille de Pommes de Terre

POTATO AND TOMATO STEW

Although the name ratatouille *is associated with the Provence dish of aubergines (eggplant), peppers, courgettes (zucchini) and tomatoes, it is also slang, or argot, for a stew, in particular vegetable stews. (See also* Ratatouille de Navets.*)*

750 g (1½ lb) new/firm old potatoes
1 large red pepper
2 large onions
1 clove garlic
500 g (1 lb) ripe, juicy tomatoes
3–4 tbsp oil
bouquet garni
salt
pepper
1 tbsp chopped parsley

Peel the potatoes and quarter or cut into moderately large pieces. Remove the stalk, core and seeds from the pepper. Peel the onions and garlic. Thinly slice the onions and pepper and crush the garlic. Chop the tomatoes coarsely (if you wish, they can be peeled first). Cook the potatoes in a pan of boiling salted water for 5 minutes. Drain well.

Heat the oil in a heavy-based pan. Add the pepper and onions and cook for 7–10 minutes until they begin to soften but do not colour. Add the potatoes, tomatoes and bouquet garni. Season to taste. Cover and cook over a gentle heat for 15–20 minutes until the vegetables are tender. If necessary add a few tablespoons of water to prevent the mixture becoming dry. Remove the bouquet garni and check the seasoning. Pile into a hot dish and sprinkle with chopped parsley just before serving.

Pommes de Terre des Vendangeurs

GRAPE-PICKERS' POTATOES

*Left: Salade Verte Mélangée
(page 157).
Right: Pommes des
Terre des Vendangeurs*

This dish is meant to be eaten during the harvesting of grapes; while everyone is in the vineyards, it is left cooking to await their return. Choose any firm potatoes available in the autumn. Eat it with roast meats or by itself, with plenty of wine.

Peel the potatoes and cut into moderately thick slices. Remove the rinds from the bacon. Line the inside of an earthenware pot with three-quarters of the smoked streaky slices, then layer the potatoes, cheese and unsmoked bacon. Season each layer with pepper (salt should not be necessary — the bacon should be salty enough). Finish with a layer of potatoes and cover with the remaining smoked bacon. Cut the butter into pieces and dot over the surface. Place in a preheated oven 230°C (450°F) (Gas Mark 8) for 20–30 minutes, then reduce the heat to 200°C (400°F) (Gas Mark 6) and cover the pot with a lid or aluminium foil and continue cooking for 2–2½ hours. If necessary remove the lid for the last 20–30 minutes so the bacon can brown, or instead, if you prefer, reserve a little of the cheese and sprinkle over the top.

750 g (1½ lb) potatoes

250 g (8 oz) thin, smoked, streaky bacon slices

250 g (8 oz) thin, unsmoked streaky bacon slices

black pepper

100 g (4 oz) (1 cup) grated Emmenthal cheese

50 g (2 oz) (¼ cup) butter

Pommes de Terre aux Anchois

POTATOES WITH ANCHOVIES

These potatoes from Rousillon are often served with aperitifs, but can also be eaten as an accompaniment to grilled meats.

24–30 *small new potatoes*
100 g (4 oz) (½ cup) *butter*
75 g (3 oz) *anchovy fillets/2–3 tbsp anchovy essence*
pepper
oil/fat for deep-frying

Scrub the potatoes and place in a pan of boiling salted water. Cook for 5 minutes. Drain, rinse and remove the skins. With the point of a small, sharp knife, make a large cavity down the centre of each. Cream the butter in a bowl. Chop the anchovy fillets finely and crush to a paste with a knife, pestle and mortar or liquidizer. Blend into the butter or add anchovy essence to taste. Season with pepper. Heat a pan of fat/oil to 180°C (370°F) or until a small cube of bread browns in 30 seconds. Fry the potatoes until soft inside and golden brown and crisp on the outside. To test if they are cooked, prick them with a large needle or fine skewer. Drain well and keep hot. Just before serving, fill each potato with anchovy butter.

Pommes de Terre Biarritz

POTATOES WITH PEPPERS AND HAM

750 g (1½ lb) *old potatoes*
1 *small red/green pepper*
100 g (4 oz) *slice ham*
40 g (1½ oz) (3 tbsp) *butter*
4–6 tbsp *milk*
1 tbsp *chopped mixed herbs (parsley, chervil, thyme, savory, etc.)*

Peel the potatoes and cut into even-sized pieces. Place in a pan of cold water, bring to the boil and cook for about 20 minutes until tender. Remove the stalk, core and seeds from the pepper. Cut into small dice and cook in a pan of boiling salted water for 10–15 minutes until tender. Drain well. Chop the ham into small pieces. When the potatoes are cooked, drain and mash until smooth, or purée. Beat in the butter a little at a time. Heat the milk and beat in enough to give a soft, fluffy consistency. Add the ham, herbs and pepper. Return to the pan and heat through for a moment or two over gentle heat, beating all the time. Pile into a hot dish.

Pommes de Terre à la Basquaise

BASQUE-STYLE POTATOES

4 *large potatoes*
3–4 tbsp *oil*
1 *medium red pepper*
1 *medium green pepper*
250 g (8 oz) *tomatoes*
100 g (4 oz) *Bayonne (Parma) ham/ smoked bacon*
2 *cloves garlic*
2 *medium onions*
1 tbsp *chopped parsley*
2–3 tbsp *breadcrumbs*
salt
black pepper

Peel the potatoes and cut in half lengthways. Scoop out some of the centre with a ball-cutter. Place in a large pan, cover with salted water and bring to the boil. Cook for 2–3 minutes only and then drain carefully. Brush inside and out with oil and place in an oiled dish. Remove the stalks, cores and seeds from the peppers and cut into small dice. Skin, seed and chop the tomatoes. Remove the rind from the bacon if used, and dice the ham/bacon. Peel the garlic and onions and chop finely. Heat 2 tablespoons of oil in a pan and cook the peppers, onions and garlic until tender. Add the tomatoes and ham/bacon. Cook for 4–5 minutes until the bacon is tender. Season to taste and stir in the chopped parsley.

Place the mixture in the prepared potato shells and cook in a preheated oven 180°C (350°F) (Gas Mark 4) for about an hour (the time will depend on the size and type of potato, so check them with a skewer after 45 minutes). Meanwhile, heat the remaining oil in a frying pan and fry the breadcrumbs, turning continuously with a spatula, until golden brown (if you prefer, the breadcrumbs can be lightly browned in the oven instead). When the potatoes are cooked, sprinkle with the breadcrumbs.

Pommes de Terre Normandes

POTATOES WITH LEEKS

A dish from Normandy, this is similar to the well-known Pommes de Terre Boulangère *but uses leeks instead of onions. It is frequently eaten on its own during Lent instead of fish.*

Peel the potatoes and slice thinly, preferably with a mandolin or the slicing attachment on a food processor or mixer. Wash well and drain. Trim the leeks and wash well. Thinly slice the white part (save the green part for soup). Peel and finely slice the onion. Butter the inside of a heatproof dish with half the butter. Layer the potatoes, leeks and onion, seasoning each layer and finishing with a layer of potatoes. Pour on sufficient stock to barely cover the potatoes. Bring to the boil. Cut the remaining butter into small pieces and dot over the surface. Cover with a lid or aluminium foil and bake in a preheated oven 180°C (350°F) (Gas Mark 4) for 1–1¼ hours. Remove the lid or foil. Bring the cream to the boil and pour over. Continue cooking for 20–30 minutes until the potatoes and leeks are soft and the top golden brown.

750 g (1½ lb) old potatoes
350 g (12 oz) leeks
1 medium onion
50 g (2 oz) (¼ cup) butter
salt
pepper
1 tbsp chopped parsley
450 ml (¾ pt) (2 cups) white stock
150 ml (¼ pt) (⅔ cup) single (light) cream

Aligot

Aligot is a country potato dish from the Auvergne. For many years it has been eaten on Fridays and Fast days instead of fish. It can be served as a first course or as an accompaniment to pork dishes, particularly sausages.

The cheese used in this dish is Tomme de Cantal, *a soft unfermented cheese which is a speciality of the Auvergne. If this is not available use* Raclette *or English Cheshire or mild Cheddar. This dish is usually cooked in an oven-to-table pan so it can be taken straight to the table and everyone can help themselves.*

Peel the potatoes and boil for 20 minutes until tender. Drain well. In the meantime, slice the cheese thinly and peel and crush the garlic. Purée the potatoes or mash them until smooth. Beat in the butter, cheese, garlic and cream. Season to taste with salt and pepper and mix well. Return to the pan and cook over gentle heat for about 15 minutes, stirring occasionally until the cheese has melted and the mixture is hot.

750 g (1½ lb) old floury potatoes
175 g (6 oz) Tomme de Cantal
1 clove garlic
50 g (2 oz) (¼ cup) butter
3 tbsp double (heavy) cream
salt
pepper

Pommes de Terre à la Provençale

POTATOES WITH GARLIC AND PARSLEY

To retain their flavour, boil the potatoes in their skins and then peel them. Choose small to medium potatoes; if they are all the same size they will cook evenly.

Scrub the potatoes and cook in boiling salted water until tender. Drain, refresh in cold water and peel. Cut into 5-mm (¼-in) slices. Peel and finely chop the garlic. Heat the oil in a frying pan and fry the potatoes, turning them occasionally until golden brown. Add the garlic during the last few minutes so it is barely cooked (there is then no danger of it becoming too brown and bitter). Season to taste, pile onto a hot dish and sprinkle with chopped parsley just before serving.

750 g (1 lb) firm old/new potatoes
3–4 cloves garlic
3–4 tbsp olive oil
salt
black pepper
1 tbsp chopped parsley

Top: Pois Chiches à la Fondue de Tomates (page 116). Bottom: Lentilles aux Épinards (page 115).

750 g (1½ lb) potatoes
3 medium onions
175 g (6 oz) bacon
4 large tomatoes
4–6 tbsp oil
salt
black pepper

Truffade

A tasty potato dish from the Massif-Central that can be served as an accompaniment, but more often is served separately with a salad.

Peel the potatoes and cut into 1-cm (½-in) dice. Peel and thinly slice the onions. Remove the rind from the bacon and dice. Peel, seed and chop the tomatoes. Heat 3–4 tablespoons oil in a frying pan. Add the potatoes and fry, turning frequently, until light golden brown on all sides. Add the bacon and onion and continue to cook until they begin to soften, then add the tomatoes. Season to taste. Heat a little more oil in a heatproof dish and transfer the mixture to this dish. Place in a preheated oven 190°C (375°F) (Gas Mark 5) for 30–45 minutes until tender.

Pommes de Terre au Gratin

BROWNED POTATOES

Peel the potatoes and slice them thinly with a mandolin or slicing attachment to a food processor or mixer. Place the slices in a buttered heatproof dish, seasoning each layer lightly. Heat the stock and pour in only enough to barely cover the potatoes. Cut the butter into small pieces and dot over the surface. Cover with a lid or aluminium foil and cook in a preheated oven 190°C (375°F) (Gas Mark 5) for 1¼–1½ hours. Remove the lid or foil for the last 20 minutes to brown. Serve in the cooking dish.

Top: Choufleur à l'Italienne (page 36).
Bottom: Choufleur aux Croûtons
(page 35).

750 g (1½ lb) old potatoes
salt
pepper
450 ml (¾ pt) (2 cups) stock
50 g (2 oz) (¼ cup) butter

Pommes de Terre à la Paysanne

COUNTRY-STYLE POTATOES

This dish is another variation of sliced potatoes cooked in stock and, like Pommes de Terre Normandes, is frequently served as a main course during Lent instead of fish.

750 g (1½ lb) potatoes
100 g (4 oz) sorrel
1 clove garlic
75 g (3 oz) (6 tbsp) butter
2 tbsp chopped chervil
450 ml (¾ pt) (2 cups) white stock
salt
black pepper

Peel and finely slice the potatoes, preferably with a mandolin or the slicing attachment to a food processor or mixer. Trim and wash the sorrel. Drain well. Peel and crush the garlic. Melt 25 g (1 oz) (2 tbsp) butter in a pan and add the sorrel. Cook gently for 7–10 minutes until the sorrel has 'melted'. Stir occasionally. Season to taste and add the garlic and chopped chervil. Mix well. Butter the inside of a heatproof dish with half the remaining butter. Layer the potato and sorrel mixture, seasoning each layer lightly and finishing with a layer of potatoes. Pour on sufficient stock to barely cover the potatoes. Cut the remaining butter into small pieces and dot over the surface. Bring to the boil, cover with a lid or aluminium foil and cook in a preheated oven 180°C (350°F) (Gas Mark 4) for about 1½ hours. Remove the lid or foil for the last 20–30 minutes so the top becomes golden brown and crisp.

LE POTIRON
Pumpkin

Pumpkins are available in the late summer and autumn and are used for both savoury and sweet dishes. They can grow to an enormous size, but it is best to buy them no more than 2.5 kg (5 lb), or a piece the weight you need. Choose firm, unblemished pumpkin, or, if it is cut, look for close-textured flesh without strings.

Purée de Potiron et Céleri

PUMPKIN AND CELERIAC PURÉE

1 kg (2 lb) pumpkin
500 g (1 lb) celeriac
600 ml (1 pt) (2½ cups) milk
¼ tsp sugar
salt
pepper
75 g (3 oz) (6 tbsp) butter
2–3 slices bread
4–5 tbsp oil
fried croûtons (page 221) (optional)

Peel the pumpkin and celeriac. Remove the seeds from the pumpkin and cut into 5-cm (2-in) cubes. Cut the celeriac into 2.5-cm (1-in) cubes and cook in boiling salted water for 30–35 minutes until tender. Drain well. Place the pumpkin in another pan with the milk and season with a little salt and black pepper and sugar. Bring to the boil, then lower the heat and simmer gently for 20–25 minutes. When the pumpkin is tender, drain well and reserve the milk.

Purée the pumpkin and celeriac through a fine vegetable mill or in a food processor. Return to a clean pan and beat in 50 g (2 oz) (¼ cup) butter, then add enough of the reserved milk to moisten the purée without making it too soft. Season to taste with salt and pepper. Meanwhile, remove the crusts from the bread and cut each slice into four triangles. Fry in the remaining butter and oil until golden brown on both sides. Drain on kitchen paper towel. Pile the purée in a hot dish and garnish with croûtons.

Palets de Potiron

PUMPKIN PANCAKES

These pancakes go well with spicy dishes, or omit the salt and pepper, sprinkle them with sugar and serve as a dessert dish.

Peel and seed the pumpkin and cut into pieces. Cook in boiling, salted water for 20–30 minutes until tender. Drain well. Purée through a vegetable mill or in a food processor. Return the pumpkin to the pan and cook over gentle heat, stirring all the time, until the purée is quite dry. Place the purée in a mixing bowl and stir in the flour, eggs, lemon rind, sugar and seasoning. Melt the butter and whisk into the mixture a little at a time. Beat until smooth and refrigerate until required.

Heat the oil in a frying pan then pour it off so the pan is lightly coated. Drop teaspoonfuls of the mixture into the pan, leaving room for them to spread and form small, flat rounds about 5 cm (2 in). Cook for about 30 seconds or until lightly coloured on both sides. Continue to oil the pan as necessary, and cook the remaining mixture in the same way. If the mixture is too thick, add a little melted butter or a few drops of milk; if the mixture is too soft and spreads too much, beat in a little more flour.

500 g (1 lb) pumpkin
65 g (2½ oz) (⅔ cup) flour
2 eggs
grated rind of 1 lemon
¼ tsp sugar
salt
black pepper
25 g (1 oz) (2 tbsp) butter
1–2 tbsp oil

Subrics de Potiron

PUMPKIN CAKES

Pumpkin cooked in this way is excellent with game. For this recipe, 250 g (8 oz) of cooked pumpkin purée is required. I found that 1 kg (2 lb) gave me just the right amount but this will depend on the size of the pumpkin, thickness of the skin and so on, so do err on the generous side when weighing the pumpkin. Subrics des Épinards can be made in the same way using 800 g (1¾ lb) spinach instead of pumpkin and omitting the garlic.

Peel and seed the pumpkin and cut into small pieces. Cook in boiling salted water for 15 minutes. Drain well and purée through a vegetable mill or in a food processor with the garlic. Return the purée to the pan and cook over gentle heat, stirring all the time, until quite dry. Make the *Sauce Béchamel.* Beat the egg yolks and eggs together and add to the sauce with the pumpkin purée and cheese. Season to taste with a pinch of cayenne pepper, nutmeg and a little salt. Butter the inside of 8 castle pudding moulds, or custard cups, well and fill with the mixture. Place in a bain-marie or roasting pan filled with hot water and bake in a preheated oven 200°C (400°F) (Gas Mark 6) for 20 minutes.

1 kg (2 lb) pumpkin
1 clove garlic
Sauce Béchamel made with:
    250 ml (8 fl oz) (1 cup) milk
    25 g (1 oz) (2 tbsp) butter
    25 g (1 oz) (¼ cup) flour
2 egg yolks
3 whole eggs
50 g (2 oz) (½ cup) grated Emmenthal cheese
cayenne pepper
nutmeg
salt

LE RUTABAGA
Swede (Rutabaga)

Swede (rutabaga) is another vegetable that is not used a great deal in France but I have found references to it in both old and modern recipe books. It is usually served as a purée. Kohl-rabi is also sometimes known as rutabaga.

Top: Palets de Potiron (page 105).
Bottom: Subrics de Potiron (page 105).

1 kg (2 lb) swede
50 g (2 oz) (¼ cup) butter
salt
black pepper

Purée de Rutabaga

MASHED SWEDE

Peel the swede thickly to remove completely the second layer under the skin, which can taste bitter. Cut the swede into large dice and cook in boiling salted water for 20–30 minutes until tender. Drain well. Return to the pan and mash with a fork or potato-masher. Add the butter and season to taste with salt and plenty of black pepper. Stir or beat over gentle heat until all excess water has evaporated and the swede is creamy and fairly smooth (a few small lumps do not matter). Check the seasoning. Pile into a serving dish and serve hot.

LES SALSIFIS
Salsify

Left: *Tomates aux Tomates* (page 112).
Right: *Salsifis à la Normande* (page 108).

Salsify is a long, tapering root with a light-brown skin. Young roots have fresh, grey-green leaves. It has a flavour slightly reminiscent of asparagus. *Scorzonera* is similar to salsify but has a black skin. When buying salsify, avoid small roots and dry or shrivelled skins. Peel the salsify and cut it into short lengths. Keep in acidulated water (page 10) until required. Cook it in acidulated water or a *blanc* (page 10) to preserve its colour.

Salsifis à la Normande

NORMANDY-STYLE SALSIFY

750 g (1½ lb) salsify
2 tbsp lemon juice
1 large onion
50 g (2 oz) (¼ cup) butter
25 g (1 oz) (¼ cup) flour
200 ml (7 fl oz) (1 cup) cider
100 ml (3½ fl oz) (½ cup) double (heavy)
  cream
salt
pepper
pinch nutmeg

Peel the salsify (page 107) and cut into 5-cm (2-in) lengths. Cook in boiling salted water with the lemon juice for 25–30 minutes or until tender. Drain well. Meanwhile, peel and finely chop the onion. Heat the butter in a pan and cook the onion until soft and lightly coloured. Add the flour and mix well. Cook together for 2–3 minutes then add the cider and the cream a little at a time. Bring to the boil, stirring continuously, and cook for 4–5 minutes. Season to taste with salt, pepper and a pinch of nutmeg. Add the salsify. Boil for another 2–3 minutes. Pour into a hot serving dish.

Salsifis au Gratin

SALSIFY IN CHEESE SAUCE

750 g (1½ lb) salsify
300 ml (½ pt) (1¼ cups) Sauce Béchamel
  (page 214)
75 g (3 oz) (¾ cup) grated Gruyère cheese
salt
pepper

Prepare the salsify (page 107) and cut into 5-cm (2-in) lengths. Cook in boiling salted water for about 30 minutes or until tender. Drain well. Make the Sauce Béchamel and add half the cheese. Heat through without boiling. Season to taste. Add the salsify and then pour into a hot dish. Sprinkle over the remaining cheese and place in a preheated oven 200°C (400°F) (Gas Mark 6) for 10–15 minutes, or under a hot grill until golden brown.

Salsifis Frits

FRIED SALSIFY

750 g (1½ lb) salsify
2 tbsp lemon juice/vinegar
Pâte à Frire (page 220)
1–2 lemons
oil/fat for deep-frying
salt
pepper

Prepare the salsify (page 107) and cut into 5-cm (2-in) lengths. Cook in boiling salted water with the lemon juice/vinegar for about 30 minutes, or until tender. Drain well. Meanwhile, make the Pâte à Frire and cut the lemons into wedges. Heat the pan of oil/fat to 190°C (380°F) or until a small cube of bread browns in 20 seconds. Dip each piece of salsify into the batter and carefully drop into the hot fat. Cook for 3–4 minutes until golden brown. Take care not to put too many in the pan at one time. Drain well on kitchen paper towel. Pile into a hot dish and, just before serving, season with salt and pepper and garnish with lemon wedges.

Salsifis à la Provençale

PROVENCE-STYLE SALSIFY

750 g (1½ lb) salsify
300 ml (½ pt) (1¼ cups) Sauce Tomate
  (page 218)
2 cloves garlic
2–3 tbsp olive oil
salt
black pepper
1 tbsp chopped parsley

Prepare the salsify (page 218) and cut into 5-cm (2-in) lengths. Cook in boiling salted water for about 30 minutes or until tender. Drain well. In the meantime, make the Sauce Tomate and peel and finely chop the garlic. Heat the oil in a frying pan and cook the salsify until golden brown. Drain off most of the oil. Stir in the Sauce Tomate and cook for 3–4 minutes. Season to taste. Pour into a hot dish and sprinkle with garlic and parsley.

LES TOMATES
Tomatoes

One of the nicest things about shopping in French vegetable markets is the wide range of tomatoes available: big fat ones or small round ones for salads or cooking, and the juicy, long plum ones that are so good for sauces. In the market you will not see boxes of evenly matched tomatoes, but piles and piles of odd-shaped ones, red or red and green, all with great flavour. Certainly there is nothing to beat the flavour of sun-ripened tomatoes; how pallid hot-house ones seem in comparison!

Don't worry about eating tomatoes if they are still slightly green. As long as they have been grown in the sun, they have a wonderful flavour and crispness and need only a little vinaigrette, salt and plenty of black pepper to make an easy but excellent hors d'oeuvre. I can make a meal of them with plenty of crisp, fresh French bread and butter. However, do make certain they are ripe if you want to cook them. Whether you are going to eat or cook tomatoes, make certain they are firm. If you are going to keep them for a few days, buy them slightly under-ripe; they will be ripe by the time you need them.

To peel tomatoes plunge them into a pan of boiling water for 30 seconds. To keep them firm, place them immediately in iced cold water. Peel the skin with a small, sharp-pointed knife. If the seeds are to be removed, cut the tomato in half and scoop them out with a ball-cutter.

Gratinée de Tomates

BAKED TOMATO AND CHEESE CUSTARD

Serve this dish with a salad or as an accompaniment to roast meats or sautées.

Peel the tomatoes and slice. Peel and finely chop the onions. Beat the eggs and milk in a large bowl. Heat most of the butter/oil in a pan and cook the onion until soft but without colour. Add the onions and tomatoes to the eggs and milk together with the herbs. Season to taste and mix thoroughly. Butter/oil the inside of a heatproof dish. Pour in the mixture and sprinkle with cheese. Place in a preheated oven 220°C (425°F) (Gas Mark 7) for 30 minutes until golden brown.

6 large tomatoes
3 large onions
2 eggs
150 ml (¼ pt) (⅔ cup) milk
50 g (2 oz) (¼ cup) butter/3–4 tbsp olive oil
1 tbsp chopped, mixed herbs (parsley, chervil, chives, basil, thyme, etc.)
50 g (2 oz) (½ cup) grated Gruyère cheese
salt
black pepper

Tomates Provençales à la Poêle

PROVENÇALE FRIED TOMATOES

Cut the tomatoes in half and season well. Heat 2 tablespoons of oil in a frying pan and fry the tomatoes on both sides until soft. Remove from the pan and arrange on a hot dish. Add the remaining oil to the pan and when hot fry the breadcrumbs until golden brown. Stir continuously so they colour evenly. Meanwhile, peel and finely chop the garlic and mix with the parsley. Sprinkle the fried breadcrumbs over the tomatoes and finish with the parsley and garlic mixture. Serve hot.

6–8 tomatoes
salt
black pepper
4 tbsp olive oil
3–4 tbsp breadcrumbs
3 cloves garlic
1 tbsp chopped parsley

Les Champignons (page 29) (clockwise): À la couche *(button),* morilles, pleurotes, girolles *and* cèpes.

Top: Gratinée Campagnarde (page 120). Bottom: Potage Neige Blanche (page 121).

Tomates aux Tomates

TOMATOES WITH TOMATOES

12 large tomatoes
2 medium onions
1 clove garlic
25 g (1 oz) (2 tbsp) butter
2 tbsp oil
½ tsp chopped fresh basil/good pinch dried
   basil
1 bay leaf
300 ml (½ pt) (1¼ cups) double (heavy)
   cream
1 tbsp chopped parsley

Peel, seed and finely chop 8 tomatoes. Peel the onions and garlic. Chop the onions and crush the garlic. Heat the butter in a pan with 1 tablespoon of oil and cook the onions until soft but without colour. Add the garlic, chopped tomatoes, basil and bay leaf. Season lightly and simmer gently for 20–25 minutes until the mixture reduces to a very thick purée. Check the seasoning and remove the bay leaf. Cut the remaining 4 tomatoes in half and remove the seeds. Season them inside with a little salt and pepper. Brush with oil and place in a preheated oven 200°C (400°F) (Gas Mark 6) for 5–10 minutes so they are heated through and just cooked. Take care not to overcook them.

In another pan bring the cream to the boil and cook for 8–10 minutes until it thickens slightly. Season to taste. Arrange the tomato halves on a hot dish and fill each with the mixture. Keep hot in a warm oven. Just before serving reheat the cream if necessary, pour over the tomato halves and sprinkle a little chopped parsley in the centre of each.

Tomates Fumées

TOMATOES WITH BACON AND MUSHROOMS

4 large/8 small tomatoes
100 g (4 oz) smoked bacon slices
100 g (4 oz) mushrooms
3 medium onions
1 egg
5 tbsp olive oil
1 tbsp chopped mixed herbs (parsley,
   chives, chervil, thyme, etc.)
salt
black pepper
3–4 tbsp breadcrumbs

Very large Continental tomatoes are best for this recipe. If they are not available, use eight smaller ones.

Cut the tomatoes in half and remove the seeds with a ball-cutter or teaspoon. Season the insides lightly. Remove the rind and chop the bacon finely. Trim and clean the mushrooms, peel the onions and chop both finely. Beat the egg. Heat 3 tablespoons of oil in a pan and add the bacon, mushrooms and onions. Cook for 10–12 minutes until tender. Remove from the pan and stir in the beaten egg and mixed herbs. Season to taste. Fill the tomatoes with the mixture and coat the tops with breadcrumbs. Place in a heatproof dish and sprinkle with the remaining oil. Cook in a preheated oven 200°C (400°F) (Gas Mark 6) for 10–15 minutes until golden brown.

LES TOPINAMBOURS
Jerusalem Artichokes

Topinambours are knobbly shaped tubers, only distantly related to the artichoke. Nor do they have anything to do with Jerusalem: it is possible that this is a corruption of *girasole*, the Italian name for the sunflower, to which they are also distantly related.

Jerusalem artichokes are easy to grow and ready to eat in the late autumn and winter. The tubers have a creamy-white or purplish skin. At one time they were very knobbly, but modern varieties are much smoother. They are best used as soon after gathering as possible because they go soft and will wither if stored for too long. Buy or dig them up as you need them. Either peel them thinly, or wash well and cook them in their skins and then peel. Keep and cook in acidulated water (page 10).

Besides the following recipes Jerusalem artichokes can also be cooked as for *Salsify au Gratin*. The sauce can be enriched by adding 2 beaten egg yolks.

Topinambours aux Fritots

JERUSALEM ARTICHOKE FRITTERS

Peel the artichokes and cook in boiling salted water for 15–20 minutes until almost tender. Drain well and slice. Cook as for *Salsify Frits* and garnish with lemon wedges.

500 g (1 lb) Jerusalem artichokes
2 tbsp lemon juice/vinegar
Pâte à Frire (page 220)
1–2 lemons
fat/oil for deep-frying

Topinambours à la Provençale

ARTICHOKES WITH TOMATOES AND HERBS

While this dish can be served alone, it goes remarkably well with fat roast meats, such as lamb and pork and, in particular, goose.

Peel the artichokes and cook in boiling salted water for 15 minutes until nearly tender. Drain and slice thickly. Meanwhile, skin, seed and chop the tomatoes. Peel and chop the garlic. Heat the oil in a pan and cook the artichokes for 2–3 minutes. Add the tomatoes, herbs and garlic and cook for 8–10 minutes until the tomatoes 'melt' and form a sauce and the artichokes are tender. Season well with salt and plenty of black pepper.

750 g (1½ lb) Jerusalem artichokes
350 g (12 oz) ripe tomatoes
1 clove garlic
3–4 tbsp olive oil
¼ tsp chopped fresh marjoram/thyme
salt
black pepper

DRIED VEGETABLES

Because such a large variety of dried vegetables are available in France, I have included a small selection of recipes for them. Although dried, these vegetables will not keep forever in your cupboard and will become very hard if stored for too long. Wash all dried vegetables well before using. With the exception of orange lentils, they all need to be soaked in cold water, and before cooking rinsed in cold water again. Cook dried vegetables without salt until they are almost tender (if salt is added in the beginning it will harden them).

Flageolets are small green beans. Lima beans can be used instead. Soak overnight and cook for 1–1¼ hours.

Haricots blancs — white (navy) beans — are one of the most popular dried vegetables. They can vary from small, white ones to large ones, sometimes called butter beans. If freshly dried they should not need soaking for more than 4–6 hours, but I always soak them overnight to be on the safe side. Cook them for 1½–2 hours.

Soissonaise is the name given to many dishes containing a purée of these beans, because they are grown widely around Soissons.

*Haricots rouge — red (kidney) beans — **must** be soaked for at least 18 hours. Rinse them, place in a pan of cold water and boil rapidly for 15 minutes before adding other ingredients. Cook for 2–2½ hours.*

Lentilles — lentils — have been eaten for thousands of years and have been found in Bronze-Age dwellings. There are two types of lentils used for cooking: a green French lentil and the orange Egyptian one. The green lentil, which is normally used in French cookery, varies in shade from bright green to greyish-green or brown. It is larger than the orange lentil and has more flavour.

Soak French lentils for at least 6 hours, or overnight, and cook them for 50–60 minutes. Orange lentils need no soaking; cook them for 30–40 minutes.

Pois cassés — split peas — can be yellow or green. They are often used in soups or can be served as a vegetable purée. Soak overnight for 1½–1¾ hours.

Pois chiches — chick-peas — are large, round, pale-yellow peas. They can be served as a vegetable or I have often eaten them as part of a mixed hors d'oeuvre with a vinaigrette or Sauce Ravigote (page 217). Soak them in cold water for at least 6 hours and cook for 1¾–2 hours.

Flageolets en Purée

FLAGEOLET PURÉE

This is excellent with roast lamb.

500 g (1 lb) (2½ cups) flageolets, soaked overnight
1 carrot
1 medium onion
2 cloves
bouquet garni
50 g (2 oz) (¼ cup) butter
3–4 tbsp double (heavy) cream

Soak the flageolets overnight. Peel the carrot and onion and stick the cloves into the onion. Rinse the flageolets and place in a pan of water with the carrot, onion and bouquet garni. Bring to the boil and cook for about 2 hours or until the flageolets are soft. Season with salt about 10 minutes before the end of the cooking time. Drain well. Discard the bouquet garni. Mash the flageolets with a fork or potato-masher. (If you prefer you can purée them through a vegetable mill or a food processor but a smooth purée is not essential, in fact, the slightly rough texture is a feature of this dish.) Return to the pan, if necessary, and beat in the butter and cream. Season to taste and reheat, stirring continuously. Pile into a hot dish.

Flageolets aux Champignons

FLAGEOLETS WITH MUSHROOMS

350 g (12 oz) (2 cups) dried flageolets, soaked overnight
1 carrot
1 onion
bouquet garni
250 g (8 oz) small button mushrooms
50 g (2 oz) (⅓ cup) butter
2 tsp lemon juice
100 ml (3½ fl oz) (½ cup) double (heavy) cream
salt and pepper

Soak the beans overnight in cold water. Drain and rinse well. Peel the carrot and onion and place in a pan of water with the beans and bouquet garni. Bring to the boil and simmer for 1–1½ hours until tender. Season with salt about 10 minutes before the end of the cooking time. Drain well and discard the carrot, onion and bouquet garni.

Trim, clean and quarter the mushrooms. Heat the butter in a pan and add the mushrooms and lemon juice. Cover and cook for 7–8 minutes until tender. Add the cream to the pan with the cooked flageolets. Bring to the boil, taste and adjust the seasoning. Pour into a hot dish.

Haricots Blancs au Gratin

BAKED HARICOT BEANS

350 g (12 oz) (2 cups) haricot beans, soaked overnight
1 onion
2 cloves
bouquet garni
2 cloves garlic
65 g (2½ oz) (⅓ cup) butter
2–3 tbsp white breadcrumbs
salt
pepper

Soak the beans overnight in cold water. Prepare and cook them as for *Haricots Blancs à la Vendéenne*. Drain well and remove the onion, bouquet garni and garlic. Melt half the butter in a pan, add the beans and mix well. Season to taste. Place in a dish and sprinkle with the breadcrumbs. Cut the remaining butter into small pieces and dot over the top. Bake in a preheated oven 200°C (400°F) (Gas Mark 6) for about 15 minutes until crisp and golden brown.

Haricots Blancs à la Vendéenne

HARICOT BEANS WITH HAM AND GARLIC

Soak the beans in cold water overnight. Peel the onion and stick the cloves into it. Peel the garlic, leave two cloves whole and crush the other two. Cut the ham/bacon into thick strips. Place the beans in a pan of water with the onion, two whole cloves of garlic and bouquet garni. Bring to the boil and cook for 1½–2 hours until the beans are tender. Add salt about 10 minutes before the end of the cooking time. Drain well and remove the onion, garlic and bouquet garni. Heat the butter in a pan and cook the ham/bacon until golden brown. Remove from the pan. Add the cream and cook until it thickens, then add the crushed garlic and chopped parsley. Cook for a moment or two, then stir in the beans, mix well and season to taste. Put in a hot dish and sprinkle with the cooked ham.

350 g (12 oz) (2 cups) dried haricot beans, soaked overnight
1 onion
2 cloves
4 cloves garlic
250 g (8 oz) smoked ham/bacon
bouquet garni
50 g (2 oz) (¼ cup) butter
100 ml (3½ fl oz) (½ cup) double (heavy) cream
salt
black pepper
1 tbsp chopped parsley

Lentilles à la Dijonnaise

DIJON-STYLE LENTILS

Serve this hot as a dish on its own or for a light lunch or supper. For the best flavour, use mustard containing whole mustard seeds (aux grains).

Soak the lentils for at least 6 hours or overnight in cold water. Drain and cook in a pan of water with 1 whole, peeled onion for about 50–60 minutes until tender. Season with salt about 10 minutes before the end of the cooking time. Drain well and discard the onion. Peel and finely chop the other onion and dice the ham/meat. Melt the butter in a pan and cook the onion until soft and golden brown. Stir in the flour and cook for a minute or two, then pour in the stock a little at a time, stirring constantly. Add the mustard and ham/meat and season to taste with salt and pepper. Cook for 2–3 minutes then add the lentils and mix well. Cook for 4–5 minutes. Pile into a hot dish.

350 g (12 oz) (1½ cups) green lentils, soaked overnight
2 onions
150 g (6 oz) ham/cold roast meat
50 g (2 oz) (¼ cup) butter
1½ tbsp flour
300 ml (½ pt) (1¼ cups) white stock
2 tbsp Dijon mustard
salt
black pepper

Lentilles aux Épinards

LENTILS WITH SPINACH

Soak the lentils for at least 6 hours or overnight. Wash the spinach well and remove the coarse stalks. Peel the onions and leave the small ones whole and finely chop the medium one. Remove the stalks, cores and seeds from the peppers and cut into thin strips. Peel and crush the garlic. Place the lentils in a large pan of cold water with the small onions and sliced peppers. Cook for 50–60 minutes until the lentils are nearly tender, then add the spinach and 1 tablespoon of salt. Continue cooking until the spinach and lentils are tender. Drain well. Heat half the butter and oil in a pan and cook the chopped onion until nearly soft. Add the remaining butter and oil with the garlic and spices and cook for 2–3 minutes. Add the lentils and spinach mixture and cook over gentle heat for 10 minutes, stirring frequently. Pile into a hot dish and serve very hot.

350 g (12 oz) (1½ cups) green lentils, soaked overnight
500 g (1 lb) spinach
6 small onions
1 medium onion
2 small red peppers
1 clove garlic
1 tbsp salt
75 g (3 oz) (6 tbsp) butter
4 tbsp oil
2 cloves
2 cardomom seeds
scant tsp powdered cinnamon
scant ½ tsp tumeric and powdered cumin

Purée de Pois Cassés

PURÉE OF SPLIT PEAS

Serve this with grilled sausages or bacon and roast pork. Some recipes suggest cooking pigs' feet with the peas. When cooked they are brushed with butter, coated with breadcrumbs, grilled until golden brown and crisp and served with the purée. Alternatively, it is traditional in some parts of France to serve the purée with a bowl of fried croûtons.

500 g (1 lb) (2½ cups) split peas, soaked overnight
1 leek
1 carrot
2 onions
bouquet garni
3 tbsp double (heavy) cream
25 g (1 oz) (2 tbsp) butter
salt
black pepper

Soak the peas overnight in cold water. Trim the leek, wash well and slice the white part (keep the green part for soup). Peel and slice the carrot and onions. Place the peas, leek, carrot and onions in a pan of cold water with the bouquet garni. Bring to the boil, cover and cook for 1½–1¾ hours until the peas are tender. About 10 minutes before the end of the cooking time remove the lid and cook until all the liquid has evaporated. Season to taste. Remove the bouquet garni and purée the peas through a vegetable mill or in a food processor. Return to the pan and heat through. Stir in the cream and butter and check the seasoning. Pile on to a hot dish.

Pois Chiches à la Fondue de Tomates

CHICK-PEAS IN TOMATO SAUCE

The tomato sauce, or fondue, in this recipe uses the shallots of Provence — the long, pinkish-red ones that have a sweet flavour. If you are unable to obtain these, use 3–4 small shallots or 2 medium onions.

250 g (8 oz) (1¼ cups) chick-peas, soaked overnight
500 g (1 lb) ripe tomatoes
2 pink Provençale shallots or 3–4 small shallots/2 medium onions
2 cloves garlic
3 tbsp olive oil
bouquet garni
salt
black pepper
1 tbsp chopped parsley

Soak the peas overnight in cold water. Cook in boiling water for 1½–2 hours until tender. Season to taste with salt about 10 minutes before the end of the cooking time. Meanwhile, peel, seed and chop the tomatoes and peel and finely chop the shallots and garlic. Heat the oil in a pan and cook the shallots for 3–4 minutes. Add the tomatoes, garlic and bouquet garni. Season to taste and cook over gentle heat for about 30 minutes. Remove the bouquet garni and check the seasoning. When the peas are cooked, drain well and mix into the sauce. Pour into a hot dish and garnish with parsley just before serving.

Pois Chiches à la Catalane

CATALONIAN CHICK-PEAS

Chorizo is a Spanish garlic sausage. If this is not available use any garlic cooking sausage.

250 g (8 oz) (1¼ cups) chick-peas, soaked overnight
100 g (4 oz) smoked, streaky bacon
200 g (6 oz) chorizo
4 tomatoes
1 clove garlic
2–3 tbsp olive oil
bouquet garni
salt
black pepper

Soak the peas in cold water overnight then cook in boiling water for 1½–2 hours until tender. Add salt to taste about 10 minutes before the end of the cooking time. Drain and reserve some of the cooking liquor. Remove the rind and dice the bacon. Slice the sausage thickly. Peel, seed and chop the tomatoes. Peel the garlic. Heat the oil in a pan and cook the bacon, sausage and garlic for a few minutes. Add the tomatoes and bouquet and cook for 5 minutes. Add the peas and sufficient cooking liquor to moisten the mixture. Cook for 7–10 minutes then remove the bouquet garni and the clove of garlic. Check the seasoning and if necessary add a little more cooking liquor to give a soft consistency.

2 SOUPS

HOT SOUPS

Consommé

A tasty consommé needs a really good meat or chicken stock. The liquid from boiled beef or poached chicken is excellent, but vegetables are also essential, not only for extra flavour but to act as a filter that clarifies the stock. For this reason I feel consommé deserves a place among soups made from vegetables.

The secrets of making a delicious consommé are quite simple. Firstly, chop all the vegetables very fine so they create greater bulk in the filter that forms on top of the stock. Secondly, stir the soup gently all the time until the stock is on the point of boiling and just about to break through the filter. If you stop stirring too soon the egg white will sink to the bottom, the filter will not form properly and the result will be cloudy. Thirdly, as soon as the filter is formed, lower the heat. The stock should not boil rapidly but must be kept simmering so the filter remains on the surface. If it stops simmering the filter will sink to the bottom.

To keep consommé hot or to reheat it, place it in a bowl over a pan of hot water. It can go cloudy if reheated over direct heat.

Trim the white part of the leek and the celery, and peel the carrot. Cut all three into very small dice or chop in a food processor (take care to run the machine for only a moment or two or the vegetables will purée). Cut the tomato into pieces (canned tomatoes or the pulp and skins from another recipe will do). Shred the shin of beef (this can also be done in a food processor) and soak in the water for 20 minutes.

Place the vegetables in a pan with the stock. Lightly whisk the egg whites into the water and meat with a fork and add to the pan of vegetables. Season to taste (it is essential to season well at this stage because the vegetables will absorb some of the seasoning). Bring to the boil over very gentle heat stirring continuously. As soon as the filter coagulates and the liquid shows signs of breaking through, stop stirring, lower the heat and leave to simmer for 30–45 minutes. Take care that it simmers constantly or the filter will sink and spoil the clarification.

Place a piece of wet muslin in a sieve over a bowl. Carefully strain the liquid through the muslin, keeping the filter in the pan with a large spoon — another pair of hands is useful here! Add the sherry and, if necessary, season with a little more salt. Add the garnish of your choice.

1 medium leek
1 stick celery
1 carrot
1 tomato
100 g (4 oz) lean shin/shank of beef (optional)
4 tbsp water
4 egg whites
1 litre (2 pt) (1 quart) good-flavoured stock
salt
pepper
3–4 tbsp sherry (to taste)

Consommé à la Julienne

CONSOMMÉ WITH VEGETABLES

1 small carrot
1 small turnip
1 small stick celery
6–8 French/snap beans
1 litre (2 pt) (1 quart) consommé

See also Consommé en Gelée and Consommé Madrilène en Gelée.

Peel and trim the vegetables and cut into very thin strips about 5 cm (2 in) long. Cook in boiling salted water until tender. Drain well and place in the bottom of a hot soup tureen. Pour the hot consommé over.

Crème à la Bruxelloise

CREAM OF BRUSSELS SPROUTS SOUP

This soup is an ideal way of using large or overgrown sprouts.

500 g (1 lb) Brussels sprouts
900 ml (1½ pt) (4 cups) chicken stock
75 g (3 oz) (6 tbsp) butter
40 g (1½ oz) (6 tbsp) flour
300 ml (½ pt) (1¼ cups) milk
150 ml (¼ pt) (²⁄₃ cup) single (light) cream
salt
pepper

Trim and wash the Brussels sprouts. If possible, reserve 8–10 very small ones for garnish. Place the sprouts in a pan with the stock. Season lightly and cook for 25–30 minutes. Purée through a vegetable mill or in a liquidizer. Melt 50 g (2 oz) (¼ cup) butter in a pan, add the flour and cook for 2–3 minutes. Add the soup and milk a little at a time, stirring continuously. Bring to the boil, still stirring, and season to taste. Meanwhile, cook the reserved sprouts in boiling salted water until tender. Drain well. Melt half the remaining butter in a pan and cook the sprouts gently until brown. Place in the bottom of a hot soup tureen. Add the cream to the soup and heat through. Check the seasoning and beat in the remaining butter a little at a time. Pour into the tureen.

Crème de Laitues

CREAM OF LETTUCE SOUP

Overgrown lettuces or those that have 'bolted' can be used with great success in this delicious soup. Trim the leaves from the thick stems and use the equivalent of two good lettuces.

2 lettuces
2 medium onions
50 g (2 oz) (¼ cup) butter
50 g (2 oz) (½ cup) flour
600 ml (1 pt) (2½ cups) chicken stock
300 ml (½ pt) (1¼ cups) milk
150 ml (¼ pt) (²⁄₃ cup) single (light) cream
2 egg yolks

Wash the lettuce and remove the coarse stalks. Take a few good leaves, roll up like a cigar and cut into very thin shreds. Put to one side. Peel and chop the onions. Heat the butter in a pan, add the onion and cook gently until soft but without colour. Meanwhile, blanch the remaining lettuce in boiling salted water for 2–4 minutes. Drain well, refresh in cold water and drain well again. When the onions are soft, add the flour and cook for 2–3 minutes. Then stir in the stock and milk and bring to the boil, stirring continuously. Add the blanched lettuce, season lightly and simmer for 25–30 minutes.

Purée the soup through a fine vegetable mill or in a liquidizer. Return to the pan and heat through. Beat the cream and egg yolks together. Pour in a little of the soup, mix well and strain back into the pan. Check the seasoning and heat through without boiling. Place the reserved shredded lettuce in the bottom of a warm soup tureen and pour the hot soup over.

Crème de Carottes

CREAM OF CARROT SOUP

Peel and slice the carrots and onion. Melt 50 g (2 oz) (¼ cup) butter in a pan and add the vegetables. Cover with greaseproof paper and a lid and cook over very gentle heat for 10–15 minutes until soft but without colour. Remove the greaseproof paper. Wash the rice and add to the pan with the stock, sugar and bouquet garni. Season lightly with salt and pepper. Bring to the boil and simmer for 30 minutes. Remove the bouquet garni. Purée the soup through a vegetable mill or in a liquidizer. Return to the pan and add enough milk to give a creamy consistency. Stir in the cream and reheat, then whisk in the remaining butter in small pieces. Check and adjust the seasoning. Pour into a hot soup tureen and sprinkle with the tarragon. Serve with fried diced croûtons.

500 g (1 lb) carrots
1 medium onion
65 g (2½ oz) (⅓ cup) butter
40 g (1½ oz) (4 tbsp) rice
1 litre (2 pt) (1 quart) stock
½ tsp sugar
bouquet garni
salt
pepper
300 ml (½ pt) (1¼ cups) milk
4 tbsp double (heavy) cream
1–2 tsp chopped tarragon
fried diced croûtons (page 221)

Crème de Haricots Frais

CREAM OF HARICOT (NAVY) BEAN SOUP

If fresh beans are not available the soup can be made with 100 g (4 oz) dried beans, soaked overnight.

Shell the beans and peel the onions and garlic. Slice the onions and crush the garlic. Peel, seed and chop the tomatoes. Heat the butter in a pan, add the onions and when they begin to colour add the beans. Cover and cook over very gentle heat for 10–15 minutes. Add the tomato to the pan with the garlic, bouquet garni and stock. Mix well. Partly cover the pan and simmer for 1–1¼ hours until the beans are soft. Discard the bouquet garni. Purée the soup through a fine vegetable mill or in a liquidizer. Add the cream and season to taste. Bring to the boil and simmer for 5 minutes. Pour into a hot soup tureen and serve with fried diced croûtons.

350 g (12 oz) (2 cups) fresh haricot (navy) beans
2 medium onions
1 clove garlic
2 tomatoes
50 g (2 oz) (¼ cup) butter
bouquet garni
1 litre (2 pt) (1 quart) chicken stock
3 tbsp double (heavy) cream
fried diced croûtons (page 221)

Crème d'Oseille

CREAM OF SORREL SOUP

Sorrel soup is a great favourite of mine, but it does tend to curdle easily, especially if it is kept hot. However, this is easily overcome by simply liquidizing the soup at high speed for a moment or two and reheating carefully. The best way to keep the soup hot is in a bowl over a pan of gently simmering water, making certain that the water does not touch the bowl. Pour into a warm, not hot, soup tureen.

Wash the sorrel and remove the coarse stalks. Roll the leaves up like a cigar and shred finely. Heat the butter in a pan, add the sorrel and cook gently, stirring occasionally, until it 'melts'. Stir in the flour and mix well. Add the stock a little at a time, stirring constantly. If potatoes are used instead of flour, peel them and cut into small pieces and add at the same time as the stock. Bring to the boil, season to taste and simmer gently for 20–25 minutes. Purée the soup through a vegetable mill or in a liquidizer. Return to the pan and heat through. Beat the egg yolks and cream together, pour on a little of the hot soup, mix well and return to the pan. Check the seasoning and reheat without boiling. Sprinkle with chopped chervil just before serving.

150 g (6 oz) sorrel
50 g (2 oz) (¼ cup) butter
50 g (2 oz) (½ cup) flour/250 g (8 oz) potatoes
1 litre (2 pt) (1 quart) well-flavoured stock
3 egg yolks
150 ml (¼ pt) (⅔ cup) single (light) cream
salt
pepper
1 tbsp chopped chervil

Gratinée Campagnarde

COUNTRY SOUP

This dish comes from Dauphiné, the beautiful region of the French Alps bordering Italy. For best results use floury potatoes.

Serves 6–8
500 g (1 lb) pumpkin
500 g (1 lb) old potatoes
2 medium onions
200 g (6 oz) Swiss chard/spinach leaves
25 g (1 oz) (2 tbsp) butter
1.5 litres (2½ pt) (6 cups) stock/water
1 litre (1¾ pt) (1 quart) milk
salt
black pepper
6–8 slices French bread
75 g (3 oz) Emmenthal cheese

Peel the pumpkin, potatoes and onions. Cut the pumpkin and potatoes into small pieces and finely chop the onion. Wash the chard/spinach leaves well and remove the centre stalks. Shred the leaves finely. Heat the butter in a large pan and cook the onions until soft but without colour. Add the pumpkin, potatoes and chard/spinach leaves. Pour on the stock or water. If necessary, add more water to cover the vegetables. Season lightly, bring to the boil and simmer for 40 minutes or until the pumpkin is tender. Strain the vegetables and keep the cooking liquor. Purée the vegetables through a fine vegetable mill, blender or food processor.

Measure the cooking liquor and make up to 2 litres (3½ pints) (2½ quarts) pints with milk. Reserve 6 tablespoons of the purée and return the rest to a pan with the liquid. Taste and adjust the seasoning. Heat through, stirring occasionally. Meanwhile, grate the cheese and grill the bread on both sides. Coat one side of each piece with the vegetable purée and sprinkle with grated cheese. Put under a hot grill until golden brown. Pour the soup into a hot soup tureen and serve the toasted cheese separately.

Potage à la Basquaise

BASQUE VEGETABLE SOUP

2 carrots
1 turnip
1 leek
1 litre (2 pt) (5 cups) stock
bouquet garni
2 small red peppers
12–18 small spring onions (scallions)
50 g (2 oz) (¼ cup) butter
4 tbsp rice
salt and pepper
1 tbsp chopped chervil

Peel the carrots and turnip and chop finely. Trim and wash the leek and slice thinly. Place in a pan with the stock and bouquet garni, season lightly and cook for 15 minutes. Meanwhile, remove the stalks, cores and seeds from the peppers and dice finely. Peel the onions. Melt the butter in a pan, add the peppers and onions and cook for 8–10 minutes. Wash the rice, add to the soup with the peppers and onions and continue cooking for 12–15 minutes until the rice is tender. Pour into a hot soup tureen and sprinkle with chopped chervil just before serving.

Potage Neige Blanche

WHITE SNOW SOUP

750 g (1½ lb) old potatoes
2 medium onions
600 ml (1 pt) (2½ cups) chicken stock
600 ml (1 pt) (2½ cups) milk
50 g (2 oz) (½ cup) grated Parmesan cheese
fried diced croûtons (page 221)

Peel and slice the potatoes and onions and cook in the stock for 20–30 minutes until tender. Purée through a vegetable mill or liquidizer. Return to the pan, add the milk, bring to the boil and season to taste. Pour into a hot soup tureen and stir in the Parmesan cheese just before serving. Serve with fried croûtons.

Potage au Cresson

WATERCRESS SOUP

Trim and wash the watercress and reserve 10–12 small sprigs for garnish. Drain the rest well and chop coarsely. Peel the onion and potatoes. Trim and wash the leek. Finely slice the onion and leek and cut the potatoes into small pieces. Melt the butter in a pan, add the onion and leek and cook gently for 7–10 minutes until tender but without colour. Add the watercress and cook for 3–4 minutes. Add the potatoes and stock, season lightly and bring to the boil. Simmer for 20–30 minutes. Purée through a fine vegetable mill or in a liquidizer. Return to the pan, add the milk and reheat. Beat the cream and egg yolks together and add a little soup. Mix well and pour back into the pan. Check and adjust the seasoning and reheat without boiling. Pour into a warm soup tureen and sprinkle with sprigs of watercress.

1 large bunch watercress
1 medium onion
2 moderately large potatoes
1 leek
50 g (2 oz) (¼ cup) butter
900 ml (1½ pt) (3¼ cups) chicken stock
300 ml (½ pt) (1¼ cups) milk
150 ml (¼ pt) (⅔ cup) single (light) cream
2 egg yolks
salt
pepper

Potage Doria

CUCUMBER SOUP

Peel the cucumber. If possible cut out a few small balls with a ball-cutter for garnish. Otherwise, cut a few small dice and put to one side. Chop the remaining cucumber coarsely. Trim the white part of the leek and slice thinly. Peel the potatoes and cut into pieces. Melt 40 g (1½ oz) (3 tbsp) butter in a pan, add the leek and cook gently until soft but without colour. Add the stock, chopped cucumber and potatoes. Season lightly, bring to the boil and simmer for 40–45 minutes.

Purée the soup through a fine vegetable mill or in a liquidizer. Strain back into the pan and reheat. Meanwhile, blanch the cucumber garnish in boiling salted water for 5 minutes. Drain well. Melt the remaining butter in a small pan, add the blanched cucumber and cook gently until tender. Beat the egg yolks and cream together and pour on a little soup. Strain back into the remaining soup. Heat through without boiling. Adjust the seasoning. Place the cucumber garnish in the bottom of a warm soup tureen and pour the soup over. Sprinkle with herbs just before serving.

1 large cucumber
1 leek
350 g (12 oz) potatoes
50 g (2 oz) (¼ cup) butter
1 litre (2 pt) (1 quart) chicken stock
2 egg yolks
100 ml (3½ fl oz) (½ cup) double (heavy) cream
salt
pepper
1 tbsp chopped chervil

Potage au Fenouil

FENNEL SOUP

Wash, trim and finely slice the fennel. Peel the potatoes and cut into small pieces. Melt the butter in a pan, add the fennel, cover with greaseproof paper and a lid and cook for 10–15 minutes until tender but without colour. Add the potatoes and stock. Bring to the boil, season to taste and simmer gently for 20–30 minutes. Purée through a vegetable mill or in a liquidizer. Return the soup to the pan. Mix the rice flour with a little water and add to the soup. Bring to the boil and cook for a few minutes. Mix the cream with the egg yolks. Pour on a little hot soup, mix well and strain back into the pan. Season to taste and heat through without boiling. Serve with fried, diced croûtons.

2 good-sized heads of fennel
250 g (8 oz) potatoes
65 g (2½ oz) (⅓ cup) butter
1 litre (2 pt) (1 quart) stock
1–2 tbsp crème de riz (rice flour)
150 ml (¼ pt) (⅔ cup) single (light) cream
2 egg yolks
salt and pepper
fried diced croûtons (page 221)

2 leeks
500 g (1 lb) potatoes
50 g (2 oz) (¼ cup) butter
900 ml (1½ pt) (3¾ cups) white stock
450 ml (¾ pt) (2 cups) milk
1 bay leaf
1 blade mace
4 tbsp double (heavy) cream (optional)
salt and white pepper
1 tbsp chopped parsley
toasted/fried croûtons (page 221)

1.5 kg (3 lb) pumpkin (750 g [1½ lb]
  flesh)
250 g (8 oz) potatoes
2 medium onions
900 ml (1½ pt) (3¾ cups) chicken stock
450 ml (¾ pt) (2 cups) milk
25 g (1 oz) (2 tbsp) butter
salt and pepper
1 tbsp chopped herbs
fried diced croûtons (page 221)

750 g (1½ lb) ripe tomatoes
2 medium onions
2 cloves garlic
4–5 tbsp olive oil
1 litre (2 pt) (1 quart) stock
bouquet garni
2 tbsp rice
1 tbsp chopped basil
50–75 g (2–3 oz) (½–¾ cup) grated
  Gruyère cheese
garlic croûtons (page 221)

2 leeks
3 large cloves garlic
250 g (8 oz) tomatoes
2 fairly large potatoes
4–5 tbsp olive oil
1 litre (2 pt) (1 quart) stock
good pinch saffron
salt and pepper
½ French loaf
50–75 g (2–3 oz) (½–¾ cup) grated
  Gruyère cheese

Potage Parmentier

POTATO SOUP

Trim the leeks, peel the potatoes and slice thinly. Heat the butter in a pan, add the leeks and cook until soft but without colour. Add the potatoes, stock, milk, bay leaf and mace. Season lightly, bring to the boil and simmer gently for 20–30 minutes. Remove the bay leaf and mace. Purée the soup through a vegetable mill or in a liquidizer. Return to the pan and reheat. Add the cream and check the seasoning. Pour into a hot soup tureen and sprinkle with chopped parsley just before serving. Serve with toasted or fried croûtons.

Potage au Potiron

PUMPKIN SOUP

Peel the pumpkin, remove the seeds and cut 750 g (1½ lb) into small pieces and peel and dice the potatoes and onions. Place in a pan with the stock, season lightly and cook for 20–30 minutes or until tender. Purée through a fine vegetable mill or in a liquidizer. Return to the pan and add enough milk to make a creamy consistency. Beat in the butter. Taste and adjust the seasoning and reheat. Pour into a hot soup tureen and sprinkle with the herbs. Serve with fried diced croûtons.

Potage à la Provençale

PROVENÇAL SOUP

Peel, seed and chop the tomatoes. Peel the onions and garlic, chop the onions and crush 1 clove garlic. Heat 2 tbsp oil in a pan and cook the onions until soft and beginning to colour. Add the crushed garlic and cook for another few minutes. Add the tomatoes and cook gently for 10 minutes. Add the stock and bouquet garni. Season lightly and simmer for 20–30 minutes. Purée through a vegetable mill or in a liquidizer. Return to the pan with the rice and cook for 15–20 minutes. When the soup is cooked, taste and adjust the seasoning. Pour into a hot tureen, sprinkle the basil over the top and serve with the croûtons and cheese.

Soupe à l'Ail Bonne Femme

HOUSEWIFE'S GARLIC SOUP

Trim, wash and slice the leeks. Peel and crush the garlic. Peel, seed and chop the tomatoes. Peel the potatoes and cut into 1-cm (½-in) dice. Heat 2 tablespoons of oil in a pan, add the leeks and cook for 7–8 minutes until soft but without colour. Add the garlic, tomatoes, potatoes, stock and saffron. Season to taste and bring to the boil. Simmer for 25–30 minutes. Meanwhile, slice the bread. Dip each side into the remaining oil. Sprinkle with grated cheese and bake in a preheated oven 200°C (400°F) (Gas Mark 6) for 10–15 minutes until golden brown. Taste the soup, adjust the seasoning and pour into a hot soup tureen. Place a piece of bread in each soup plate and pour the soup over.

Soupe au Pistou

PISTOU SOUP

French cooks have always been happy to borrow and adapt good recipes from their neighbours. Soupe au Pistou is the French version of the Italian Minestrone alla Genovese, which is flavoured with pesto — a paste made from pine nuts, basil, cheese and oil. This has been adapted and given the Provence name of pistou and the soup has become a speciality of Nice. Canned red (kidney) beans can be used to save time.

Soak the beans in cold water overnight. Rinse and drain and place in a large pan with 2 litres (4 pints) (2 quarts) water. Bring to the boil and simmer for about 2½ hours (fresh beans need 1½–1¾ hours). Meanwhile, peel or trim the vegetables. Cut the turnip, carrots, potatoes and celery into small dice. Slice the leeks, onions and courgettes (zucchini). Cut the French (snap) beans into 1-cm (½-in) lengths and chop the tomatoes. When the beans are almost tender, add the vegetables (except the garlic), season lightly and cook for 30 minutes. Check the seasoning, add the pasta and cook for 10–12 minutes.

To prepare the *pistou*, chop the garlic and put in a mortar or liquidizer with the basil and cheese. Grind or blend to a paste. When reasonably smooth, add a little oil and grind until smooth. Then add the rest of the oil a little at a time as for mayonnaise. When the pasta is tender, add the *pistou* to the soup and mix well. Boil for a moment or two and pour into a hot soup tureen. If you wish, serve extra Parmesan cheese separately.

100 g (4 oz) dried haricot (navy) or red (kidney) beans, soaked overnight or 150 g (6 oz) fresh shelled beans
1 small turnip
2 carrots
2–3 firm medium potatoes
1 stick celery
2 small leeks (optional)
2 medium onions
2 courgettes (zucchini)
75 g (3 oz) (⅔ cup) French (snap) beans
3 large tomatoes
50 g (2 oz) vermicelli/pasta

Pistou:
4–5 cloves garlic
2–3 tbsp chopped basil
50 g (2 oz) (½ cup) grated Parmesan cheese
3 tbsp olive oil
salt and pepper

Soupe Meusienne

ARDENNES-STYLE VEGETABLE SOUP

Use an unsmoked bacon (ham) hock if possible and soak it for 2–3 hours. Otherwise, use a smoked hock and soak it overnight. A ham hock does not need soaking.

Soak the hock of bacon/ham. Peel and slice the onions. Wash the lettuce and shred finely. Peel the celeriac and cut into small dice. Melt the butter in a large pan, add the onions and celeriac/celery and cook until soft but without colour. Add the lettuce and cook for a further 2–3 minutes. Pour the water into the pan and add the peas, bacon hock, bouquet garni and clove. Bring to the boil and simmer gently for about 1½ hours until the bacon is tender.

Remove the bacon, bouquet garni and clove from the soup. Cut and dice half of the meat from the bacon/ham hock (use the remainder in a dish which requires chopped ham). Purée the rest of the soup through a vegetable mill or in a liquidizer. Return to the pan, add the cream and simmer for 2–3 minutes, then add the bacon. Taste and adjust the seasoning. Pour into a hot soup tureen and sprinkle with chopped parsley just before serving.

1 bacon (ham) hock
3 medium onions
1 large lettuce
1 small celeriac/2 sticks celery
50 g (2 oz) (¼ cup) butter
1.5 litres (2½ pt) (6 cups) water
75 g (3 oz) shelled/frozen peas
bouquet garni
1 clove
100 ml (3½ fl oz) (½ cup) double (heavy) cream
salt and pepper
1 tbsp chopped parsley

Soupe Savoyarde

SAVOY SOUP

2 leeks
1 large onion
2 small turnips
1 small celeriac
500 g (1 lb) potatoes
50 g (2 oz) (¼ cup) butter
600 ml (1 pt) (2½ cups) white stock
600 ml (1 pt) (2½ cups) milk
salt and pepper
100 g (4 oz) Gruyère cheese
fried diced croûtons (page 221)

Peel or trim the vegetables. Slice the white part of the leeks and the onion. Cut the turnips, celeriac and potatoes into small dice. Heat the butter in a pan, add the leeks, onion, turnips and celeriac. Cover with greaseproof paper and a lid and cook gently for 10–15 minutes until soft but without colour. Add the potatoes and stock, season lightly and cook for 30 minutes. Heat the milk, add to the soup and taste and adjust the seasoning. Slice the cheese thinly. Just before serving, place the croûtons in the bottom of a hot soup tureen, cover with the sliced Gruyère cheese and pour the hot soup over. Serve immediately.

Soupe Tourangelle

TOURRAINE-STYLE VEGETABLE SOUP

1 large onion
3 small leeks
100 g (4 oz) turnips
100 g (4 oz) celeriac
100 g (4 oz) cauliflower
50 g (2 oz) French (snap) beans
50 g (2 oz) (¼ cup) butter
1.5 litres (2½ pt) (6 cups) stock/water
salt and white pepper
50 g (2 oz) shelled fresh/frozen peas
2 tbsp double cream
1 tbsp chopped parsley/chervil

Peel or trim the vegetables. Thinly slice the onion and leeks. Cut the turnips and celeriac into small dice and break the cauliflower into small florets. Top and tail the beans and cut into 1-cm (½-in) lengths. Melt the butter in a pan and cook the onions and leeks until soft but without colour. Add the turnips, celeriac and cauliflower and continue cooking gently until the butter is absorbed. Add the stock/water and season with salt and white pepper. Simmer for 35–40 minutes. Add the beans and peas, if they are fresh, and simmer for 20 minutes. If frozen peas are used, add them about 10 minutes before the end of the cooking time. Check the seasoning and pour into a hot soup tureen. Swirl the cream on top and garnish with chopped parsley and chervil just before serving.

Velouté de Tomate à l'Orange

TOMATO AND ORANGE SOUP

750 g (1½ lb) ripe/canned tomatoes
100 g (4 oz) (½ cup) orange lentils
1 orange
1 medium carrot
1 large onion
25 g (1 oz) (2 tbsp) butter
bouquet garni
1 litre (2 pt) (1 quart) stock
salt
pepper

Cut the tomatoes into pieces. Wash the lentils. Peel the rind thinly from the orange (a potato peeler is ideal because it is important that none of the pith is used). Press the juice from the orange and put to one side. Peel the carrot and onion and chop finely. Heat the butter and cook the carrot and onion slowly for 7–10 minutes until soft but without colour. Then add the tomatoes, orange rind, lentils, bouquet garni and stock. Bring to the boil and simmer for about 1 hour until the lentils are tender. Season with salt and pepper to taste. Remove the bouquet garni and purée the soup through a vegetable mill or in a liquidizer. Stir in the orange juice, check the seasoning and reheat.

To serve cold: cool then refrigerate for at least 2 hours before serving. If it is necessary to adjust the consistency of the soup when it is cold add more stock and a little more orange juice to taste.

COLD SOUPS

Consommé en Gelée

JELLIED CONSOMMÉ

Consommé en Gelée is clarified in the same way as *Consommé*. A good-flavoured stock is essential: one that is made with veal bones or raw chicken carcases is best because it will set naturally in a light jelly, which is the consistency you need. It should not be too stiff but half way between a jelly and a liquid. In an emergency, soften 2–3 teaspoons of powdered gelatine in a little water and add to 1 litre (2 pints) (1 quart) of stock before you begin to clarify. Season well before clarification. Serve chilled in individual cups or glasses. When set garnish with a thin slice of lemon, a swirl of lightly soured cream or a few chopped herbs — tarragon is very good.

Consommé Madrilène en Gelée

JELLIED CONSOMMÉ MADRILÈNE

Prepare the consommé as for *Consommé en Gelée* but flavour the stock with 1–2 teaspoons of tomato purée. Skin and seed 2 tomatoes, shred finely and place in the bottom of individual cups or glasses. Pour on the clarified consommé and serve chilled.

Potage Glacé aux Avocats

CHILLED AVOCADO SOUP

Blend the creams with 2 tablespoons of lemon juice and leave for 20–30 minutes until they begin to thicken. Cut the avocados in half, remove the stones, peel and dice. Peel and finely chop the shallot and dice the cucumber finely. Mix 1 tablespoon lemon juice and stock with the avocados. Purée through a vegetable mill, food processor or liquidizer. Strain into a bowl, add the cream and season to taste with salt, pepper and more lemon juice if required. Chill well before serving. Pour into a soup tureen or individual bowls and sprinkle with a few herbs.

150 ml (¼ pt) (⅔ cup) single (light) cream
100 ml (3½ fl oz) (½ cup) double (heavy) cream
4–5 tbsp lemon juice
2 large, ripe avocados
1 shallot
50 g (2 oz) cucumber
450 ml (¾ pt) (2 cups) chicken stock
salt and pepper
mixed chopped herbs

Potage Glacé à la Catalane

CHILLED CATALAN SOUP

Soak the breadcrumbs in the vinegar. Peel, seed and chop the tomatoes. Trim the celery, courgette (zucchini) and cucumber. Peel the aubergine (eggplant), onion and garlic. Cut all the vegetables into small pieces and mix with the bread. Purée the vegetables through a very fine vegetable mill or in a food processor. Stir in the oil and stock. Season to taste with salt only. Cover and refrigerate for 24 hours. Check the soup. If it is too thick add a little more stock/water until it is the consistency of thin cream. Season to taste with black pepper and more salt if required. Serve well chilled.

50 g (2 oz) (1 cup) breadcrumbs
4 tbsp wine vinegar
350 g (12 oz) tomatoes
1 stick celery
1 small courgette (zucchini)
¼ cucumber
½ small aubergine (eggplant)
1 small onion
1 clove garlic
4 tbsp olive oil
600 ml (1 pt) (2½ cups) chicken stock/water
salt and black pepper

1 carrot
1 medium onion
1 clove garlic
1 leek
1 litre (2 pt) (1 quart) chicken stock
bouquet garni
1 small celeriac
1 tbsp lemon juice/vinegar
4 tomatoes
200 ml (7 fl oz) (1 cup) tomato juice
salt and pepper
chopped chives

1 cucumber
600 ml (1 pt) (2½ cups) plain yogurt
2 cloves garlic
100 ml (3 fl oz) (½ cup) water
3–4 tbsp lemon juice
1 tsp chopped tarragon
2 tsp chopped parsley
salt and pepper

Potage Monaco

MONACO SOUP

Peel the carrot, onion and garlic. Trim and wash the leek. Slice the carrot, onion and leek finely and crush the garlic. Place in a pan with the stock and bouquet garni. Season lightly, bring to the boil and simmer gently for 1 hour. Strain. Reserve the liquor and discard the vegetables. Meanwhile, peel the celeriac and dice finely. Cook in boiling salted water with the lemon juice/vinegar until tender. Drain, refresh and drain well again. Peel, seed and chop the tomatoes. Add the tomato juice, celeriac and tomatoes to the prepared liquor as soon as it is cool. Pour into a soup tureen and chill well. Sprinkle with chopped chives.

Soupe Glacée au Concombre

CHILLED CUCUMBER SOUP

Cut several thin slices from the cucumber and put to one side. Peel and coarsely chop the remaining cucumber and the garlic. Purée the garlic and cucumber with the yogurt. Strain and mix with the water and lemon juice. Season to taste. Strain into a soup tureen and chill for at least 1 hour. Garnish with the cucumber slices and sprinkle with herbs.

3 HORS D'OEUVRE & SALADS

COLD HORS D'OEUVRE

Aïoli Garni

From Provence comes the traditional dish Aïoli Garni, an assortment of lightly cooked or raw vegetables with fish and meat served with a marvellous Aïoli Sauce — a mayonnaise heavily flavoured with garlic. This is not a dish for the fainthearted, but if you love garlic, this is an excellent excuse to enjoy it.

The beauty of Aïoli is that it is so easy to prepare: no recipe is needed, just use the vegetables you have to hand and adjust the quantities to the number of people. Excellent as an hors d'oeuvre, Aïoli Garni is also an ideal lunch or supper dish, particularly on a hot summer's day.

Morue (dried cod) is used in traditional recipes, but smoked cod, haddock or pieces of white fish, such as monkfish, fresh cod, etc. — cooked without soaking — can be used. Ham and other cooked meats can also be included. Dried or fresh haricot beans are often used: about 100–175 g (4–6 oz) will be sufficient. Soak dried beans overnight before cooking them. Use all or a selection of the following to serve 6–8 people.

Wash the cod several times and soak in cold water overnight. Drain and remove the skin. Cut into pieces and place in a shallow pan of cold water with the bay leaves. Cover, bring to the boil and simmer for about 15 minutes. Drain and cool. Roll up the slices of ham/cold meats and cut in half if large. Hard-boil the eggs and cut in half. Make the *Aïoli* sauce. Trim or peel the vegetables. Quarter the courgettes, or zucchini, carrots, artichokes and fennel. Break the cauliflower into florets and scrub the potatoes. Cook the carrots, courgettes, beans, cauliflower, artichokes and fennel in separate pans of boiling salted water for 8–10 minutes until just tender and slightly crisp. Cook the potatoes until tender. Drain all the vegetables and skin the potatoes. Cut the tomatoes in half or quarters. Arrange the fish, meat and vegetables on a plate and serve with the sauce.

350 g (12 oz) dried cod, soaked overnight
2 bay leaves
250 g (8 oz) ham/other cold meats
2–3 eggs
300 ml (½ pt) (1¼ cups) Aïoli sauce (page 213)
2 small courgettes (zucchini)
3 carrots
3 small young artichokes (poivrades, page 11)
175 g (6 oz) French (snap) beans
2 small heads fennel
1 small cauliflower
6–8 new potatoes
3 tomatoes

Artichauts à la Vinaigrette

ARTICHOKES WITH VINAIGRETTE

Prepare and cook the artichokes (page 10). Refresh under cold water and drain well. Pull out the centre leaves — they come out in one piece — and carefully remove all the feathery 'choke' in the middle with a teaspoon. Keep the centre leaves and chill the artichokes. Place each artichoke on a dish and fill the centre with a little vinaigrette. Replace the leaves upside down. Serve the remaining sauce separately.

Serves 4
4 large artichokes
150 ml (¼ pt) (⅔ cup) vinaigrette (page 218)

Serves 4

4 large artichokes
300 ml (½ pt) (1¼ cups) mayonnaise
(page 216)
1–2 tsp tomato purée
2–3 drops Tabasco sauce
salt and pepper
½ lettuce
2–3 medium tomatoes
1–2 small lemons
250 g (8 oz) shelled prawns (shrimp)
4 whole prawns (shrimp)
1 tbsp chopped chives

Fonds d'Artichauts aux Crevettes

ARTICHOKES WITH PRAWNS (SHRIMP)

Prepare and cook the artichoke bases (page 10). Make the mayonnaise and add the tomato purée and tabasco sauce. Salt and pepper to taste. Wash the lettuce, remove the coarse stalks, roll the leaves up like a cigar and cut into thin strips. Quarter the tomatoes and cut the lemons into wedges. Remove the shells from the tails of the whole prawns (shrimp), leaving the heads on the edible tails. Place a bed of lettuce on each plate with an artichoke base in the centre. Fill the artichoke with shelled prawns and coat with mayonnaise. Arrange pieces of tomato round the artichoke and sprinkle a few chopped chives in the centre. Garnish with the whole prawns and refrigerate until required. Serve the remaining sauce separately.

Serves 4

750 kg (1½ lb) asparagus
4 thin slices Morvan/Parma ham/250 g
(8 oz) smoked salmon
2 small tomatoes
½ lettuce
1–2 tsp chopped parsley
a few sprigs parsley
300 ml (½ pt) (1¼ cups) mayonnaise
(page 216)

Asperges au Jambon ou Saumon Fumé

ASPARAGUS WITH HAM OR SMOKED SALMON

Choose young, tender asparagus for this dish.

Prepare and cook the asparagus (page 13). Drain and refresh under cold water until cold, then drain well again. Trim the asparagus stems so they are about 5 cm (2 in) longer than the width of the ham. Divide the asparagus into 4 portions and wrap each portion in a slice of ham/salmon. Slice or quarter the tomatoes. Wash and trim the lettuce and arrange on a plate. Place the asparagus and ham on top and garnish with tomatoes. Sprinkle a little chopped parsley on the tips of the asparagus and place a small bunch of parsley sprigs in the centre of the dish. Chill until required and serve with the mayonnaise.

Serves 4

1 kg (2 lb) asparagus
2 eggs
salt
pepper
150 ml (¼ pt) (⅔ cup) vinaigrette
(page 218)

Asperges à la Vinaigrette

ASPARAGUS WITH VINAIGRETTE

Prepare and cook the asparagus (page 13). Hard-boil the eggs. Sieve the yolks and finely chop the whites. Mix together carefully and season to taste. When the asparagus is cooked, refresh under cold water and drain well. Arrange on a plate or on individual dishes. Sprinkle the chopped eggs over the asparagus heads and pour a little vinaigrette over. Serve the remaining vinaigrette separately.

Serves 4

2 large, ripe avocados
1 tbsp lemon juice
100 g (4 oz) Roquefort cheese
100 ml (3½ fl oz) (½ cup) double (heavy)
cream
1 tbsp strong mustard
salt and pepper
4 black olives

Avocats au Roquefort

AVOCADOS WITH ROQUEFORT

Cut the avocados in half, remove the stones and scoop out all the flesh with a teaspoon. Place in a bowl and sprinkle with a little lemon juice. Crumble the cheese into the bowl and add the cream, mustard and a little pepper. Beat/whisk together until smooth. Add more lemon juice and season to taste. Refill the skins with the mixture and place a black olive in the centre of each. Serve individually.

Avocats aux Moules

AVOCADOS WITH MUSSELS

Scrub the mussels well, scrape off the barnacles and remove the beards. Discard any damaged mussels or those that remain open after they have been given a sharp tap or put into cold water. Peel and finely chop the onion. Put in a pan with the mussels and 1–2 tbsp of water. Cover and place over a good heat for about 5 minutes, shaking the pan occasionally. If any mussels remain closed, replace the lid and cook for a little longer. Discard any which fail to open. Drain the mussels and when cold remove from their shells. Cut the avocados in half and remove the stones. Scoop out a little flesh from the centre of each with a teaspoon. Brush the inside of each half with lemon juice. Chop the avocado flesh which has been removed and mix with a little lemon juice and the mussels. Season to taste. Pile the mixture back into the avocados and serve on individual dishes with mayonnaise or *Sauce Andalouse*.

Serves 4
1 kg (2 lb) mussels
1 medium onion
2 large, ripe avocados
2–3 tbsp lemon juice
300 ml (½ pt) (1¼ cups) mayonnaise
(page 216)/Sauce Andalouse (page 214)

Bagna Cauda

Bagna Cauda *is an Italian dish from Piedmont that has slipped over the border into France, where it is sometimes called* Fondue des Légumes. *Vegetables other than those given here, such as spring onions (scallions), radishes, young artichokes (poivrades, page 10), small cauliflower florets, mushrooms, tomatoes and cos (Romaine) lettuce can also be served — just choose a colourful selection. Everyone helps themselves, dipping pieces of vegetable into the hot garlic and anchovy sauce.*

Trim the fennel and celery, peel the carrots and remove the stalks, cores and seeds from the peppers. Cut into small finger-length slices and place in iced water for about 30 minutes so they become really crisp. Trim the chicory and wash quickly. Drain well. Drain the other vegetables and arrange in piles on a dish, leaving room in the middle for a fondue stand. Make the sauce and place on a spirit stove in the middle of the dish.

1 head fennel
4–5 sticks celery
4–5 young carrots
1 small green pepper
1 small red pepper
1–2 heads Belgian chicory
Bagna Cauda sauce (page 214)

Betteraves à la Provençale

PROVENÇALE BEETROOT (BEETS)

Peel the beetroot and onions. Slice the beetroot thinly and finely chop the onions. Heat the oil in a pan and cook the onions until soft and just beginning to colour. Purée the onions with the mustard, vinegar and anchovies in a food processor or liquidizer. Season to taste with pepper and leave for at least 30 minutes to allow the flavours to blend. Pour the mixture over the beetroot, mix well and sprinkle with parsley.

500 g (1 lb) cooked beetroot
2 large onions
4 tbsp olive oil
½ tsp strong mustard
1 tbsp vinegar
6–8 anchovy fillets
pepper
1 tbsp chopped parsley

Champignons Crus à la Crème

RAW MUSHROOMS IN ACIDULATED CREAM

Trim and clean the mushrooms (avoid washing unless absolutely necessary because they will discolour). Slice thinly. Peel and crush the garlic in a little salt. Mix with the mushrooms and acidulated cream. Season to taste. Pile on to a dish and sprinkle with chopped herbs.

500 g (1 lb) small white button mushrooms
1 small clove garlic
150 ml (¼ pt) (⅔ cup) Crème au Citron
(page 215)
salt and pepper
1 tbsp chopped parsley/tarragon

Above, top: Artichauts à la Vinaigrette (page 127). *Bottom: Asperges Hollandaise* (page 149).

Above left: Soupe au Pistou (page 123).

Left, top: Crème de Carottes (page 119). *Bottom: Potage Glacé aux Avocats* (page 125).

Carottes Râpées aux Anchois

GRATED CARROTS WITH ANCHOVIES

1 egg
350 g (12 oz) carrots
5–6 tbsp vinaigrette (page 218) made with
    lemon juice
4–5 anchovy fillets
12 green olives

Hard-boil the egg. Peel and finely grate the carrots and mix with 2 tablespoons of vinaigrette dressing. Leave for 1 hour. Meanwhile, separate the yolk from the white of the hard-boiled egg. Sieve the yolk and chop the white. Stir the yolk into the remaining vinaigrette until smooth, then stir in the white. Pour over the carrots and mix well. Stone the olives and cut the anchovies into thin strips. Pile the carrots on to a dish, garnish with a lattice of fillets and place an olive in each space.

Champignons à la Grecque

MARINATED MUSHROOMS

350 g (12 oz) small button mushrooms
2 lemons
1 tomato
6–8 onions
100 ml (3½ fl oz) (½ cup) olive oil
100 ml (3½ fl oz) (½ cup) white wine
1 tsp coriander seeds
½ tsp peppercorns
2 tsp tomato purée
bouquet garni
salt and pepper

Serve well chilled in individual ramekins, or as part of a mixed hors d'oeuvre.

Squeeze the juice from one lemon. Cut the other in half and then quarter each piece and the tomato. Peel the onions. Place all the ingredients except the mushrooms in a pan. Season lightly, bring to the boil and simmer for 10–15 minutes. Remove from the heat and leave for 15 minutes. Trim and quickly wash the mushrooms. Add to the pan, bring to the boil and simmer for 7–8 minutes. Remove the mushrooms and put in a bowl. Discard some of the coriander seeds and peppercorns and, if necessary, boil the sauce rapidly until it is of coating consistency. Pour over the mushrooms. When cold, remove the bouquet garni and check the seasoning.

Céleri à la Grecque

MARINATED CELERY

1 head celery
10 small onions/spring onions (scallions)
2 cloves garlic
100 ml (3½ fl oz) (½ cup) water
100 ml (3½ fl oz) (½ cup) dry white wine
1 tbsp lemon juice
3 tbsp olive oil
bouquet garni
½ tsp coriander seeds
4–5 peppercorns
salt
1 tbsp chopped parsley

Trim the celery and cut into 3-cm (1½-in) sticks. Blanch in boiling salted water for 4–5 minutes. Drain, refresh in cold water and drain well again. Peel the onions and garlic. Crush the garlic with a little salt. Place all the ingredients in a pan, season lightly, bring to the boil and simmer gently for 15–20 minutes, or until tender. Place the vegetables in a dish and pour the marinade over. Leave until cold and then remove the bouqet garni. Sprinkle with chopped parsley and serve well chilled.

Céleri au Paprika

CELERY IN PAPRIKA SAUCE

Serves 4
2 small heads celery
300 ml (½ pt) (1¼ cup) mayonnaise
    (page 216)
1 tbsp sweet paprika
1 tbsp tomato purée
cayenne pepper
2 tbsp double (heavy) cream
salt

Trim the celery heads and keep some of the leaves from the heart. Cut each head in half and cook in boiling salted water for 20–30 minutes until tender. Drain, refresh under cold water and drain well again. Fold the top end of the celery over to make a neat shape and chill well. Mix the mayonnaise with the paprika. Add enough tomato purée to give good colour. Flavour and season with a pinch of cayenne pepper and salt. Stir in the cream. Arrange the celery in the centre of a dish and coat with mayonnaise. Sprinkle a little paprika down the length of each piece of celery and garnish with the celery leaves. Serve chilled.

Choufleur aux Crevettes

CAULIFLOWER WITH PRAWNS (SHRIMP)

Trim the cauliflower and break into small florets. Cook in boiling salted water for 10–12 minutes. Drain, refresh under cold water and drain well again until quite dry. Mix the crabmeat with the cauliflower and arrange in a deep, round dish. Season to taste. Adjust the mayonnaise to a coating consistency and pour over the cauliflower. Sprinkle the prawns (shrimp) in the centre and serve chilled.

1 cauliflower
100 g (4 oz) white crabmeat
200 ml (7 fl oz) (1 cup) mayonnaise
  (page 216)
175 g (6 oz) shelled prawns (shrimp)
salt and pepper

Concombres ou Choufleur à la Grecque

MARINATED CUCUMBERS OR CAULIFLOWER

For this dish use the same ingredients as for Courgettes à la Grecque *but substitute 1–2 cucumbers, or cauliflower, for the courgettes (zucchini).*

Peel the cucumbers, cut in half lengthways and remove the seeds with a ball-cutter or teaspoon. Cut the cucumber into 1-cm (½-in) slices and blanch in boiling salted water for 2–3 minutes. Drain, refresh under cold water and drain well again. Prepare the marinade and cook the cucumbers as for the courgettes. To prepare cauliflower: break into florets, blanch for 2–3 minutes and cook for 5–6 minutes only.

Concombres Farcis Alsacienne

ALSACE STUFFED CUCUMBERS

This is a good way to use the last piece from a joint of boiled bacon or leftover ham.

Peel the cucumbers and cut off the ends. Cut in half and then cut again in half lengthways. Remove the seeds with a ball-cutter or teaspoon. Blanch in boiling salted water for 5 minutes, then drain, refresh under cold water and drain well again. Mince or finely chop the ham. Mix with the acidulated cream and horseradish. Season to taste with salt and pepper. Fill the cucumber shells with the mixture. Wash and dry the lettuce and arrange on a plate. Thinly slice the lemon or cut into wedges. Arrange the cucumber on top of the lettuce and garnish with lemon. Serve chilled.

1–2 cucumbers
250 g (8 oz) ham
200 ml (7 fl oz) (1 cup) Crème au Citron
  (page 215)
1 tsp grated horseradish
salt
pepper
few lettuce leaves
1 lemon

Concombres Farcis au Poisson

CUCUMBER STUFFED WITH FISH

Prepare and blanch the cucumber as for *Concombres Farcis Alsacienne*. Hard-boil the eggs. When cooked, mash or sieve the yolks and chop the whites. Drain the fish, remove any skin or bones and flake with a fork. Mix well with the egg yolks, mustard and cheese. Season to taste with lemon juice, salt and pepper. Stir in most of the herbs. Wash and dry the lettuce leaves and arrange on a dish. Fill the cucumber cases with the fish and cheese mixture and sprinkle with the egg white and remaining herbs. Place on top of the lettuce and chill until required. Serve with mayonnaise.

Serves 4–8
1–2 cucumbers
2 eggs
250 g (8 oz) poached/canned salmon or
  tuna/other fish
1 tsp mustard
100 g (4 oz) (½ cup) cream cheese
1–2 tbsp lemon juice
salt and pepper
1 tbsp chopped parsley or chives
few lettuce leaves
300 ml (½ pt) (1¼ cups) mayonnaise
  (page 216) (optional)

Top: Concombres Farcis au Poisson (page 133). *Bottom: Chartreuse de Légumes* (page 141).

Mousse de Concombre et Fromage Blanc

CUCUMBER AND CREAM CHEESE MOUSSE

Chill a 20-cm (8-in) ring mould or 15-cm (6-in) soufflé dish. Cut a few slices from the centre of the cucumber and keep for decoration. Coarsely grate the rest and leave in a sieve for 30 minutes to drain. Place the gelatine in a bowl with 4 tablespoons of water and leave to soften. Peel and finely grate the carrots and mix with a little of the lemon juice. Peel and seed the tomatoes. Press the seeds in a sieve to extract the juice and put to one side. Chop the remaining tomatoes finely. Remove the stalk, core and seeds from the pepper and chop finely. Wash and pick the watercress. Mix the cream cheese and milk until smooth. Blend in the mayonnaise. Stand the bowl of gelatine over a small pan of boiling water and stir until completely dissolved. Add to the cheese mixture with the juice from the tomato seeds. Stir occasionally until it starts to thicken.

Sprinkle about one-quarter of the chopped pepper in the base of the mould/dish. Press the cucumber to remove excess water. When the cheese mixture has thickened, add the cucumber, carrots, tomatoes and remaining pepper. Mix carefully together and when the mixture is on the point of setting, pour into the chilled mould. Refrigerate until set. Turn the mould out on to a plate or serve straight from the soufflé dish. Garnish with the slices of cucumber and watercress. Serve chilled.

Mousse de Concombre et Fromage Blanc.

1 small cucumber
15 g (½ oz) (1 tbsp) gelatine
2 medium carrots
2–3 tbsp lemon juice
6 medium tomatoes
1 small red pepper
½ bunch watercress
100 g (4 oz) (½ cup) cream cheese
100 ml (3½ fl oz) (½ cup) milk
125 ml (4 fl oz) (½ cup) mayonnaise
   (page 216)
salt
pepper

Courgettes Farcies Froides

COLD STUFFED COURGETTES (ZUCCHINI)

1 egg
4–6 small courgettes (zucchini)
2 small lemons
1 tbsp oil
25 g (1 oz) walnuts
100 g (4 oz) (½ cup) cream/cottage cheese
2–3 tsp chopped mint
paprika
salt and pepper
few lettuce leaves
few sprigs of mint

Hard-boil the egg. Trim the ends from the courgettes and cut in half lengthways. Cook in boiling salted water for 5 minutes, drain, refresh under cold water and drain well again. With a ball-cutter or teaspoon carefully remove some of the flesh from the centre and keep. Place the courgettes in a shallow dish. Grate the rind from 1 lemon and squeeze out the juice. Cut the other lemon into wedges. Beat the oil and lemon juice together and pour over the courgettes. Leave for 1 hour, turning occasionally. Coarsely chop the walnuts and mix with the cheese, lemon rind and mint. Drain the marinade from the courgettes and stir into the cheese mixture. Season with a little paprika and salt and pepper. Fill the courgette shells with the mixture. Wash the lettuce and arrange on a dish. Place the courgettes on top. Sprinkle a little more paprika on each courgette and garnish the dish with the sprigs of mint and the lemon wedges.

Courgettes à la Grecque

MARINATED COURGETTES (ZUCCHINI)

500 g (1 lb) courgettes (zucchini)
3 large tomatoes
2 cloves garlic
1 medium onion
100 ml (3½ fl oz) (½ cup) olive oil
100 ml (3½ fl oz) (½ cup) white wine/water
bouquet garni
4–5 peppercorns
½ tsp coriander
4 tbsp lemon juice
salt and pepper

Trim the ends from the courgettes and slice thickly. Peel and chop the tomatoes and crush the garlic with a little salt. Peel and slice the onion. Put all the ingredients into a pan except the courgettes. Season to taste, bring to the boil and simmer for 15 minutes. Add the courgettes and cook for 7–8 minutes. Remove the courgettes and place in a bowl. If necessary reduce the sauce until it thickens. Remove the peppercorns and bouquet garni. Pour over the courgettes and leave until cold. Chill well.

Crudités

RAW VEGETABLE HORS D'OEUVRE

Few French menus are complete without crudités. These are vegetables, mostly raw, which are grated, sliced or diced and mixed with vinaigrette or mayonnaise. Cooked beetroot (beets), potatoes and blanched red cabbage are also included. Usually at least four to six different vegetables are served, but on more than one occasion we have helped ourselves generously to about half a dozen large dishes, only to find them whipped away, thinking we had finished, and replaced by another mouthwatering selection.

Choose from the following and arrange on hors d'oeuvre dishes or on individual plates: grated carrots with vinaigrette, sliced cucumber with vinaigrette, sliced cucumber with yogurt, sliced tomatoes with vinaigrette, finely shredded celeriac with mayonnaise, diced potatoes with vinaigrette or mayonnaise, blanched red cabbage with vinaigrette, cooked artichoke hearts, or poivrades, with vinaigrette, French (snap) beans with vinaigrette, Salade Russe or chick-peas with Sauce Ravigote.

Crudités à l'Anchoïade

CRUDITÉS WITH ANCHOVY SAUCE

Provence has its own variation of crudités served with Anchoïade — *an anchovy and garlic purée.*

Trim or peel the vegetables. Slice the tomatoes, quarter the artichokes and brush with lemon juice. Cut the peppers and fennel into strips. Slice or dice the cucumber and celery, grate the carrots and slice the mushrooms.

Arrange the vegetables on a large dish so their colours and shapes contrast. Serve with *Anchoïade*.

2–3 firm tomatoes
4–6 small young artichokes (poivrades)/
cauliflower florets
2–3 tbsp lemon juice
1 small green pepper
1 small red pepper
½–1 head fennel
½ cucumber
3–4 sticks celery
2–3 carrots
4–6 button mushrooms
Anchoïade (page 213) made with 125 g
(5 oz) anchovy fillets

Aïllade

In the south of France, Aïllade *is the name given to foods prepared with a lot of garlic.* Pain d'Aïllade *is toasted bread flavoured heavily with garlic which is sometimes dipped in olive oil.* Aïllade Albigeoise *is similar to* Aïoli, *and the following dish,* Aïllade Toulousaine, *which comes from the Languedoc and Dordogne regions, is made with walnuts. Fresh walnuts, before they are dried, are essential to this dish, so it can only be made during a few weeks in autumn. Do try it — it really is delicious.*

Peel the walnut skins with a small, pointed knife. Peel and crush the garlic with a little salt, then pound with the walnuts until smooth using a pestle and mortar or liquidizer. When the mixture is smooth, whisk or blend in the oil a little at a time in the same way as for mayonnaise (page 216). When the sauce is thick, taste and season. Serve as an hors d'oeuvre with raw vegetables and crusty French bread.

75 g (3 oz) (¾ cup) shelled fresh walnuts
3–4 cloves garlic
salt
75–100 ml (2½–3 fl oz) (⅓–½ cup)
walnut/olive oil

Endives et Fenouil au Bleu

CHICORY AND FENNEL WITH BLUE CHEESE

Hard-boil the eggs. Trim the chicory, separate the leaves, wash quickly and drain well. Keep enough even-sized leaves to arrange round the inside edge of a salad bowl. Chop the rest. Trim the fennel and slice thinly or chop into medium-sized pieces. Remove the stalk, core and seeds from the pepper and cut into thin strips. Chop the hard-boiled eggs and crumble the cheese. Mix the chicory, fennel and pepper together and pile into a salad bowl. Pour the vinaigrette into the bottom. Arrange the reserved chicory leaves round the edge of the bowl and sprinkle the cheese in the centre. Toss well just before serving.

2 eggs
2–3 heads chicory
1 medium head fennel
1 medium green pepper
100 g (4 oz) blue cheese
8 tbsp vinaigrette (page 218) made with
olive oil

Top: Haricots Verts à la Côte d'Azur (page 139). Bottom: Fèves à la Croque au Sel.

Opposite: Aïoli Garni (page 127).

Fèves à la Croque au Sel

BROAD (LIMA) BEANS WITH SALT

In Provence raw broad (lima) beans are served as an hors d'oeuvre or as a snack with drinks. The beans must be freshly picked and only very young, tender ones are suitable, so this is a dish to serve if you have your own vegetable garden.

Shell the beans, if possible, just before you serve them and remove the skins — or let your guests do this as they eat them. Dip the beans into a pot of coarse salt and eat with bread (preferably coarse brown bread — *pain de campagne*) and butter.

Haricots Verts à la Côte d'Azur

CÔTE D'AZUR-STYLE FRENCH (SNAP) BEANS

Trim the beans. If long break into 2–3 pieces. Cook in boiling salted water until just tender. Drain, refresh under cold water and drain well again. Peel, seed and chop the tomatoes. Peel and crush the garlic. Heat the oil in a pan, add the tomatoes, garlic and bouquet garni. Cook for 7–10 minutes, season lightly, remove the bouquet garni and cool. Stone the olives, cut the ham/tongue into strips and add to the sauce with the capers and most of the tarragon and chives. Check the seasoning. Place the beans in a dish and pour the sauce over. Sprinkle with the remaining herbs and serve well chilled.

500 g (1 lb) French (snap) beans
500 g (1 lb) tomatoes
3–4 cloves garlic
2 tbsp olive oil
bouquet garni
10–12 olives (to taste)
1 slice ham/tongue
1 tbsp capers
1 tbsp chopped tarragon
1 tbsp chopped chives
salt and pepper

Haricots Verts au Fromage Blanc

FRENCH (SNAP) BEANS WITH CREAM CHEESE

500 g (1 lb) French (snap) beans
2 eggs
1–2 small red peppers
6 tbsp vinaigrette (page 218)
250 g (8 oz) (1 cup) cream cheese
salt
pepper

Trim the beans and cook in boiling salted water until tender. Drain, refresh under cold water and drain well again. Meanwhile, hard-boil the eggs. Remove the stalks, cores and seeds from the peppers. Cut 3–4 whole rings from one of the peppers and cut the rest into small strips. Cut the eggs into wedges. When the beans are cold, toss in vinaigrette and season to taste. Pile into a salad bowl and place the cheese in the centre. Garnish the top with the pepper rings and arrange the pieces of egg and small piles of pepper alternately round the cheese.

Vegetables in Aspic

Moulded vegetables, or vegetables with egg, ham or smoked salmon in aspic, are very popular in France and a selection is always found in any charcuterie. They are relatively simple to make, but do require a little time and patience. Homemade aspic is, of course, best but if you prefer, or if time is short, use one of the proprietary brands of aspic crystals. The addition of a tablespoon or two of sherry will give it good flavour. A can of consommé with the addition of 25 g (1 oz) (2 tbsp) gelatine is a quick substitute. Soften the gelatine in 2–3 tablespoons of cold water. Heat the consommé, mix in the gelatine and heat until it has dissolved. Add a little sherry if you wish. Chill and use as required.

To make your own aspic, follow the instructions for Consommé but before you start, soften 50 g (2 oz) (¼ cup) gelatine in a little water and add it to the pan at the same time as the raw ingredients. Stir well as the stock heats so it is completely dissolved, then stir gently until a filter forms, etc.

When the aspic is cold but still liquid, mask, or coat, the moulds with aspic. To do this, fill chilled moulds or ramekins with aspic. Stand them in a bowl of ice and water, and when the aspic starts to set round the sides, pour it out, leaving a thin covering of aspic on the sides and bottom.

The great secret about moulding vegetables in aspic is to let one layer set at a time in a thin coating of aspic. If you pour in too much, the vegetables will float and you will get a thick, uninteresting layer of aspic. So, after you have masked the mould, place a layer of vegetables in a decorative pattern in the base. Pour in only sufficient aspic to set the vegetables in place. When this has set pour in a little more aspic, let this set and repeat until the mould is filled. Keep the aspic liquid by standing the bowl in a pan of warm water. If it begins to set and go lumpy it must be completely re-melted before being used again. Conversely, standing the mould or ramekins in a roasting pan of ice water helps to speed the setting process. Any selection of cooked vegetables can be used, as, for example, those used in the following recipe.

2–3 carrots
2–3 small turnips
50 g (2 oz) French (snap) beans
1–2 small tomatoes
75 g (3 oz) shelled/frozen peas
600 ml (1 pt) (2½ cups) aspic

Peel the carrots and turnips and dice finely. Top and tail the French (snap) beans and cut into 1-cm (½-in) pieces. Skin the tomatoes. Cook the carrots, turnips, beans and peas separately in boiling salted water until tender. Drain, refresh under cold water and drain again until completely dry. Coat the mould/ramekins with aspic and then fill them with the vegetables as explained above. To turn out the moulds, dip them briefly in hot water and turn out on to a large plate or individual plates. If you wish, when the moulds are in place, pour a coating of liquid aspic on to the large plate and set in the refrigerator. Ramekins can be served as they are or unmoulded.

Chartreuse de Légumes

VEGETABLE MOULD IN ASPIC

Mask a chilled 19-cm (7½-in) tart ring, or similar-sized pan or mould with aspic (page 140).

Meanwhile, scrape the carrots and slice thinly. Trim the beans and cut diagonally into 2.5-cm (1-in) pieces. Trim the asparagus. Cook the vegetables separately in boiling salted water until just tender. Drain, refresh under cold water and drain again until dry.

Peel and slice the tomatoes. Choose even-sized slices and dip them into a little liquid aspic and arrange round the sides of the tin. Cut the tips of the asparagus and arrange in a neat pattern in the base of the tin. Cover with a thin layer or aspic and leave to set. Arrange the other vegetables in layers, coating each with aspic and allowing it to set before arranging the next layer. Continue until all the vegetables are used and finish with a layer of aspic. Refrigerate until set. Turn out on to a serving dish. Garnish with the parsley.

1 litre (2 pt) (1 quart) chicken aspic (page 140)
250 g (8 oz) young carrots
175 g (6 oz) French (snap) beans
100 g (4 oz) shelled, small broad (lima) beans
100 g (4 oz) shelled/frozen peas
500 g (1 lb) fresh asparagus/350 g (12 oz) can
250 g (8 oz) small tomatoes
sprigs of parsley

Jambon en Gelée

HAM IN ASPIC

If you prefer, for this dish a thin layer of Salade Russe can be used in place of the tomatoes, or smoked salmon in place of ham.

Cut each slice of ham into a square and then diagonally to form two triangles. Wrap the long points over each other to form a cone. Fill with a little *Salad Russe* and place fold-side down on a plate. Chill until required. Slice the tomatoes and blanch the tarragon for a moment or two in boiling salted water. Fill the moulds or ramekins in the same way as for *Oeufs en Gelée.*

2–3 thin slices cooked ham
3–4 tbsp Salade Russe (page 148)
1–2 tomatoes (optional)
few leaves tarragon (optional)
600 ml (1 pt) (2½ cups) aspic (page 140)

Oeufs en Gelée

EGGS IN ASPIC

Boil the eggs for 7 minutes and then place in cold water until completely cold. Remove the shells (the yolks will be slightly runny, so care is needed in shelling. If they prove difficult, hold them under a gentle stream of cold water and let the water fall between the egg and shell as you ease the shell away). Blanch the tarragon leaves for a moment or two in boiling salted water. Trim, clean and finely slice the mushrooms. Heat the butter in a pan, add the mushrooms and cook gently for 5–7 minutes. Season to taste and drain on kitchen paper. Chill until required.

Mask the mould with aspic (page 140) and decorate the base with a pattern of tarragon leaves. Cover with a little aspic. Place an egg in each mould and cover with aspic. Finish with layers of cooked mushrooms and sliced tomatoes. If ramekins are used and are not to be turned out, reverse the order: place the tomatoes in the base and finish with the decoration of tarragon leaves on top. In each case, pour on a final layer of aspic and refrigerate to set. Unmould, if desired (page 140).

4–6 eggs
few tarragon leaves
100 g (4 oz) white button mushrooms
40 g (1½ oz) (3 tbsp) butter
salt
pepper
2–3 small tomatoes
600 ml (1 pt) (2½ cups) aspic

Above, top: Crudités à l'Anchoïade (page 137). Bottom: A selection of crudités (page 136).

Left, top: Choufleur aux Crevettes (page 133). Bottom: Avocats aux Moules (page 129).

Left: Fonds d'Artichauts aux Crevettes (page 128). Right: Avocats au Roquefort (page 128).

500 g (1 lb) small onions
100 ml (3½ fl oz) (½ cup) wine vinegar
4 tbsp olive oil
300 ml (½ pt) (1¼ cups) water
4 peppercorns
4 tomatoes
50 g (2 oz) (⅓ cup) sultanas (golden
 raisins)
bouquet garni
salt
pepper
½ tsp sugar

Oignons à la Niçoise

NICE-STYLE ONIONS

Peel the onions and place in a heavy-based pan with the vinegar, oil and water. Bring to the boil, and cover and cook gently for 10 minutes. Meanwhile, crush the peppercorns. Skin the tomatoes and slice thinly. Add to the pan with the sultanas (raisins), bouquet garni, a little seasoning and the sugar. Bring to the boil again, reduce the heat and cook gently for 30–40 minutes. When cooked, remove the onions from the sauce and place in a dish. If necessary, boil the sauce rapidly until it is of a coating consistency. Remove the bouquet garni, check the seasoning and pour over the onions. Serve well chilled.

Poireaux à la Grecque

MARINATED LEEKS

Use the same ingredients as for Céleri à la Grecque but substitute 5–6 small leeks for the celery and onions.

Wash and trim the leeks and cut into 2.5-cm (1-in) pieces. Blanch and cook in the same way as the celery. The green part of the leeks takes longer to cook than the white part so check after 10–12 minutes and remove the white pieces as soon as they are tender. Continue cooking until the rest of the leeks are tender. Finish in the same way as for the celery.

750 g (1½ lb) small leeks
250 g (8 oz) ripe tomatoes
1 clove garlic
4 tbsp olive oil
1 tbsp chopped parsley
3 tbsp lemon juice
salt
pepper

Poireaux à la Niçoise

NICE-STYLE LEEKS

Trim the leeks and cook in boiling salted water for 10–12 minutes. Drain well, refresh under cold water and drain well again. Skin the tomatoes and quarter. Peel and finely chop the garlic. Heat the oil in a large pan, lay the leeks in the bottom and cook, turning occasionally until golden brown on all sides. Cover with greaseproof paper and a lid and cook gently for 10 minutes or until tender. Drain on kitchen paper towel. Pour off all but 1 tablespoon of the oil from the pan. Add the tomato, garlic and parsley and cook for 5–7 minutes. Stir gently so the pieces of tomato retain their shapes. Season to taste and add the lemon juice. Arrange the leeks in a row on a serving dish. Pour the tomato mixture in the middle and chill.

Poivrades à la Croque au Sel

YOUNG ARTICHOKES WITH SALT

Small young artichokes (poivrades, page 10) can be eaten raw with coarse salt in the same way as broad (lima) beans.

Remove the stalks and, if necessary, trim the tips of the leaves. The artichokes can be left whole, halved or quartered. Allow 2 per person.

Poivrades à la Sauce Ravigote

YOUNG ARTICHOKES WITH RAVIGOTE SAUCE

Remove the stalks from the artichokes and, if necessary, trim the tips of the leaves. Leave whole or halve or quarter. Serve with *Sauce Ravigote* (page 217). Allow 2 per person.

Ratatouille à la Niçoise

NICE-STYLE RATATOUILLE

Serve this cold with crusty French bread as an hors d'oeuvre, or hot with roast or grilled meats, or grilled or poached fish.

Remove the stalks and cut the aubergines (eggplant) into medium-sized dice. Sprinkle with a little salt and leave for 30 minutes. Wash and drain well. Remove the stalks, cores and seeds from the peppers and cut into thin strips. Peel and slice the onions. Trim the courgettes (zucchini) and slice thickly. Quarter the tomatoes. Chop the anchovy fillets and peel and crush the garlic in a little salt.

    Heat the oil in a pan and cook the anchovy fillets until golden brown. Add the onions and cook until soft, then add the aubergines, peppers, garlic and bouquet garni. Cover and cook for 15–20 minutes. Add the tomatoes and courgettes and continue cooking gently for 15–20 minutes until all the vegetables are tender. If the mixture is very juicy, remove the lid for the last few minutes to allow some of the liquid to evaporate. Pour into a dish and sprinkle with chopped basil.

350 g (12 oz) aubergines (eggplant)
1 medium green pepper
1 medium red pepper
3 moderately large onions
350 g (12 oz) courgettes (zucchini)
350 g (12 oz) tomatoes
2 anchovy fillets (optional)
3 cloves garlic
4 tbsp olive oil
bouquet garni
salt
pepper
1 tbsp basil

Ratatouille aux Olives Noires

RATATOUILLE WITH BLACK OLIVES

Serve this dish cold as an hors d'oeuvre with crusty French bread, or as an accompaniment to cold meats and poultry. If you wish you can stone the olives, but because this is a country recipe, it is not necessary.

Remove the stalks and cut the aubergines (eggplant) into 2.5-cm (1-in) dice. Peel and coarsely chop the tomatoes. Remove the stalks, cores and seeds from the peppers and cut into strips about 1 cm ($\frac{1}{2}$ in) wide. Peel and slice the onions. Trim and slice the celery and peel and crush the garlic with a little salt. Stone the olives if desired. Heat 2 tablespoons of oil in a pan and cook the onions, celery and garlic for 5 minutes. Remove from the pan, add the rest of the oil and when it is hot cook the peppers and aubergines over gentle heat for 10 minutes. Stir occasionally. Return the onions, celery and garlic to the pan and add the tomatoes. Season to taste, cover the pan and cook gently for 30–40 minutes until the vegetables are tender. Add the olives and cook for 3–4 minutes, then pour into a serving dish. When cold, sprinkle with parsley and chill.

3 small aubergines (eggplant)
6 large ripe tomatoes
2 small red peppers
2 small green peppers
2 large onions
3–4 sticks celery
75 g (3 oz) black olives
5 tbsp olive oil
salt
pepper
1 tbsp chopped parsley

Clockwise: Choufleur à la Grecque (page 133); Poivrons à la Grecque; Poireaux à la Grecque (page 144); Champignons à la Grecque (page 132).

4–6 *small green/red peppers*
10–12 *small onins/large spring onions (scallions)*
1 *lemon*
350 g (12 oz) *tomatoes*
3 *cloves garlic*
100 ml (3½ fl oz) (½ cup) *olive oil*
100 ml (3½ fl oz) (½ cup) *white wine*
1 tsp *coriander seeds*
1 *bouquet garni*
salt
pepper
1 tbsp *chopped parsley*

Poivrons à la Grecque

MARINATED PEPPERS

Remove the stalks, cores and seeds from the peppers and cut into large pieces. Peel the onions and squeeze the juice from the lemon. Peel the tomatoes and chop coarsely. Peel and crush the garlic. Heat 4 tablespoons of oil in a pan, add the peppers and onions and cook gently for 5–6 minutes, taking care that they do not colour. Add the lemon juice, tomatoes, garlic, wine, coriander seeds and bouquet garni together with the remaining oil. Season to taste with salt and pepper and bring to the boil. Simmer gently for 20 minutes until the peppers are soft. Pour into a dish, leave until cold and then remove the bouquet garni. Sprinkle with chopped parsley and serve well chilled.

Terrine de Légumes Monsieur Vaugnoux

MR VAUGNOUX'S VEGETABLE TERRINE

Monsieur Vaugnoux is the chef-patron at Le Praline, a small restaurant at Praz-sur-Arly, high in the mountains of the Haute-Savoie. We had a most pleasant meal there one evening, and I so enjoyed the terrine I asked for the recipe, which Monsieur Vaugnoux kindly gave me. The recipe was for double the amount I have given, so if you wish make a larger quantity. I found it freezes very well. If sorrel is not available, spinach can be used. However, because spinach does not have the acidity of sorrel, add a little lemon juice to taste. Also, blanch the spinach in boiling salted water for 2–3 minutes before cooking in the butter.

Butter the inside of a 500-g (1-lb) terrine/loaf pan. Line the base with greaseproof paper. Trim the courgettes (zucchini) and cook in boiling salted water for 7–8 minutes. Drain, refresh under cold water and drain well again. Quarter each courgette lengthwise and slice thickly. Remove the coarse stalks from the sorrel and wash well. Melt the butter in a pan, add the sorrel and cook very slowly until it 'melts' and softens to a purée. Beat the eggs well and mix with the cheese, courgettes and sorrel. Season to taste. Pour into the prepared terrine and bake in a preheated oven 180°C (350°F) (Gas Mark 4) for 35–40 minutes or until the terrine is firm and shrinking slightly from the sides of the dish. Remove from the oven and cool, then refrigerate. Turn the terrine out and slice. Serve on individual plates with a little *Fondue* on either side.

Terrine de Légumes Monsieur Vaugnoux.

500 g (1 lb) courgettes (zucchini)
125 g (5 oz) sorrel
40 g (1½ oz) (3 tbsp) butter
2 eggs
50 g (2 oz) (½ cup) grated Gruyère cheese
salt
pepper
Fondue de Trois Légumes (page 215)

Salade Russe

RUSSIAN SALAD

If used as a separate hors d'oeuvre, this salad can be garnished with diced, cooked beetroot (beets) and wedges of hard-boiled egg. Sometimes black caviar or lumpfish roe is placed in a hollow in the centre of the salad.

Trim, peel/scrape the vegetables. Cut the beans into 1-cm ($\frac{1}{2}$-in) pieces and cut the turnips, carrots and potatoes into small dice. Cook the beans, turnips, carrots, potatoes and peas separately in boiling salted water until tender. Drain, refresh under cold water and drain again until completely dry. Slice the mushrooms thinly and mix with the other vegetables and mayonnaise. Serve as part of a mixed hors d'oeuvre or as required.

100 g (4 oz) French (snap) beans
100 g (4 oz) turnips
100 g (4 oz) carrots
100 g (4 oz) firm potatoes
100 g (4 oz) shelled/frozen peas
50 g (2 oz) white button mushrooms
150 ml (¼ pt) (⅔ cup) mayonnaise (page 216)

Tomates au Fromage Blanc

CHEESE-FILLED TOMATOES

If cream cheese is used for this recipe it may be necessary to soften it with a tablespoon or two of milk.

Cut a slice off the top of each tomato. Scoop out the seeds with a ball-cutter or teaspoon and season the inside lightly with salt and pepper. Turn upside down and leave to drain for 20–30 minutes. Mix the cheese with the herbs and season to taste. Fill the centres of the tomatoes with the cheese. Cut the tomato lids in half and place in a 'v' on top of each. Garnish the centre with a small sprig of parsley. Arrange on a plate or on individual dishes and serve chilled.

Serves 4
4 tomatoes
salt and pepper
250 g (8 oz) (1 cup) cottage/cream cheese
1–2 tbsp chopped mixed herbs (parsley, chives, chervil, tarragon, etc.)
few small sprigs of parsley

Tomates à la Sévigné

TOMATOES WITH CHICKEN AND MUSHROOMS

Prepare the tomatoes as for *Tomates au Fromage Blanc*. Trim and clean the mushrooms and slice thinly. Heat the butter in a pan and cook the mushrooms for 5–7 minutes until tender. Drain on kitchen paper towel. Dice the chicken. Remove the stalk, core and seeds from the pepper and dice finely. If you wish, blanch the diced pepper in boiling salted water for 2–3 minutes. Drain, refresh under cold water and drain again until completely dry. Mix the mushrooms, chicken, pepper and mayonnaise together. Season to taste. Generously fill the tomatoes with the mixture and replace the 'lids'. Arrange a bed of lettuce on a plate. Place the tomatoes on top and serve with the remaining mayonnaise.

Serves 4
4 large tomatoes
100 g (4 oz) mushrooms
40 g (1½ oz) (3 tbsp) butter
200 g (6 oz) cooked chicken
1 small green pepper
300 ml (½ pt) (1¼ cups) mayonnaise (page 218)
few lettuce leaves

HOT HORS D'OEUVRE

Artichauts Hollandais ou Maltais

ARTICHOKES HOLLANDAISE OR MALTAISE

Trim and cook the artichokes (page 10). Pull out the centre leaves and carefully scrape away all the feathery 'choke' from the centre. Keep the artichokes hot in a steamer over a pan of hot water. Make the *Sauce Hollandaise* or *Maltaise*. Place the artichokes on individual plates. Put a spoonful or two of sauce in the centre and serve the rest separately.

Asparagus can also be served in this way. Use 1 kg (2 lb) asparagus.

4–6 large artichokes
Sauce Hollandaise (page 216)/Sauce Maltaise (page 217)

Cassolettes aux Champignons

MUSHROOM RAMEKINS

Trim and clean the mushrooms. Remove the stalks and chop finely. Place the mushroom caps in a bowl with the lemon juice and mix well. Heat 15 g (½ oz) (1 tbsp) butter in a pan and cook the chopped stalks for 4–5 minutes until tender. Meanwhile, coarsely chop the ham and add to the pan with the parsley. Season lightly. Divide into individual dishes and keep hot. Heat the remaining butter in another pan, add the mushroom caps and season lightly. Cover with greaseproof paper and a lid and cook gently for 7–8 minutes. Warm the brandy, pour over the mushrooms and flambé. Add the cream, bring to the boil and simmer for 5 minutes. Season to taste. Place the mushrooms on top of the ham mixture in the ramekins. Pour the sauce on and sprinkle with grated cheese. Place under a hot grill until golden brown.

500 g (1 lb) small button mushrooms
2 tsp lemon juice
50 g (2 oz) (¼ cup) butter
175 g (6 oz) ham
1 tbsp chopped parsley
salt
pepper
2 tbsp brandy
150 ml (¼ pt) (⅔ cup) double (heavy) cream
75 g (3 oz) (¾ cup) grated Gruyère cheese

Petits Chaussons aux Champignons

SMALL MUSHROOM TURNOVERS

Make the pastry and refrigerate for 30 minutes. Clean and trim the mushrooms and slice finely. Heat 25 g (1 oz) (2 tbsp) butter in a pan and cook the mushrooms for 5–7 minutes or until tender. Season lightly. Melt the remaining butter in another pan and make a thick *Sauce Béchamel* with the flour and milk. Boil for 4–5 minutes, stirring continuously. Season to taste with salt, pepper and a pinch of paprika. Beat the egg yolk, pour in a little hot sauce, mix well and return to the pan. Heat through without boiling. Add enough of the sauce to the mushrooms to bind them. Leave to cool.

Roll the pastry out on to a lightly floured board and cut out 9-cm (3½-in) circles. Beat the egg and brush a 1-cm (½-in) border round each. Place some of the mushroom mixture in each circle (don't overfill or it will ooze out while cooking). Fold the pastry over and flute the edges. Brush with beaten egg and cook in a preheated oven 220°C (425°F) (Gas Mark 7) for about 15 minutes until crisp and golden brown. Serve hot.

Pâte Demi-feuilletée made with 350 g (12 oz) (3 cups) flour (page 220)
250 g (8 oz) small button mushrooms
50 g (2 oz) (¼ cup) butter
Sauce Béchamel (page 214) made with:
25 g (1 oz) (¼ cup) flour
150 ml (¼ pt) (⅔ cup) milk
salt
pepper
pinch paprika
1 egg yolk
1 whole egg

Tomates à la Sévigné (page 148).

Rissoles au Cresson

WATERCRESS RISSOLES

In French cookery, rissoles are small, savoury turnovers that are deep-fat fried. Sometimes, as in this recipe, they are coated with egg and breadcrumbs before they are fried. Very fine vermicelli is often used as well. These rissoles are also excellent to serve as cocktail savouries because they can be made in advance and frozen until needed.

Pâte Brisée made with 175 g (6 oz)
   (1½ cups) flour (page 219)
2 bunches watercress
50 g (2 oz) (¼ cup) butter
15 g (½ oz) (2 tbsp) flour
75 ml (2½ fl oz) (⅓ cup) milk
25 g (1 oz) (½ cup) grated Gruyère cheese
salt
pepper
3–4 tbsp fine breadcrumbs
fat-oil for deep-frying

Make the pastry and refrigerate for 30 minutes. Meanwhile, strip the leaves from the watercress and wash well. Dry on kitchen paper and chop finely. Melt the butter in a pan, add the watercress and cook gently for 4–5 minutes. Stir in the flour, mix well and cook for 2–3 minutes, stirring continuously. Add the milk a little at a time and bring to the boil. Cook for 2–3 minutes, still stirring continuously. Beat in the grated cheese, season to taste and leave until quite cold.

Roll out the pastry on to a lightly floured board and cut out 7.5-cm (3-in) circles. Beat the egg and brush a border round the edge of each circle. Place a little of the filling in the centre, fold over and seal well. Dip the turnover into the beaten egg and then into the breadcrumbs. Press the breadcrumbs in firmly and, if possible, refrigerate for 30 minutes to set. Heat the pan of fat/oil to 180°C (370°F), or until a small piece of bread browns in 30 seconds. Fry the *rissoles* for 5–6 minutes until golden brown. Drain well on kitchen paper towel and serve hot.

Left: Rissoles de Fromage Blanc et Maïs. Right: Gnocchi à l'Alsacienne (page 152).

Rissoles de Fromage Blanc et Maïs

CHEESE AND SWEETCORN RISSOLES

Make the pastry and refrigerate for 30 minutes. Meanwhile, drain the sweetcorn and cheese. Peel the spring onions (scallions) and finely chop the onions and the tender part of the stalks. Mix the sweetcorn, cheese and onions together and season to taste with salt and pepper.

Roll the pastry out on to a lightly floured board to a 40 × 20 cm (16 × 8 in) rectangle. Cut in half and then cut each side in 4 to make a total of 8 squares. Beat the egg and brush a border round the edge of each square. Place some filling in the centre of each. Fold over diagonally and seal firmly. Crimp the edges. Heat the pan of fat/oil to 180°C (370°F) and cook the *rissoles* for 5–6 minutes until crisp and golden brown. Drain on kitchen paper towel and serve hot with *Sauce Tomate* or *Sauce Portugaise*.

Pâte Demi-feuilletée made with 250 g (8 oz) flour (page 220)

200 g (7 oz) can sweetcorn

100 g (4 oz) curd/cottage cheese

4 spring onions (scallions)

salt and pepper

fat/oil for deep-frying

300 ml (½ pt) (1¼ cup) Sauce Tomate (page 218)/Sauce Portugaise (page 217)

Gnocchi à l'Alsacienne

ALSATIAN POTATO-DUMPLINGS

Although gnocchi *is considered an Italian dish, potato dumplings are popular in other European countries as well, particularly Germany. In the Alsace, which has seen many changes of authority in its history, much of the food has a strong German influence. This is a very popular dish from that region and is often known by the German name Grumbeereknepfle. These gnocchi can also be served with stews, in which case serve them without the cream and cheese; a little melted butter can be poured over them instead if you wish.*

750 g (1½ lb) floury potatoes
50 g (2 oz) (½ cup) flour
1 egg
salt
pepper
pinch nutmeg
4 tbsp double (heavy) cream
75 g (3 oz) (¾ cup) grated Gruyère cheese

Peel the potatoes and boil one-third until tender. Drain well and mash until smooth. Meanwhile, grate the remaining potatoes very finely and then squeeze in a dish towel until dry. Mix the grated and cooked potatoes and beat in half the flour and the egg. Mix well and add as much flour as is necessary to bind the mixture. Season well with salt and pepper and add a pinch of nutmeg.

Bring a large pan of salted water to the boil. With two dessert spoons mould the mixture into small egg shapes; about half a spoonful will suffice. Drop these into the boiling water and reduce the heat until it simmers gently. Cook the *gnocchi* for about 7–8 minutes. (The exact time will depend on how finely the potatoes are grated. I always take one out of the water, cut it in half and taste it to see if it is cooked.) If the *gnocchi* break apart while simmering, a little more flour is needed in the mixture.

When the *gnocchi* are cooked, lift them out with a draining spoon and drain quickly on kitchen paper towel. Place in a hot serving dish and keep hot until all the mixture has been used. Pour the cream over the *gnocchi* and cover with the grated cheese. Place under a hot grill or in a preheated oven 200°C (400°F) (Gas Mark 6) for 15–20 minutes until golden brown.

SALADS AS HORS D'OEUVRE

Salade de Haricots Rouges au Thon

RED (KIDNEY) BEAN AND TUNA FISH SALAD

Choose sharp green eating apples, such as Granny Smiths.

250 g (8 oz) red haricot (kidney) beans, soaked for 18 hours
1–2 eggs
2 green eating apples
2 tbsp lemon juice
200 g (7 oz) can tuna fish
1 medium onion
1 bunch watercress
6 tbsp vinaigrette (page 218)
salt
pepper

Soak the beans. Drain and rinse well. Place in a pan of cold water, bring to the boil for 15 minutes and simmer for 1½ hours or until tender. Add salt about 10 minutes before the end of the cooking time. Meanwhile, hard-boil the eggs. Quarter the apples, remove the core and seeds and slice thinly. Mix with the lemon juice. Drain the tuna fish (if you wish you can use the oil in the vinaigrette) and flake coarsely. Finely chop the onion and slice the cucumber thinly. Wash and pick the watercress. Cut the eggs into wedges.

Mix the fish, apples, onion, cucumber and vinaigrette together. Season to taste with salt and pepper and leave for 30 minutes. When the beans are cooked, drain and refresh under cold water. Drain well again and mix with the fish mixture. Check the seasoning. Pile into a salad bowl and garnish with the watercress and eggs. Chill until required.

Salade au Cidre

CIDER SALAD

Only the white leaves from an escarole heart are needed for this recipe. Curly endive (chicory) can be used instead, or a very crisp lettuce.

Scrub the potatoes and cook in their jackets in boiling salted water until tender. Peel and slice. Bring the cider to the boil and add the potato slices. Toss the potatoes for a few moments, then remove from the heat and leave to cool. Meanwhile, wash and trim the escarole and celery. Break the escarole into pieces and thinly slice the celery. Cut the chicken/ham into mouth-sized pieces. Peel the apple, quarter, remove the core and seed and slice thinly. Cut the slices in half and toss in the lemon juice. When the potatoes are cold, mix the ingredients together with the exception of the chopped herbs. Put on a serving dish and sprinkle with the parsley/chives. Chill before serving.

350 g (12 oz) firm old/new potatoes
5–6 tbsp dry cider
1 heart very white escarole
2–3 sticks celery
175 g (6 oz) cooked chicken/ham
1 large eating apple
2 tbsp lemon juice
150 ml (¼ pt) (⅔ cup) mayonnaise (page 216)
1–2 tsp chopped parsley/chives

Salade de Choufleur à la Crème

CAULIFLOWER SALAD WITH ACIDULATED CREAM

Trim the cauliflower and break into small florets. Cook in boiling salted water for 5–7 minutes until barely tender— the cauliflower should still be slightly crisp. Drain well and refresh under cold water until completely cold (take great care: if hot cauliflower is not completely chilled it develops a very strong flavour.) Make the acidulated cream and season to taste with salt and pepper. Arrange the cauliflower in a dish and pour on the cream before it begins to thicken. Sprinkle with chopped parsley and chill before serving.

1 cauliflower
300 ml (½ pt) (1¼ cups) Crème au Citron (page 215)
salt
pepper
1 tbsp chopped parsley

Mâche au Roquefort et aux Noix

LAMB'S LETTUCE WITH ROQUEFORT AND WALNUTS

Lamb's lettuce, mâche, or corn salad, can be found growing in corn fields. It is a very hardy plant and easy to cultivate. It is an ideal winter salad although it grows throughout the year. Just pick a few leaves from each plant and it will continue growing.

Walnut oil is delicious and is used in many salads from the Auvergne and Dordogne. Buy it in small quantities because the flavour deteriorates if kept too long. However, it will keep for several months if tightly sealed. If walnut oil is not available use a good vegetable oil. Using a smaller amount of cheese, this salad can also be served as an accompaniment.

Wash the lettuce well and remove any roots or discoloured leaves. Drain well and place in a salad bowl. Slice the cheese thinly and coarsely chop the walnuts. Mix together with the lettuce. Peel the onions and chop finely. Make a vinaigrette dressing with the oil, lemon juice, seasoning and mustard. Stir in the onions. Just before serving, pour in the vinaigrette and toss well.

100–200 g (4–6 oz) lamb's lettuce
75 g (3 oz) Roquefort/other blue cheese
50 g (2 oz) (½ cup) walnuts
3 spring onions (scallions)
6 tbsp walnut oil
2 tbsp lemon juice
salt
pepper
¼ tsp mustard

Left: Mâche au Roquefort et aux Noix (page 153). Right: Épinards au Lard (page 157).

Salade Midinette

Salade Midinette.

MIDINETTE'S SALAD

A midinette is an office worker, shop girl or young dressmaker, so this is a good slimming lunch.

Hard-boil the eggs and peel and slice. Wash and trim the watercress. Peel and dice the beetroot (beets) and cut the anchovy fillets into strips. Mix the beetroot with the vinaigrette. Arrange a border of watercress round the edge of a dish. Pile the beetroot in the centre and garnish with a trellis of anchovy strips. Sprinkle with chopped parsley and arrange the sliced eggs round the beetroot.

2 eggs
1 bunch watercress
6 small globe beetroots (beets)
3–4 anchovy fillets
2–3 tbsp vinaigrette (page 218)
1–2 tsp chopped parsley

Salade Alsacienne

ALSACE SALAD

175 g (6 oz) red cabbage
1 tbsp vinegar
4–6 tbsp vinaigrette (page 218)
175 g (6 oz) cervalas/other Continental
　sausage
100 g (4 oz) Gruyère cheese
2–3 small tomatoes

Remove the coarse stalks from the cabbage and shred finely. Blanch in a pan of boiling salted water with the vinegar for about 30 seconds. Drain, refresh under cold water and drain well again. Mix with the vinaigrette. Slice the sausage and cut the cheese into 1-cm (½-in) dice. Peel and quarter the tomatoes. Toss the ingredients together and pile into a salad bowl, or serve on individual plates.

Salade de Navets à la Crème

TURNIPS WITH ACIDULATED CREAM

500 g (1 lb) young, small turnips
　(preferably long)
200 ml (7 fl oz) (1 cup) Crème au
　Citron (page 215)
salt and pepper
paprika

Peel the turnips and slice thinly. Blanch in boiling salted water for 1–2 minutes. Drain, refresh under cold water and drain well again. Arrange the turnips neatly in a shallow dish. Make the acidulated cream, season to taste with salt and pepper and pour a thin coating over the turnips before it begins to thicken. Chill and sprinkle with a little paprika just before serving.

Salade Panachée

CABBAGE AND TONGUE SALAD

100 g (4 oz) red cabbage
100 g (4 oz) white cabbage
1 tbsp vinegar
4–6 tbsp vinaigrette (page 218)
250 g (8 oz) cooked, sliced tongue
salt
pepper
4–5 gherkins

Remove the coarse stalks and shred the cabbages thinly. Blanch the red cabbage in boiling salted water with the vinegar for 30 seconds. Drain, refresh under cold water and drain well again. Mix the red and white cabbages separately with the vinaigrette and season well. Cut the tongue into strips or dice. Slice the gherkins. Arrange the red and white cabbage and the tongue in contrasting circles on a plate, finishing with some tongue in the centre. Decorate with sliced gherkins round the edge of the tongue and round the outside of the plate.

SALADS AS ACCOMPANIMENTS

Batavia aux Croûtons

BATAVIA (CHICORY) WITH CROÛTONS

Other salads, such as mâche *(lamb's lettuce),* feuilles de chien *(dog's tooth lettuce) and* chicorée frisée *(curly endive) can be used in the same way.*

1 batavia (chicory)
4 tbsp vinaigrette
garlic croûtons (page 221) made with 2–3
　slices bread
2–3 tbsp grated Parmesan cheese

Wash the batavia (chicory) and break into pieces. Drain well. Place in a salad bowl and pour the vinaigrette into the bottom. Meanwhile, fry the croûtons and drain on kitchen paper towel until cold. Sprinkle the Parmesan cheese over the salad and pile the croûtons in the middle. Toss well before serving.

Pissenlit ou Épinards au Lard

DANDELION OR SPINACH LEAVES WITH BACON

There are several varieties of dandelion that can be grown easily in the garden. When cultivated the plants are blanched in the same way as for curly endive (chicorée frisée), but it is quite usual for the young leaves of wild dandelions to be used. In the country it is a common sight to see people picking them from fields or grass edges along the roads. Young spinach leaves can be used also.

Wash and drain the dandelion leaves and place in a salad bowl. Remove the rind and dice the bacon. Just before serving heat the oil in a pan and cook the bacon until golden brown. Add the vinegar and mix well. Pour on to the dandelion leaves and serve immediately.

350 g (12 oz) dandelion leaves
175 g (6 oz) piece smoked, streaky bacon
2 tbsp oil
2 tbsp vinegar
salt
pepper

Salade Chaude de Haricots Rouges

HOT RED (KIDNEY) BEAN SALAD

After soaking the beans, rinse well and place in a pan of cold water, bring to the boil and boil rapidly for 15 minutes. Then lower the heat and cook for about 1½ hours or until tender. Add salt about 10 minutes before the end of the cooking time. Meanwhile, peel the onions, slice into rings and separate the layers. Make the vinaigrette dressing (this one has more vinegar than usual). Pour over the onion rings and stir in 1 tablespoon of herbs. Leave for at least 30 minutes. When the beans are cooked, drain well. Drain the vinaigrette dressing from the onions and stir into the beans. Pile into a hot dish and just before serving mix in the onions and sprinkle with the remaining herbs.

350 g (12 oz) (2 cups) red (kidney) beans
*   soaked*
*   for 18 hours*
2–3 medium onions
vinaigrette dressing (page 218) made with
*   6 tbsp oil and 4 tbsp vinegar*
2 tbsp chopped mixed herbs (parsley,
*   chervil, tarragon, chives, etc)*
salt
pepper

Salade Verte Mélangée

MIXED GREEN SALAD

Wash the vegetables. Break the lettuce and endive into pieces. Trim the watercress and finely slice the cucumber. Remove the stalk, core and seeds from the pepper and cut into thin strips. Peel and trim the onions. Pour the vinaigrette into the bottom of a large salad bowl, arrange the vegetables on top and toss well just before serving.

½ lettuce
¼ curly endive
½ bunch watercress
¼ cucumber
1 small green pepper
6–8 small spring onions (scallions)
6–8 tbsp vinaigrette (page 218)

Salade de Betteraves à la Menthe.

150 ml (¼ pt) (⅔ cup) plain yogurt
2 tbsp chopped mint
1 tbsp brown sugar
1 tbsp lemon juice
1 bunch spring onions (scallions)
1 large green eating apple
1 large raw beetroot (beets) approx.
  250 g (8 oz)
2 tbsp sultanas (golden raisins)
1 bunch watercress
1 lemon
salt
pepper

Salade de Betteraves à la Menthe

BEETROOT (BEET) SALAD WITH MINT

This is a delicious salad to serve with cold meats.

Put 1–2 tablespoons of yogurt and a little mint to one side. Mix the remaining yogurt and mint with the brown sugar and lemon juice. Season to taste with salt and pepper. Peel and thinly slice the onions. Quarter the apple, remove the core and seeds and chop into small pieces. Stir the apple into the sauce. Peel and coarsely grate the beetroot (beets) and stir into the sauce with the onions and sultanas (golden raisins). Mix well. Cover the bowl with cling-film and refrigerate for 1 hour. Meanwhile, wash and pick the watercress and cut the lemon into thin wedges.

Pile the beetroot mixture into a bowl and arrange sprigs of watercress round the edges. Make a well in the centre of the beetroots, pour in the reserved yogurt and sprinkle with mint. Garnish with lemon wedges.

Left: Roulade aux Épinards (page 176). Right: Soufflé aux Courgettes (page 173).

4 VEGETABLES WITH EGGS

Artichauts à la Reine

QUEEN'S ARTICHOKES

Prepare the artichoke hearts (page 10) and cook in boiling salted, acidulated water (page 10) until tender. Keep hot in a steamer over a pan of boiling water. Make the mushroom sauce but do not add the eggs and cream.

To poach the eggs heat a pan of water with the vinegar. When boiling, reduce the heat so the water is barely moving. Break 1 egg into a saucer. With a whisk or fork create a whirlpool in the water and slide the egg into it. As the egg starts to set, fold over the white to enclose the yolk completely. Add a second egg and cook each one for $3\frac{1}{2}$–4 minutes. Lift out with a draining spoon and keep hot in a bowl of warm water.

Beat the uncooked eggs and cream together. Pour on a little sauce, mix well, return to the pan and heat through without boiling. Check the seasoning. Place the artichoke hearts in individual deep dishes. Pour on a little sauce. Place a poached egg on top and cover with the remaining sauce. Serve immediately.

Serves 4

4 large artichokes

2 tbsp lemon juice

300 ml (½ pt) (1¼ cups) Sauce aux Champignons (page 214) made with 2 egg yolks and 4 tbsp double (heavy) cream

4 eggs

1 tbsp vinegar

salt

pepper

Oeufs Froids à la Maltaise

MALTESE EGGS

Hard-boil or poach the eggs (above). Shell the hard-boiled eggs and cut in half. Peel the celeriac and grate coarsely or cut into very fine strips. Keep in water with lemon juice until required. Remove the stalk, core and seeds from the pepper and dice finely. If you wish, blanch the pepper in boiling salted water for a moment or two, then drain/refresh. With a small, sharp knife — a serrated one is best — cut a slice from each end of an orange. Place the orange cut-end down and carefully cut away all the skin and pith. Cut out the segments and cut each into 2–3 pieces. Thinly slice the other orange and then cut the slices in half.

Make the *Sauce Maltaise*. Drain the celeriac (and the pepper if it has been blanched) and dry on kitchen paper towel or a dish towel. Mix the vegetables and orange segments together with a tablespoon or two of *Sauce Maltaise* and season to taste. Place the mixture on a serving dish and the eggs on top. Carefully coat each egg with *Sauce Maltaise* and sprinkle a little paprika on top of each. Arrange the orange slices round the edge of the dish and serve chilled.

4–6 eggs

1 large celeriac

2 tbsp lemon juice

1 green pepper

2 oranges

300 ml (½ pt) (1¼ cups) Sauce Maltaise Froide (page 216)

salt

pepper

a little paprika

Flan à la Ratatouille

VEGETABLE CUSTARD

This dish can be served as a light meal with a salad. If the bacon is omitted, it makes an excellent vegetarian dish.

Peel and chop the tomatoes and garlic. Heat the oil in a pan, add the tomatoes, garlic, basil and bouquet garni. Season lightly and cook until the tomatoes are soft. Trim and dice the courgettes (zucchini). Remove the stalk, core and seeds from the pepper and cut into thin strips. When the tomatoes are soft, add the courgettes and pepper. Mix well, cover and cook gently for 20–25 minutes until the vegetables are tender. If necessary remove the lid for the last few minutes to allow the liquid to evaporate. Check the seasoning and allow to cool slightly.

Meanwhile, remove the rind from the bacon and cut into thin strips. Heat the remaining oil in a pan and fry the bacon until golden brown. Beat the eggs well, add the cheese, bacon and vegetables. Mix well. Season to taste with salt, pepper and a pinch of nutmeg. Pour the mixture into a well-buttered 18-cm (7-in) tart ring, deep sandwich tin or small cake pan, or a 500 g (1 lb) loaf tin or terrine. Bake in a preheated oven 180°C (350°F) (Gas Mark 4) for 1–1¼ hours until the custard is set and starts to shrink from the sides of the tin. Remove from the oven and leave until cold, then turn out on to a plate and garnish with cucumber and tomatoes.

500 g (1 lb) tomatoes
2 cloves garlic
2 tbsp oil
3 tbsp olive oil
1 tbsp finely chopped basil
bouquet garni
salt
pepper
3 small courgettes (zucchini)
1 green pepper
100 g (4 oz) bacon
6 eggs
50 g (2 oz) (½ cup) grated Gruyère cheese
pinch nutmeg
Garnish:
  ¼ cucumber
  2–3 small tomatoes

Oeufs à la Niçoise

EGGS WITH NIÇOISE SALAD

Hard-boil or poach the eggs (page 160). Trim the beans and cut into pieces. Scrub the potatoes. Cook the beans and potatoes in separate pans of boiling salted water until tender. Drain, remove the potato skins and slice. Mix with the beans and vinaigrette. Peel and quarter the tomatoes. Mix the mayonnaise with sufficient tomato purée to colour it pale pink. Season to taste. Cut the anchovy fillets into strips and stone the olives. Place the beans and potatoes in the middle of a serving dish and arrange the eggs on top (hard-boiled eggs can be halved). Carefully coat each egg with mayonnaise and arrange a lattice of anchovies over the dish. Place an olive on top of each egg and arrange the tomatoes round the edge. Chill until required.

4–6 eggs
350 g (12 oz) French (snap) beans
250 g (8 oz) small, new potatoes
2–3 tbsp vinaigrette (page 218)
2–3 small tomatoes
300 ml (½ pt) (1¼ cups) mayonnaise (page 216)
5–6 anchovy fillets
4–12 black olives

Oeufs à la Portugaise

PORTUGUESE EGGS

If you wish, this dish can be prepared in advance. Cover with aluminium foil or a lid and reheat in a preheated oven 200°C (400°F) (Gas Mark 6) for 20 minutes.

Hard-boil the eggs and make the *Sauce Portugaise*. Peel the eggs. If necessary keep them hot in a bowl of hot water. When the sauce is ready, check the seasoning. Cut the eggs in half and place in a hot, buttered dish. Pour the sauce over and sprinkle with chopped parsley just before serving.

4–6 eggs
300 ml (½ pt) (1¼ cups) Sauce Portugaise (page 217)
1 tbsp chopped parsley

Top: *Pipérade Basquaise* (page 164).
Bottom: *Oeufs Pochés au Petits Légumes.*

Oeufs Pochés aux Petits Légumes

POACHED EGGS WITH VEGETABLES

The new style French cookery avoids the use of flour in sauces. The eggs in this recipe are coated with a hot, acidulated cream sauce.

Serves 4

175 g (6 oz) French (snap) beans

175 g (6 oz) carrots

2 onions

100 g (4 oz) turnips

75 g (3 oz) (6 tbsp) butter

4 shallots

100 ml (3½ fl oz) (½ cup) wine vinegar

200 ml (7 fl oz) (1 cup) double (heavy) cream

8 eggs

salt

white pepper

Trim the beans and peel the carrots and onions. Cut all the vegetables into *julienne* — very thin, finger-length strips. Peel and finely chop the shallots. Cook the beans, carrots and turnips in separate pans of boiling, salted water for about 10 minutes or until tender. Drain well. Heat 50 g (2 oz) (¼ cup) of butter in a pan and toss the cooked vegetables until coated with butter. Keep hot.

Meanwhile, cook the shallots and vinegar in a pan over gentle heat until the shallots are soft and the vinegar is reduced to about 1 tablespoonful. Add the cream and boil until it thickens. Taste and season. Poach the eggs (page 160). Cut the remaining butter into small pieces and whisk a few at a time into the hot sauce. Divide the vegetables into 4 portions and place on individual plates. Place 2 eggs on each plate and coat with the sauce. Serve immediately.

Oeufs Pochés Parmentier

POACHED EGGS IN POTATO NESTS

Make the potato mixture and place in a bag with a large star nozzle. Pipe out large 'nests' on to a greased baking sheet. Make certain the centre of each is large enough to hold a poached egg. Place in a preheated oven 200°C (400°F) (Gas Mark 6) for 10 minutes. Beat one egg well and brush over the nests. Return them to the oven for 10–15 minutes or until golden brown. Keep hot. Make the *Sauce Mornay* and poach the remaining eggs (page 160). Place an egg in the centre of each nest and coat with the *Sauce Mornay*. Serve any remaining sauce separately.

Aumônières aux Champignons (page 177).

Pommes de Terre Duchesse (page 95) made with 750 g (1½ lb) potatoes
5–7 eggs
300 ml (½ pt) (1¼ cups) Sauce Mornay (page 217)

Oeufs à la Tripe

EGGS IN ONION SAUCE

2 large onins
50 g (2 oz) (1/4 cup) butter
4–6 eggs
300 ml (1/2 pt) (1 1/4 cups) Sauce Béchamel
 (page 214)
salt
pepper
1 tbsp chopped parsley

In the days when French children were not given meat, eggs prepared in this way were served instead of tripe.

Peel the onions and slice thinly. Melt the butter in a pan and cook the onions until soft but without colour. Season to taste. Hard-boil the eggs. When cooked, shell and keep hot in a bowl of hot water. Make the *Sauce Béchamel*, stir in the onions and adjust the seasoning. Quarter the eggs, arrange in a hot dish and pour the sauce over. Sprinkle with chopped parsley just before serving.

Pipérade Basquaise

BASQUE-STYLE EGGS

This is a great favourite of mine and a good standby for unexpected lunches. I find canned tomatoes and frozen, chopped peppers quite acceptable in an emergency. If you wish, 100 g (4 oz) of ham can be chopped and added at the same time as the eggs, or serve it with grilled or fried bacon or ham, although I am quite happy to eat it on its own.

2 green peppers
1 red pepper
1 large onion
500 g (1 lb) tomatoes
4 tbsp olive oil
6–8 eggs
salt
pepper
fried croûtons (page 221, optional)

Remove the stalks, cores and seeds from the peppers and cut into thin strips. Peel and finely slice the onion. Peel the tomatoes and chop coarsely. Heat the oil in a pan and cook the onions for 5 minutes over gentle heat. Add the peppers and continue to cook gently until both vegetables are soft but without colour. Add the tomatoes and continue cooking until the sauce thickens. Season to taste. Meanwhile, make the croûtons, if used. Beat the eggs well and add to the mixture. Cook gently, stirring all the time, until the eggs scramble lightly. Taste and adjust the seasoning. Serve immediately. Garnish with triangular croûtons or serve with crusty French bread and butter.

Tartelettes Mimosa

MIMOSA TARTLETS

Pâte Demi-feuilletée made with 100 g
 (4 oz) (1 cup) flour (page 220)
4 eggs
4–6 tbsp Salade Russe (page 148)
150 ml (1/4 pt) (2/3 cup) mayonnaise
 (page 216)

Make the pastry and refrigerate for 30 minutes. Roll out and line 6 deep tartlet tins. Line these with greaseproof paper and fill with baking beans and cook in a preheated oven 220°C (425°F) (Gas Mark 7) for 15–20 minutes. Cook on a wire rack. Meanwhile, hard-boil the eggs. Place a layer of salad in each tartlet case. Cut 3 eggs in half and place a half, cut-side down, in each case. Adjust the mayonnaise to a coating consistency and coat the eggs. Sieve the yolk, chop the white of the remaining egg and sprinkle on top of the mayonnaise. Serve chilled.

OMELETTES

Omelettes are best eaten as soon as they are cooked, so it is a good idea to use two pans or, if you have a pan of the right size, make one or two larger ones and cut them at the table. Keep a pan especially for making omelettes and pancakes; it should not be washed but wiped with kitchen paper towel after use.

Omelettes à la Forestière

FORESTER'S OMELETTES

Clean and trim the mushrooms. Slice half of them and finely chop the rest. Peel and finely chop the shallots. Melt 40 g (1½ oz) (3 tbsp) butter in a pan and cook the mushrooms for 5–6 minutes until tender. Season lightly, remove from the pan and keep hot. Add a little more butter if necessary and cook the shallots until tender but without colour. Add the chopped mushrooms and cook for 2–3 minutes. Add the lemon juice and cream and boil until it thickens slightly.

To make the omelettes, beat 2 eggs with a teaspoon of water and seasoning. Heat a good knob of butter in a pan, and when it foams, pour in the egg. Stir rapidly over good heat for a moment or two and then, using a fork, bring the egg from the sides of the pan into the centre. Tip the pan to allow any liquid egg to run to the outside of the pan and continue until it is set on the bottom but creamy in the centre. Place a portion of the sliced mushrooms in the omelette, fold in three and roll on to a plate. Keep hot until all the omelettes are cooked and, just before serving, pour a little mushroom sauce over each.

Serves 4

350 g (12 oz) mushrooms
2 shallots
75 g (3 oz) (6 tbsp) butter
1 tbsp lemon juice
150 ml (¼ pt) (⅔ cup) double (heavy) cream
salt
pepper
8 eggs

Omelettes à l'Arlésienne

ARLESIENNE OMELETTES

Cut the stalk from the aubergine (eggplant) and dice finely. Sprinkle lightly with salt and leave on a wire rack for 30 minutes. Wash and dry well. Peel and finely chop the onion, tomatoes and garlic. Heat 2 tablespoons of oil in a pan and cook the onions gently for 5–6 minutes. Add the aubergines and more oil if needed. When the aubergine starts to soften, add the tomatoes and garlic. Season to taste and simmer until nearly all the liquid has evaporated and the mixture is quite dry. Keep hot. Make the omelettes (above) and fill each with some of the aubergine mixture. Fold in three and turn out on to a hot plate.

Serves 4

1 aubergine (eggplant) approx. 350 g (12 oz)
1 medium onion
100 g (4 oz) tomatoes
1 clove garlic
3–4 tbsp olive oil
salt and pepper
8 eggs
50 g (2 oz) (¼ cup) butter
1 tbsp chopped parsley

Omelettes d'Avocats

AVOCADO OMELETTES

Cut the avocados in half and remove the stones. Cut a few slices as a garnish if you wish. Peel one and cut the flesh into small dice. Sprinkle with a little lemon juice and mix gently. Scoop the flesh from the other with a teaspoon and mash to a purée with a fork. Melt 25 g (1 oz) (2 tbsp) butter in a pan, add the diced avocado and cook for 2–3 minutes, then add the purée and cream. Heat through, stirring carefully. Season to taste and keep hot. Make the omelettes (above), fill with a portion of avocado, then roll up.

Serves 4

2 ripe avocados
1–2 tbsp lemon juice
75 g (3 oz) (6 tbsp) butter
2 tbsp double (heavy) cream
salt and pepper
8 eggs

Left: Omelette Basquaise (page 168).
Right: Omelette Solognote.

Omelettes Solognote

ASPARAGUS OMELETTES

This recipe may seem extravagant, but it is delicious. Small, thin asparagus can be used if they are tender. For a less rich sauce, use milk instead of cream.

Trim and cook the fresh asparagus (page 13) if used, or heat canned asparagus in their liquid. Drain well, reserving some of the cooking liquor. Cut 3–5 cm (2–3 in) off the tips. Keep hot. Purée the rest through a vegetable mill or in a food processor. Melt half the butter in a small pan, add the purée, sprinkle in the flour and mix well. Cook for 2–3 minutes, then add the cream and 3–4 tablespoons of the cooking liquor or liquid from the tin. Bring to the boil, stirring all the time, and boil for 8–10 minutes. Season to taste.

Make the omelettes (page 165) and turn out unfolded on to a plate. Pour some of the sauce into the centre of each and arrange the tips so they overlap the outer edge of the omelette. Fold in half so the sauce and cut ends of the asparagus are covered and pour the remaining sauce over.

Serves 4

500 g (1 lb) small green asparagus/350 g (12 oz) can

75 g (3 oz) (6 tbsp) butter

1 tbsp flour

200 ml (7 fl oz) (1 cup) double (heavy) cream

salt

pepper

8 eggs

Above, top: *Pâté de Cépes à la Limousine*
(page 184). Bottom: *Quiche au Petits Pois*
(page 184).

Top: *Tourte aux Asperges* (page 189).
Bottom: *Flamiche* (page 181).

Omelette Basquaise

BASQUE-STYLE OMELETTE

You will need a fairly large pan for this omelette — about 18 cm (7 in) — as the omelette should be a good 2.5-cm (1-in) thick when cooked. If necessary, you can make two smaller ones. The omelette is not folded — just slide it out on to a plate and cut into wedges to serve. This type is often eaten cold with a salad.

1 small green pepper
1 small red pepper
1 medium onion
250 g (8 oz) tomatoes
100 g (4 oz) bacon
3–4 tbsp olive oil
6–8 eggs

Remove the stalks, cores and seeds from the peppers and cut into small dice. Peel and finely slice the onion. Peel the tomatoes and chop coarsely. Remove the rind and cut the bacon into small strips. Heat 2 tablespoons of oil in a pan and cook the bacon until golden brown. Remove from the pan and add the peppers and onion. Cook gently until soft and lightly coloured, then add the tomatoes and cook for 2–3 minutes and season well. Beat the eggs, and stir in the vegetable mixture and bacon.

Heat 1 tablespoon oil in a large omelette pan. Add the egg mixture and cook over fairly good heat. With a fork draw in the cooked egg from the sides of the pan into the centre once or twice. As the omelette starts to set on the outside, tip the pan and lift the edges of the omelette so any liquid egg can run underneath. When the egg is set in its base, turn the omelette over and cook for a moment or two. Take care not to overcook — it is nicer when soft in the middle.

Omelette Paysanne

COUNTRY-STYLE OMELETTE

175 g (6 oz) small potatoes
100 g (4 oz) bacon
50 g (2 oz) sorrel
100 g (4 oz) (½ cup) butter
6–8 eggs
salt
pepper

Scrub the potatoes, peel and dice. Remove the rind and cut the bacon into strips. Wash the sorrel well and remove the coarse stalks. Heat 25–50 g (1–2 oz) (2–4 tbsp) butter in a large omelette pan and fry the potatoes until golden brown. Remove from the pan and add the bacon and cook until golden brown. In the meantime, heat another 25 g (1 oz) (2 tbsp) butter in another pan and cook the sorrel until it 'melts'. Beat the eggs and add the vegetables and bacon. Season well. Make and serve the omelette as for *Omelette Basquaise*.

SOUFFLÉS

Contrary to popular belief, it is possible to make and refrigerate most soufflés for 20 minutes before cooking, which eliminates the problem of trying to cook and entertain guests at the same time.

Before starting the soufflé, prepare the dish: butter the inside of a soufflé dish well and coat it with fine white breadcrumbs or grated Parmesan cheese. Tie a band of buttered greaseproof paper round the top edge so it stands about 5-cm (2-in) higher than the dish. Individual soufflés can be made in ramekins. Prepare them in the same way as for large soufflé dishes; they take about 10–12 minutes to cook. Once cooked, serve the soufflé without delay.

Vegetable soufflés are very popular in France served as a separate vegetable dish or as an accompaniment to the main course. There are two basic methods: one uses a very thick Sauce Béchamel called panada with a vegetable purée (below). The other is used for firm vegetables, such as potatoes, in which the vegetable purée provides the base (page 173).

Method 1

To make the *panada*, melt the butter in a pan and add the flour. Cook for 3–4 minutes, then stir in the milk a little at a time. Bring to the boil, stirring continuously, and cook for 7–8 minutes. Add the vegetable purée to the sauce and leave for a few minutes to cool. Separate the egg yolks and whites and add the yolks to the mixture. Stir until evenly mixed and season well. Whisk the 4 egg whites until stiff and dry. Fold 1 tablespoon thoroughly into the mixture, then very carefully fold in the remaining whites in three batches. Pour into the soufflé dish and cook in a preheated oven 200°C (400°F) (Gas Mark 6) for 20–25 minutes. Serve immediately.

50 g (2 oz) (¼ cup) butter
50 g (2 oz) (½ cup) flour
300 ml (½ pt) (1¼ cups) milk
vegetable purée (see recipes)
3 eggs
1 extra egg white
salt
pepper

Soufflé aux Carottes

CARROT SOUFFLÉ

Prepare a soufflé dish (page 168). Peel the carrots and cut into even-sized pieces. Cook in boiling salted water until tender. Drain well. Purée through a vegetable mill or in a food processor and return the purée to a saucepan. Cook over gentle heat, stirring all the time, until any surplus moisture in the purée has evaporated. Add to the *panada* with the cheese, if used, and continue as for Method 1.

500 g (1 lb) carrots
2–3 tbsp grated Parmesan cheese (optional)
ingredients as for Method 1

Soufflé aux Champignons

MUSHROOM SOUFFLÉ

Prepare a soufflé dish (page 168). Trim and clean the mushrooms. Remove the stalks and finely chop 100 g (4 oz). Finely slice the rest. Melt the butter in a pan and add the sliced mushrooms and cook until tender. Season lightly and remove from the pan. Add the chopped mushrooms and cook until tender. Season as well. Make the *panada*. Add the chopped mushrooms to the *panada* with the cheese, if used, and continue with the recipe as for Method 1. Place one-third of the mixture in the soufflé dish. Spread half the sliced mushrooms on top, cover with another layer of soufflé mixture and the remaining mushrooms. Cover with the remaining soufflé mixture.

350 g (12 oz) mushrooms
50 g (2 oz) (¼ cup) butter
ingredients as for Method 1
2–3 tbsp grated Parmesan cheese (optional)
pinch nutmeg

Soufflé aux Oignons

ONION SOUFFLÉ

The preparation of the onions will take about an hour. If you wish, this part of the recipe can be prepared well in advance.

Prepare a soufflé dish (page 168). Peel and finely slice the onions. Melt the butter in a heavy-based pan, add the onions and season lightly. Cover and cook gently until the onions are soft but without colour, stirring occasionally so they do not brown on the bottom of the pan. (While the onions are cooking, a lot of liquid will seep from them. As soon as they are soft, remove the lid and continue cooking until all the liquid has evaporated. The heat can be raised slightly but take care not to colour the onions.) Make the *panada*. Add the onions to the *panada* and continue with the recipe as for Method 1, adding a little paprika and seasoning.

1 kg (2 lb) onions
50 g (2 oz) (¼ cup) butter
salt
pepper
ingredients as for Method 1
a little paprika

Above: Filets de Maquereaux aux Courgettes (page 195).

Left, top: Moules aux Champignons (page 195).

Left, bottom: Bar à la Portugaise (page 193).

Soufflé au Choufleur

CAULIFLOWER SOUFFLÉ

1 large cauliflower
2–3 tbsp grated Parmesan cheese (optional)
ingredients as for Method 1 (page 169)

Prepare a soufflé dish (page 168). Break the cauliflower into florets and wash well. Cook in boiling salted water until just tender — about 15 minutes. Drain well, refresh under cold water and drain until completely dry, or dry on kitchen paper towel. Make the *panada*. Purée the cauliflower through a food processor or vegetable mill. Add to the *panada* with the cheese (if used) and continue with the recipe as for Method 1.

Soufflé a l'Oseille

SORREL SOUFFLÉ

1 kg (2 lb) sorrel
50 g (2 oz) (¼ cup) butter
ingredients as for Method 1 (page 169)

Prepare a soufflé dish (page 168). Wash the sorrel well and remove the coarse stalks and ribs. Heat the butter in a pan, add the sorrel and cook until it softens and 'melts' into a purée. Continue cooking until the purée is as dry as possible. Season to taste. Make the *panada*. Add the sorrel to the *panada* and continue as for Method 1.

Soufflé aux Poireaux

LEEK SOUFFLÉ

8 large leeks, approx. 1 kg (2 lb)
25 g (1 oz) (2 tbsp) butter
ingredients as for Method 1 (page 169)

Prepare a soufflé dish (page 168). Wash and trim the leeks and cut into 2.5-cm (1-in) pieces. Cook in boiling salted water until just tender. Drain well. Chop finely. Heat the butter in a pan, add the leeks and cook over gentle heat until tender and dry. Make the *panada*. Add the leeks to the *panada* and continue as for Method 1.

Soufflé de Potiron

PUMPKIN SOUFFLÉ

500 g (1 lb) pumpkin
75 g (3 oz) (¾ cup) grated Gruyère cheese
ingredients as for Method 1 (page 169)

Prepare a soufflé dish (page 168). Peel the pumpkin and remove the seeds. Cut into even-sized pieces and cook in boiling salted water until tender. Drain well. Make the *panada*. Purée the pumpkin through a vegetable mill or in a food processor and mix into the *panada* with the grated cheese. Continue as for Method 1.

Petits Soufflés aux Tomates

SMALL TOMATO SOUFFLÉS

4 large tomatoes
150 ml (¼ pt) (⅔ cup) Sauce Béchamel
  (page 214)
2 eggs
2 tbsp grated Parmesan cheese
salt
pepper

Cut a thin slice from the top of each tomato. Scoop out the centre with a ball-cutter or teaspoon, sprinkle with a little salt, turn upside down and drain on a wire rack for 20–30 minutes. Make the *Sauce Béchamel*. Separate the eggs and stir the yolks and most of the cheese into the sauce. Season well. Whisk the egg whites until stiff and dry and carefully fold into the mixture in three batches. Fill the tomatoes with the soufflé and sprinkle the cheese on top. Place in a buttered dish and bake in a preheated oven 200°C (400°F) (Gas Mark 6) for 15–18 minutes.

Method 2

In Method 2 the vegetable purée forms the base of the soufflé.

Soufflé de Pommes de Terre

POTATO SOUFFLÉ

Prepare a soufflé dish (page 000). Peel the potatoes, cut into even-sized pieces and cook in boiling salted water until tender. Drain well and purée through a vegetable mill or in a food processor. Weigh the potatoes and return 350 g (12 oz) to the pan. Beat in the butter and cream and cook over gentle heat for 3–4 minutes, stirring all the time. Turn out into a large bowl. Separate the eggs and beat the yolks into the potato. Season well with salt and pepper and a pinch of nutmeg. Whisk the egg whites until stiff and dry and carefully fold into the mixture. Place the mixture in the prepared soufflé dish and cook in a preheated oven 200°C (400°F) (Gas Mark 6) for 20–25 minutes. Serve immediately.

500 g (1 lb) old potatoes
65 g (2 ½ oz) (⅓ cup) butter
3 tbsp double (heavy) cream
3 eggs
1 extra white
salt
pepper
pinch nutmeg

Soufflé aux Topinambours

JERUSALEM ARTICHOKE SOUFFLÉ

Prepare a soufflé dish (page 168). Peel the artichokes and cook in boiling salted water with the lemon juice until tender. Drain well and purée through a vegetable mill or food processor. Return to the pan and cook over gentle heat until the purée is dry, stirring continuously. Weigh the artichoke purée and mix the cream and butter with 350 g (12 oz) of the purée. Continue as for Method 2.

750 g (1 ½ lb) Jerusalem artichokes
1 tbsp lemon juice
ingredients (except potatoes) as for Method 2

Soufflé aux Courgettes

COURGETTE (ZUCCHINI) SOUFFLÉ

This soufflé is quite different from others as it is made in a ring mould and turned out before serving. It can also be eaten cold and served with either a Fondue de Trois Légumes or Sauce Tomate Crue instead of the hot Sauce Tomate.

Butter the inside of an 18-cm (7-in) ring mould. Trim and wash the courgettes (zucchini) and grate coarsely. Place in a colander and sprinkle with a little salt. Leave for 30 minutes, then press out as much liquid as possible (the liquid is very good if added to vegetable soups). Heat 50 g (2 oz) (¼ cup) butter and add the courgettes. Cook for 7–8 minutes, stirring frequently. Melt 25 g (1 oz) (2 tbsp) butter in another pan, add the flour, mix well and cook for 2–3 minutes. Add the milk a little at a time, stirring constantly. Bring to the boil, still stirring, and cook for 3–4 minutes. Separate the eggs and add the yolks to the sauce with the courgettes. Mix well and season with salt and pepper.

Whisk the egg whites until stiff and dry and carefully fold into the mixture in three batches. Pour into the prepared mould and cook in a preheated oven 190°C (375°F) (Gas Mark 5) for 35–40 minutes. Turn out on to a hot plate and fill with *Sauce Tomate*. If served cold, turn out while hot, cool quickly and refrigerate until required.

1 kg (2 lb) courgettes (zucchini)
115 g (4½ oz) (⅔ cup) butter
25 g (1 oz) (¼ cup) flour
200 ml (7 fl oz) (1 cup) milk
3 eggs
salt
pepper
300 ml (½ pt) (1¼ cups) Sauce Tomate (page 218) (optional)

Poulet aux Champignons (page 202).

Left: Paupiettes de Boeuf aux Carottes (page 200). *Right: Poivrons Farcis* (page 201).

Roulade aux Épinards

SPINACH ROULADE

Roulades are excellent for dinner parties because they can be prepared in advance and reheated. Serve them as a separate vegetable dish or as an hors d'oeuvre.

1 kg (2 lb) spinach
600 ml (1 pt) (2½ cups) Sauce Béchamel (page 214)
4 eggs
salt
pepper
pinch nutmeg
75–100 g (3–4 oz) (¾–1 cup) grated Gruyère cheese
25 g (1 oz) (2 tbsp) butter

Grease a 33 × 23 cm (13 × 9 in) Swiss roll tin, or jelly roll pan, and line with greaseproof paper. Wash the spinach and remove the coarse stalks and ribs. Cook in boiling salted water for 12–15 minutes until tender, then drain and press until dry or squeeze in a cloth. Chop very finely. Make the *Sauce Béchamel*. Measure out 300 ml (½ pt) (1¼ cups) and reserve the rest. Separate the eggs. Beat the egg yolks and spinach into the sauce and season well with salt and pepper and a pinch of nutmeg. Whisk the egg whites until stiff and dry and fold into the mixture in three batches.

Pour the mixture into the prepared tin, tipping the tin from side to side so it is filled evenly. Avoid spreading it with a spatula because this breaks down the air bubbles. Bake in a preheated oven 180°C (350°F) (Gas Mark 4) for 15 minutes, or until the mixture is set and springy like a sponge. Remove the *roulade* from the oven and turn out on to a large dish towel. Carefully lift the tin off the *roulade* and leave for 5 minutes, then strip off the paper. Trim off 1 cm (½ in) of the *roulade* on one of the shorter sides.

Heat the reserved sauce and whisk until smooth. Add 50–75 g (2–3 oz) (½–¾ cup) cheese to taste and season well, adding a pinch of nutmeg. Spread the sauce over the *roulade*, taking care to leave a margin all round the edge so the filling does not run out when it is rolled up. Place the *roulade* with the long side in front of you. Lift the edge of the dish towel nearest to you and pull it away from you so the action rolls up the *roulade* without direct pressure. Try to roll it as tightly as possible so there is no gap in the middle. Place the *roulade* in a buttered heatproof dish with the edge underneath. Melt the butter and brush over the top and sprinkle on a thin coating of cheese. When required, place in a preheated oven 180°C (350°F) (Gas Mark 4) for 10–12 minutes until the cheese forms a light crust on top. Cut into thick slices and serve.

Roulade aux Champignons

MUSHROOM ROULADE

100 g (4 oz) (½ cup) butter
50 g (2 oz) (½ cup) flour
450 ml (¾ pt) (2 cups) milk
4 eggs
100 g (4 oz) (1 cup) grated Gruyère cheese
salt
pepper
pinch nutmeg
150 ml (¼ pt) (⅔ cup) chicken stock
75 g (3 oz) lean bacon
250 g (8 oz) mushrooms
1 tbsp finely chopped parsley

Grease a 33 × 23 cm (13 × 9 in) Swiss roll tin, or jelly roll pan, and line with greaseproof paper. Melt 25 g (1 oz) (2 tbsp) butter in a pan, add 25 g (1 oz) (¼ cup) flour and mix well. Cook for 2–3 minutes and then add the milk a little at a time, stirring constantly. Bring to the boil, still stirring, and cook for 3–4 minutes. Separate the eggs. Add the yolks and 75 g (3 oz) (¾ cup) cheese to the sauce and season well with salt, pepper and a pinch of nutmeg. Whisk the egg whites until stiff and dry and fold carefully into the sauce in three batches. Pour into the prepared tin. Tip the tin from side to side until the mixture is spread evenly in the tin. Cook in a preheated oven 200°C (400°F) (Gas Mark 6) for 15 minutes. Remove the *roulade* from the oven and turn out on to a large dish towel.

In the meantime, make the filling. Make a sauce in the same way as for *Roulade aux Épinards*, using the remaining milk and chicken stock. Remove the rind and cut the bacon into strips. Melt 15 g (½ oz) (1 tbsp) butter in another pan and cook the bacon until tender and a golden colour. Remove from the pan. Trim, clean and slice the mushrooms. Add another 15 g (½ oz) (1 tbsp) butter to the pan and cook the mushrooms until tender. Season lightly. Reserve half the mushrooms if possible keeping back the best shaped slices. Stir the remainder into the sauce with the bacon. Fill the *roulade*, roll up and finish in the same way as for *Roulade aux Épinards*. Just before serving, reheat the reserved mushrooms and arrange down either side of the *roulade*.

PANCAKES

Aumônières aux Champignons

MUSHROOM PURSES

Make the pancakes and keep hot over a pan of hot water (page 221). Trim, clean and quarter the mushrooms. Heat 45 g (1½ oz) (3½ tbsp) butter in a pan, add the mushrooms and lemon juice and cook for 7–8 minutes until tender. Add the tomato purée and season to taste with tabasco sauce, salt, pepper and a little sugar. Mix well and cook over gentle heat for 2–3 minutes. Keep hot. Quarter the tomatoes. Melt the remaining butter in a small frying pan and cook the tomatoes until just heated through. Keep hot. Just before serving place a portion of the mushrooms in the centre of each pancake. Gather up the edges of the pancakes and tie with string about 2–3 cm (1–1½ in) from the top, so they look like string purses. Place on a hot dish and garnish with the tomato.

Serves 4
4 × 23-cm (9-in) pancakes (page 221)
250 g (8 oz) button mushrooms
50 g (2 oz) (¼ cup) butter
2 tbsp lemon juice
2 tbsp tomato purée
2–3 drops tabasco sauce
salt
pepper
1 tsp caster/superfine sugar
2 tomatoes

Crêpes Fourrées

STUFFED PANCAKES

Make 6 large or 8 small pancakes and keep hot over a pan of boiling water (page 221). Peel the celeriac and cut into 1-cm (½-in) dice. Cook in boiling salted water with the lemon juice/vinegar for 7–10 minutes. Drain well. Trim and wash the leeks and slice thinly. Heat the butter in a pan, add the leeks and celeriac and season lightly with salt and pepper. Cover and cook over gentle heat for 20–25 minutes until tender. Meanwhile, peel and crush the garlic and mix with the cream cheese and herbs. Soften with a little milk, season with celery salt and pepper, mix well and leave for 20–30 minutes. When the celeriac and leeks are cooked, add the peas and heat through. Remove from the heat and stir in the cheese mixture. Place a portion of the filling on each pancake, roll up and place in a hot dish. Sprinkle with the grated cheese and almonds and cook in a preheated oven 200°C (400°F) (Gas Mark 6) for 10–15 minutes, or under a hot grill, until brown.

Pâte à Crêpes (page 221)
500 g (1 lb) celeriac
1 tbsp lemon juice/vinegar
3 small leeks
25 g (1 oz) (2 tbsp) butter
1 clove garlic
75 g (3 oz) (6 tbsp) cream cheese
1 tbsp chopped parsley and chervil
1–2 tbsp milk
salt
celery salt
pepper
20 g (2 oz) cooked peas
50 g (2 oz) (½ cup) grated Gruyère cheese
25 g (1 oz) (¼ cup) flaked almonds

Cassoulet Toulousain (page 198).

Sauté de Mouton aux Haricots Rouges (page 199).

Crêpes au Gratin à la Ligurienne

LIGURIAN PANCAKES

If the anchovies are very salty, soak them in a little milk for 10–15 minutes.

Pâte à Crêpes (page 221)
500 g (1 lb) ripe tomatoes
1 tbsp olive oil
1 sprig tarragon
8–10 anchovy fillets
3 eggs
pepper
50 g (2 oz) (¼ cup) butter
2–3 tbsp white breadcrumbs

Make 6 large or 8 small pancakes. Keep hot over a pan of boiling water (page 221). Peel, seed and chop the tomatoes. Place in a pan with the oil and tarragon and cook gently until the mixture thickens. Remove the tarragon. Meanwhile, chop the anchovy fillets. Hard-boil the eggs and when cooked, shell and chop coarsely. Add the anchovies and eggs to the sauce and season with pepper. Spread a little of the mixture on each pancake. Fold in half and spread a little more on one side. Fold in half again and place in a hot dish. Spread any remaining mixture over the top and cover with a layer of breadcrumbs. Melt the butter and pour over the top. Grill until golden brown.

Crêpes à la Normandes

NORMANDY PANCAKES

Pâte à Crêpes (page 221)
350 g (12 oz) small button mushrooms
1–2 tsp lemon juice
50 g (2 oz) butter
2 tbsp Calvados
300 ml (½ pt) (1¼ cups) Sauce à la Crème (page 215)
1 egg yolk
2–3 tbsp milk
salt
pepper

Make 6 large or 8 small pancakes. Keep hot over a pan of boiling water (page 221). Trim, clean and quarter the mushrooms. Heat the butter in a pan and add the mushrooms and lemon juice. Cook gently for 8–10 minutes until tender. Warm the Calvados by standing it in hot water for a minute or two. Pour over the mushrooms and flambé. Make the *Sauce à la Crème*. Beat the egg yolk with a little milk. Pour in a little of the sauce, mix well, return to the pan and heat through without boiling. Add the mushrooms and taste and adjust the seasoning. Place some of the filling inside each pancake, roll up and arrange down the centre of a hot dish.

Crêpes à la Provençale

PROVENÇALE PANCAKES

Pâte à Crêpes (page 221)
750 g (1½ lb) tomatoes
2 medium onions
2 cloves garlic
4 tbsp oil
2 tsp tomato purée
1 sprig thyme
1 sprig tarragon
1 tbsp chopped parsley
salt
pepper
100 g (4 oz) mushrooms
50–75 g (2–3 oz) (½–¾ cup) grated Gruyère cheese

Make 6 large or 8 small pancakes. Keep hot over a pan of boiling water (page 221). Peel, seed and chop the tomatoes. Peel and finely chop the onions and garlic. Heat 2–3 tablespoons of oil in a pan, add the onions and garlic and cook until soft but without colour. Add the tomatoes, tomato purée, thyme, tarragon and chopped parsley. Season lightly and cook until the mixture thickens. Remove the thyme and tarragon and check the seasoning. Meanwhile, clean and trim the mushrooms and slice thickly. Heat 1 tablespoon of oil in a pan and cook the mushrooms for 5–7 minutes until tender. Season lightly and stir into the sauce. Spread a little sauce on each pancake and fold in half. Repeat. Place the pancakes down the centre of a hot dish. Sprinkle with the cheese and brown under a hot grill, or in a preheated oven 200°C (400°F) (Gas Mark 6) for 10–15 minutes.

5 VEGETABLE QUICHES, TARTS & PIES

Flamiche

LEEK AND BACON TART

Flamiche *are leek tarts that are a speciality of Burgundy and Picardy. In Picardy they are often called* flamique. *Usually they are made as open flans but also can be covered with pastry and made into pies. In Picardy the flan usually is made with leeks, cream and eggs, while in Burgundy ham or bacon are included. In the eighteenth century flamiche were made from bread dough and were rather like biscuits. When cooked they were spread with butter and eaten immediately. In later recipes flamiche were made as pastry sticks flavoured with Brie or Camembert. In some parts of France a sweet variation is still made from a yeast dough enriched with eggs and sugar and flavoured with rum.*

Make the pastry and refrigerate for 30 minutes then roll out and line a 20-cm (8-in) flan ring. Refrigerate until needed. Trim, wash and finely slice the leeks. Remove the rind and cut the bacon into strips. Melt three-quarters of the butter in a pan. Cook the bacon for 3–4 minutes, remove from the pan, add the leeks and cook over gentle heat for 20–30 minutes until soft but not coloured. Season to taste and leave to cool.

Beat the egg yolks and cream together and season lightly. Place the leeks in the pastry case, cover with the bacon strips and pour on the eggs and cream. Cut the remaining butter into small pieces and dot over the top. Place in a preheated oven 220°C (425°F) (Gas Mark 7) for *Pâte Demi-feuilletée* and 200°C (400°F) (Gas Mark 6) for *Pâte Brisée*. Cook for 25–30 minutes until crisp and golden brown. Serve hot or warm.

Variation: Prepare the pastry case as before and bake blind for 20 minutes. Cook the leeks in the same way as above. Make 300 ml (½ pint) (1¼ cups) *Sauce Béchamel* (page 214), mix with 2 egg yolks, 3–4 tablespoons double (heavy) cream and the leeks. Bake in a preheated oven 180°C (350°F) (Gas Mark 4) for 20 minutes.

Pâte Demi-feuilletée (page 220)/Pâte Brisée (page 219) made with 175 g (6 oz) (1½ cups) flour
500 g (1 lb) leeks
4 slices lean, streaky bacon
75 g (3 oz) (6 tbsp) butter
3 egg yolks
100 ml (3½ oz) (½ cup) single (light) cream
salt

Quiche

Quiche *originated in France in the Lorraine, although it is thought it may have been first made in Germany and, like so many other good things from neighbouring countries, strayed across the border. In early recipes bread dough was used with a savoury egg and custard filling. It was only later that pastry was used for the tart, and bacon and cheese added to the filling. Now there are several variations, each district in the Lorraine and Alsace claiming their own recipe as the true one.*

Sauté de Veau Printanier (page 201).

Choucroute à l'Alsacienne (page 197).

Pâté de Cèpes à la Limousine

LIMOUSIN CÈPE PIE

If Bayonne or other raw ham is not available, use thin gammon slices.

Pâté Demi-feuilletée (page 220) made with
  175 g (6 oz) (1½ cups) flour
750 g (1½ lb) cèpes/other mushrooms
1 medium onion
75 g (3 oz) (6 tbsp) butter
salt
pepper
300 ml (½ pt) (1¼ cups) Sauce Béchamel
  (page 214)
4 tbsp cream
4 thin slices Bayonne/other ham
1 egg

Make the pastry and refrigerate for 30 minutes. Trim and wash the *cèpes* and slice thickly. Peel and finely chop the onion. Heat the butter in a pan and cook the onions until soft and golden brown. Add the *cèpes* and cook for 4–5 minutes. Season to taste. Make the *Sauce Béchamel*, stir in the cream and mix in the onions and *cèpes*. Butter a 900-ml (1½-pint) (3¾ cups) pie dish and line the inside with half the raw ham. Cover with the *cèpe* and onion sauce and remaining ham.

Roll out the pastry. Line the edge of the dish with a narrow strip of pastry and brush with water. Cover the top with the rest of the pastry and seal well. Trim any surplus pastry and flute the edge. Cut leaves or crescents from the pastry trimmings. Beat the egg and brush over the top of the pie, garnish with the leaves or crescents and glaze these as well. Bake in a preheated oven 220°C (425°F) (Gas Mark 7) for 20 minutes then reduce the heat to 180°C (350°F) (Gas Mark 4) and continue cooking for 20–30 minutes. If the pastry begins to brown too much, cover with a piece of greaseproof paper. Serve hot.

Quiche aux Petits Pois

PEA AND BACON QUICHE

The following recipe is adapted from the traditional quiche. Other vegetables can be used instead of peas, for example I am very fond of sliced courgettes (zucchini): use 3–4 medium-sized courgettes (zucchini) and blanch them in boiling salted water for 4–5 minutes.

Pâte Brisée made with 175 g (6 oz)
  (1½ cups) plain flour (page 219)
250 g (8 oz) shelled/frozen peas
150 g (5 oz) lean bacon
150 ml (¼ pt) (⅔ cup) single (light)
  cream/milk
2 eggs
salt
pepper
pinch nutmeg
50 g (2 oz) (½ cup) grated Gruyère cheese

Make the pastry and refrigerate for 20 minutes. Roll out and line a 23-cm (9-in) flan tin. Prick the base lightly, line with greaseproof paper and fill with baking beans. Refrigerate until needed. Cook the peas. Remove the rind, cut the bacon into strips and blanch in boiling water for 5 minutes. Drain well and mix with the peas. Cook the pastry case for 10 minutes in a preheated oven 220°C (425°F) (Gas Mark 7). Meanwhile, beat the eggs and cream together and season with salt, pepper and a pinch of nutmeg. Stir in the cheese. Remove the baking beans and greaseproof paper from the pastry case. Place the peas and bacon in the base and pour the egg and cream mixture over. Lower the heat to 190°C (375°F) (Gas Mark 5) and bake for 35–40 minutes. If the top begins to brown too much cover with a piece of greaseproof paper. Serve hot or warm.

Tarte aux Champignons au Vin Blanc

MUSHROOM AND WHITE WINE TART

Sift the flour with ½ teaspoon salt on to a board or into a bowl. Cut the butter into small pieces and rub into the flour. Add the egg and 3 tablespoons of wine. Blend well until the mixture forms a ball. Knead lightly until smooth. Wrap in cling-film or place in a plastic box and refrigerate for 30 minutes. Roll out and line a 23-cm (9-in) flan ring. Refrigerate until required.

Trim, clean and slice the mushrooms. Place in a bowl and stir in the lemon juice. Peel and thinly slice the onions. Melt the butter in a pan and cook the onions until soft but without colour. Add the mushrooms and cook for 3–4 minutes. Add the bouquet garni and the remaining wine. Season lightly and cook for 10 minutes. Raise the heat and cook until most of the liquid has evaporated. Remove the bouquet garni. Beat the eggs and cream together, stir in the mushroom mixture and season to taste. Pour into the prepared pastry case and bake in a preheated oven 200°C (400°F) (Gas Mark 6) for 35–40 minutes. Serve hot.

Pastry:
225 g (8 oz) (2 cups) flour
100 g (4 oz) (½ cup) butter
1 egg
250 ml (8 fl oz) (1 cup) dry white wine

Filling:
500 g (1 lb) white button mushrooms
2 tbsp lemon juice
175 g (6 oz) onions
50 g (2 oz) (¼ cup) butter
bouquet garni
200 ml (7 fl oz) (1 cup) double (heavy) cream
3 eggs
salt and pepper

Tarte aux Herbes

VEGETABLE TART

If Swiss chard is not available, use large spinach leaves. Spinach could also be used instead of the sorrel, but the acidity of the sorrel does give a special flavour.

Make the pastry and refrigerate for 30 minutes. Roll out and line a deep 23-cm (9-in) flan dish. Prick the base lightly and refrigerate until required. Wash the leeks well and slice thinly. Melt half the butter in a pan and cover and cook the leeks for about 15–20 minutes until soft but without colour. Wash the chard and sorrel leaves well and shred finely. Wash or wipe and slice the mushrooms. Heat the remaining butter in another pan, add the chard, sorrel and mushrooms and cook for 15–20 minutes until all the liquid has evaporated. Beat the eggs, milk and cream together and mix with the cooked vegetables. Season well. Pour into the prepared pastry case and bake in a preheated oven 200°C (400°F) (Gas Mark 7) for 35–40 minutes. Serve hot or warm.

Pâte Brisée made with 225 g (8 oz) (2 cups) flour (page 219)
3 small leeks
75 g (3 oz) (6 tbsp) butter
4–5 leaves Swiss chard
100 g (4 oz) sorrel
100 g (4 oz) mushrooms
4 eggs
150 ml (¼ pt) (⅔ cup) milk
6 tbsp double (heavy) cream
salt
black pepper

Tarte aux Oignons

ONION TART

Make the pastry and refrigerate. Roll out and line a 23-cm (9-in) flan ring. Prick the base lightly. Peel and slice the onions finely. Cut the bacon into strips. Melt the butter in a pan and add the onion and bacon. Cover and cook over gentle heat for 15–20 minutes until the onions are soft but without colour. Stir in the flour. Beat the eggs and milk together. Mix well with the onions and bacon and season to taste. Pour into the prepared pastry case and cook in a preheated oven 220°C (425°F) (Gas Mark 7) for 25–30 minutes. If the pastry begins to brown too much cover with a piece of greaseproof paper. Serve hot.

Pâte Demi-feuilletée made with 100 g (4 oz) (1 cup) plain flour (page 220)
500 g (1 lb) onions
3 slices lean bacon
50 g (2 oz) (¼ cup) butter
25 g (1 oz) (¼ cup) flour
2 eggs
200 ml (7 fl oz) (1 cup) milk
salt
pepper

Nouilles aux Aubergines (page 203).

Gougère Garnie à la Ratatouille (page 206).

Beignets des Légumes et Sauce Aigre Douce
(page 204).

Tarte à la Moutarde

MUSTARD TART

This recipe has a bread-dough base. Because larger quantities of bread are just as easy to make as small, when I cook this tart I use three times the amount of flour, salt, oil and water with the same amount of yeast and use the remaining dough for bread rolls: divide the dough into 10–12 pieces, mould the rolls and place on a greased baking sheet. Leave in a warm place until double in size, then glaze with beaten egg and bake in a preheated oven 230°C (450°F) (Gas Mark 8) for approximately 15 minutes.

175 g (6 oz) (1½ cups) strong (bread) flour

¼ tsp salt

15 g (½ oz) (1 tbsp) fresh yeast/2 tsp dried yeast and 1 tsp sugar

1½ tsp oil

6 tbsp tepid water, approx.

4 tomatoes

2 tbsp Dijon mustard

3 tbsp double (heavy) cream

salt

pepper

Sift the flour and salt into a bowl and make a well in the centre. Mix the yeast and sugar, if used, with 2–3 tablespoons of tepid water. Leave the dried yeast and sugar in a warm place until the yeast starts to froth. Add the oil and remaining tepid water and pour into the centre of the bowl of flour. Work in the flour, adding a little more water if necessary to obtain a soft, but not sticky, dough. Knead well, cover and leave in a warm place for about 1 hour until double in size.

Turn the dough out on to a lightly floured board and knead well until the dough is pliable. Roll out and line the base of a 23-cm (9-in) lightly greased flan tin. Press the dough up the sides of the tin and lightly prick the base. Slice the tomatoes and arrange on the dough. Mix the mustard and cream together and season to taste. Spread over the tomatoes. Place in a preheated oven 220°C (425°F) (Gas Mark 7). After 20 minutes lower the heat to 190°C (375°F) (Gas Mark 5) for 15–20 minutes. Serve warm or cold.

Tarte aux Poireaux à la Bière

LEEK AND BEER TART

Leek tarts are a speciality of northeastern France. This one comes from the Ardennes and is unusual in that the leeks are stewed in beer, which gives them a most distinctive flavour. The result is surprisingly good. The original recipe called for 'blond' beer; I use pale ale but any other light beer can be used. Milk can be substituted for cream, if preferred.

Pâte Brisée made with 175 g (6 oz) (1½ cups) plain flour (page 219)

6–7 leeks, approx. 350 g (12 oz) after trimming

50 g (2 oz) (¼ cup) butter

500 ml (18 fl oz) (2⅓ cups) pale ale

1 slice Ardennes ham/100 g (4 oz) smoked, streaky bacon

3 egg yolks

150 ml (¼ pt) (⅔ cup) single (light) cream

salt

black pepper

pinch nutmeg

Make the pastry and refrigerate for 30 minutes. Trim the leeks and discard the green parts (save for soup). Wash the leeks well and cut into 5-cm (2-in) lengths. If thick, slice down the middle. Melt the butter in a pan, add the leeks and cook for 3–4 minutes, stirring occasionally. Season lightly. Pour in the beer and partially cover and cook over gentle heat for about 1 hour until the leeks are soft and all the liquid has evaporated. Dice the ham/bacon finely. Beat the egg yolks and cream together and season to taste with salt, pepper and a pinch of nutmeg.

Roll out the pastry and line a 20-cm (8-in) flan tin. Refrigerate for 15–20 minutes. Prick the base, line the case with a piece of greaseproof paper and fill with baking beans. Bake for 15 minutes in a preheated oven 220°C (425°F) (Gas Mark 7). Remove the baking beans and paper from the case. Arrange the leeks in the pastry case, pour the egg and cream mixture over and sprinkle with chopped ham. Lower the heat to 190°C (375°F) (Gas Mark 5) and return the tart to the oven. Cook for 35–40 minutes until set and golden brown. Serve hot or warm.

Tourte aux Asperges

ASPARAGUS TART

Canned or bottled asparagus can be used instead of fresh asparagus.

Make the pastry and refrigerate for 30 minutes. Roll out and line a 20-cm (8-in) flan ring. Line with greaseproof paper and fill with baking beans. Refrigerate until needed. Trim and cook the asparagus (page 000). Drain well. Cut about 7 cm (3 in) off the tip ends and chop the rest. Hard-boil the eggs then slice two, reserving the best slices for garnishing. Chop the remaining slices and the other egg. Make the *Sauce Béchamel*. Add the cream, chopped asparagus, chopped egg and parsley. Season to taste. Bake the prepared pastry case in a preheated oven 220°C (425°F) (Gas Mark 7) for 20 minutes. Remove the beans and paper. Pour in the sauce and arrange the asparagus tips and slices of egg on top. Sprinkle with the cheese and return to the oven for 10–15 minutes until golden brown.

Pâte Demi-feuilletée made with 175 g (6 oz) (1½ cups) flour (page 220)
500 g (1 lb) small asparagus
3 eggs
300 ml (½ pt) (1¼ cups) Sauce Béchamel (page 214)
3 tbsp double (heavy) cream
1 tbsp chopped parsley
salt
pepper
50 g (3 oz) (½ cup) grated Gruyère cheese

Tourte Comtoise

COMTOISE TART

In mountainous regions, such as the Franche-Comté, where people are likely to be snowbound during the winter months, many dishes use basic ingredients which are kept in store. Emmanthal cheese may be used instead of Comté.

Make the pastry and refrigerate for 30 minutes, then roll out and line a 20-cm (8-in) flan ring. Refrigerate until required. Peel the potatoes and cook in boiling salted water for 15 minutes. Drain and slice thinly. Slice the cheese thinly and dice the ham. Place a layer of cheese in the pastry case, cover with a layer of potato and some ham. Repeat the layers, keeping enough cheese for the final layer. Beat the eggs and cream together and season to taste with salt, pepper and a pinch of nutmeg. Strain into the flan and cover with the remaining cheese. Bake in a preheated oven 220°C (425°F) (Gas Mark 7) for 20 minutes, then reduce the heat to 190°C (375°F) (Gas Mark 5) and continue cooking for 15–20 minutes until the tart is golden brown. Serve hot.

Pâte Demi-feuilletée made with 175 g (6 oz) (1½ cups) flour (page 220)
500 g (1 lb) potatoes
75 g (3 oz) Comté/Emmanthal cheese
100 g (4 oz) ham
3 eggs
200 ml (7 fl oz) (1 cup) single (light) cream/milk
salt and pepper
pinch nutmeg

Above top: Confiture de Tomates Rouges (page 211). *Right: Confiture de Tomates Vertes* (page 211).
Left: Confiture de Potiron (page 210).

Right: Soufflé Glacé aux Avocats (page 210).

Top: Flan de Carottes à la Flamande (page 208). Bottom: Cheveaux d'Ange (page 207).

6 VEGETABLES WITH FISH & MEAT

VEGETABLES WITH FISH

Cabillaud en Pot au Feu

COD HOT-POT

750 g (1½ lb) cod fillet/firm white fish
6–8 thin slices smoked streaky bacon
4 medium onions
750 g (1½ lb) potatoes
2 green peppers
500 g (1 lb) ripe tomatoes
75 g (3 oz) (6 tbsp) butter
salt
pepper

Wash and skin the fish and cut into 5–8-cm (2–3-in) pieces. Remove the bacon rind. Peel the onions and potatoes. Thinly slice the onions and thickly slice the potatoes. Remove the stalks, cores and seeds from the peppers and cut into thin strips. Peel and slice the tomatoes. Melt half the butter in a deep heatproof casserole, add the onions and cook for 5–7 minutes until nearly tender but without colour. Remove the onions from the pan. Add the remaining butter and when melted pour off and reserve.

Place half the bacon in the base of the casserole and the onions. Continue with a layer of peppers, fish, potatoes and tomatoes. Season each layer and repeat, ending with a layer of tomatoes. Add enough water to fill half the pan. Pour over the melted butter with any left from cooking the onions. Cover and cook over gentle heat for 50–60 minutes until the vegetables are tender. During the cooking time, if necessary add a little water. Serve in the cooking dish.

Rôti de Cabillaud aux Petits Pois

ROAST COD WITH PEAS

Serves 4–5
1 kg (2 lb) piece of cod
500 g (1 lb) shelled fresh/frozen peas
12–15 small onions
4 tomatoes
175 g (6 oz) smoked streaky bacon
50 g (2 oz) (¼ cup) butter
100 ml (3½ fl oz) (½ cup) dry white wine
salt
pepper

Remove the bones from the cod, season well, roll up and tie with string. Blanch fresh peas in boiling salted water for 8–10 minutes. Drain. If frozen peas are used add them about 15 minutes before the end of the cooking time. Peel the onions and blanch in boiling salted water for 5–6 minutes. Drain well. Peel and quarter the tomatoes. Remove the rind and cut the bacon into thin strips. Heat the butter in a deep heatproof dish. Cook the bacon for 2–3 minutes then add the onions and cook for 5–7 minutes. Place the fish in the dish and baste with butter. Stir in the peas and tomato and pour on the wine. Season lightly. Cover the pan with a lid/aluminium foil and place in a preheated oven 180°C (350°F) (Gas Mark 4) for 40–45 minutes until the fish and vegetables are tender. Check the seasoning. Remove the string. Serve hot in the cooking dish or place the fish on a hot plate and pour the vegetables and liquor over.

Bar à la Portugaise

PORTUGUESE SEA BASS

Salmon and trout can also be cooked in this way. It is a most attractive dish for a special dinner party and is easy to cook because the garnishes and Sauce Portugaise *can be prepared in advance.*

Clean and scale the fish, season well inside and out and place in a dish or roasting pan. Pour on the wine and water. Peel and finely slice the onion and place round the fish with the bay leaf. Cover with aluminium foil and cook in a preheated oven 180°C (350°F) (Gas Mark 4) for approx. 30–35 minutes (if the flakes separate slightly under the skin when pressed and the flesh feels firm, the fish is cooked). Keep hot.

Meanwhile, remove 3–4 layers of the leek and cook in boiling, salted water until tender. Make the *Sauce Portugaise.* When the sauce has been brought to the boil, simmer gently for 20 minutes until it thickens slightly. Hard-boil the egg and peel and slice the tomatoes, reserving the end pieces. Heat half the butter in a frying pan and cook the tomato slices and end pieces until heated through. Season well and keep hot. Slice the lemons (if you wish they can be decorated with a canelle knife first). Cut each slice in half. Shell and slice the egg (keep 3–4 slices from the middle and use the rest in another dish). Mash some of the reserved ends of tomato to a purée and cover the yolks of the sliced egg. Cover and keep hot.

When the fish is cooked, remove the skin and place the fish on a long serving dish. Pour the *Sauce Portugaise* around, arrange the tomato slices on top of the sauce. Cover and keep hot. Strain the liquor from the fish into a pan and boil over good heat until 2–3 tablespoons remain. Cut the remaining butter into small pieces and whisk into the pan a little at a time. Taste and season. Pour over the fish. Cut the leeks into thin strips and arrange a few on top of the fish to simulate leaves and stems. Place the prepared egg slices on top of each stem to form 'flowers'. Just before serving garnish the edge of the dish with sliced lemon.

1 sea bass, approx. 1 kg (2 lb) gutted
200 ml (7 fl oz) (1 cup) white wine
150 ml (¼ pt) (⅔ cup) water
1 small onion
1 bay leaf
1 small leek
salt
pepper
300 ml (½ pt) (1¼ cups) Sauce Portugaise (page 217)
1 egg
500 g (1 lb) tomatoes
2 lemons
75 g (3 oz) (6 tbsp) butter

Colin Bohémienne

BOHEMIAN HAKE

Wash and trim the fish. Peel the carrots and celeriac, trim and wash the leek and cut all these vegetables into very thin strips. Melt half the butter in a pan, add the prepared vegetables and cook until soft but without colour. Season to taste and place in the bottom of a heatproof dish. Lay the fillets/cutlets on top and season lightly. Pour on the wine and cover with greaseproof paper/aluminium foil. Cook in a preheated oven 200°C (400°F) (Gas Mark 6) for about 20 minutes. In the meantime, remove the stalks, cores and seeds from the peppers and dice finely. Heat the remaining butter in a pan, add the peppers and cook gently until tender but without colour. Season to taste and keep hot. Make the *Sauce à la Crème/Sauce Béchamel.*

When the fish is cooked, arrange on a hot dish and keep hot. Strain the cooking liquor into a pan and boil until reduced by half. Beat the egg yolk, pour on the reduced liquor and mix well. Add to the sauce, mix well and heat through without boiling. Stir in the vegetables and peppers. Taste and adjust the seasoning. Pour over the fish and serve.

4–6 fillets/cutlets hake/other white fish, approx. 200 g (6 oz) each
1 large carrot
¼ celeriac
1 leek
50 g (2 oz) (¼ cup) butter
150 ml (¼ pt) (⅔ cup) dry white wine
2 small red peppers
300 ml (½ pt) (1¼ cups) Sauce à la Crème (page 215)/Sauce Béchamel (page 214)
1 egg yolk
salt
pepper

Daurade Farcie aux Laitues

SEA-BREAM STUFFED WITH LETTUCE

Serves 4

1 sea-bream, approx. 750 g (1½ lb) gutted
2 firm hearts of lettuce
75 g (3 oz) (6 tbsp) butter
2 medium onions
150 ml (¼ pt) (⅔ cup) water
salt
pepper
1 egg
100 g (4 oz) sausage meat
2–3 slices fat bacon
2 tbsp double (heavy) cream
1 tbsp chopped chervil

Discard any damaged lettuce leaves. Remove the remaining large leaves and wash well. Drain, cut out the coarse stalks, roll the leaves up like a cigar and shred finely. Quarter the lettuce hearts. Peel and finely chop the onions. Blanch the lettuce quarters in boiling salted water for 5–7 minutes. Drain well and fold into a neat shape.

Heat 50 g (2 oz) (¼ cup) butter in a heatproof dish. Place the lettuce hearts in the dish, cover and cook over gentle heat for 15 minutes, then add the chopped onion and water. Season well, cover with greaseproof paper and replace the lid. Cook over very gentle heat or in a preheated oven 200°C (400°F) (Gas Mark 4) for 45–50 minutes or until tender. In the meantime, hard-boil the egg. Remove the shell and chop coarsely. Melt the remaining butter in a pan and add the shredded lettuce. Cook for 7–10 minutes then mix in the sausage meat and chopped egg.

Wash the fish and remove the backbone. Season well inside and out. Place the sausage meat and lettuce mixture evenly inside the fish. Remove the rinds from the bacon and wrap the slices round the fish. When the lettuce are nearly cooked, grill the fish under good heat for 10–12 minutes on each side. Place on a hot dish and arrange the lettuce garnish round. Keep hot. Mix any juices from the grill pan with the cooking liquor from the lettuce. Boil until reduced by one-third. Add the cream and chervil, check the seasoning and pour over the lettuce. Serve immediately.

Filets de Daurade Monaco

MONACO SEA-BREAM

500 g (1 lb) mussels, soaked overnight
750–1 kg (1½–2 lb) fillets sea-bream/
  other white fish
salt
pepper
75 g (3 oz) (6 tbsp) butter
2 medium carrots
2 medium onions
2 shallots
¼ celeriac
100 g (4 oz) mushrooms
250 g (8 oz) cockles
2–3 tbsp dry white wine
6–8 whole prawns (shrimp)
100 ml (3½ fl oz) (½ cup) Madeira
300 ml (½ pt) (1½ cups) double (heavy)
  cream

Soak the mussels in water with a tablespoon of flour or oatmeal overnight. Wash the fish and lay the fillets in a buttered dish. Season well. Cut half the butter into small pieces and dot over the fish. Cover with greaseproof paper/aluminium foil and refrigerate until required. Peel the carrots, onions, shallots and celeriac. Trim and clean the mushrooms. Cut the carrots and celeriac into very thin strips about 4 cm (1½ in) long. Thinly slice the onions, shallots and mushrooms. Remove the beards from the mussels and scrub the mussels and cockles well. Discard any which are damaged or remain open after being immersed in cold water or tapped hard. Remove the shell from the tails of the prawns (shrimp), leaving the edible tail on the head.

Bake the fish in a preheated oven 200°C (400°F) (Gas Mark 6) for 15–20 minutes. At the same time, melt the remaining butter in a pan, add the vegetables, cover with a piece of greaseproof paper and a lid and cook over gentle heat until tender but without colour. Season to taste, add the Madeira and cook for another 3–4 minutes. Place the mussels and cockles in a pan with the wine. Cover and cook over good heat for 5–7 minutes or until they are all open. Boil the cream for 4–5 minutes, add the vegetables and check the seasoning. Arrange the fish on a hot dish, pour the sauce over and garnish with the mussels, cockles and prawns.

Filets de Maquereaux aux Courgettes

MACKEREL FILLETS WITH COURGETTES (ZUCCHINI)

Remove the backbones, heads and tails from each fish and cut in half down the back. Place the fillets in a large buttered dish, season with salt and pepper and pour on the wine and water. Peel and thinly slice the onion, scatter over the fish and add the bouquet garni. Cover the dish with aluminium foil and cook in a preheated oven 190°C (375°F) (Gas Mark 5) for 15–20 minutes. Discard the onion and bouquet garni and place the fish in the centre of a large dish. Cover and keep hot. Reserve the cooking liquor.

In the meantime, trim and slice the courgettes (zucchini). Peel, seed and chop the tomatoes. Peel and crush the garlic. Heat the oil in a frying pan and cook the courgettes until golden brown. Add the tomatoes and garlic and cook for 3–4 minutes. Season to taste. Arrange the courgettes down each side of the fish. Boil the mackerel cooking liquor until reduced to a thin syrup. Pour over the fish and sprinkle with parsley.

Serves 4
4 mackerel 250 g (8 oz) each
200 ml (7 fl oz) (1 cup) dry white wine
100 ml (3½ fl oz) (½ cup) water
1 small onion
bouquet garni
500 g (1 lb) courgettes (zucchini)
3–4 tomatoes
2–3 cloves garlic
2–3 tbsp olive oil
salt and pepper
chopped parsley

Morue `a la Basquaise

BASQUE SALT COD

Smoked haddock or cod can be used in place of salt cod and does not need to be soaked overnight.

Wash the cod and place in a bowl. Cover with cold water and leave overnight, changing the water 3–4 times. If smoked cod/haddock are used which are very salty, soak in cold water for 20–30 minutes. Remove the stalks, core and seed from the peppers and cut into thin strips. Peel, seed and chop the tomatoes. Peel and finely slice the onions. Heat the oil in a pan and cook the onions and peppers until soft but without colour. Add the tomatoes, season lightly and cook for a further 20 minutes over gentle heat. Remove the skin from the fish and cut into large pieces. Place in a shallow pan, cover with water and bring to the boil. Lower the heat and poach gently for 10–15 minutes until tender. Remove the fish carefully and place in a hot dish. Pour the sauce over. Serve hot.

Serves 4–5
1 kg (2 lb) salt cod, soaked overnight
1 small green pepper
1 small red pepper
4 large ripe tomatoes
2 large onions
4 tbsp olive oil
salt
black pepper

Moules aux Champignons

MUSSELS WITH MUSHROOMS

Serve this dish as a first course or as an hors d'oeuvre.

Prepare the mussels (page 000). Peel and finely chop the onion. Trim, clean and slice the mushrooms. Place the mussels in a large pan with the onion and white wine. Cover and cook over good heat for 5–6 minutes until the mussels open. Drain and reserve the cooking liquor. In the meantime, make the *Sauce Béchamel*. Heat the butter in a pan and cook the mushrooms until tender. Season to taste. Remove the mussels from their shells and place in a hot dish. Cover with the mushrooms and keep hot. Strain the mussel liquor into a pan and boil until reduced by half. Add to the *Sauce Béchamel* with the cream and bring to the boil. Season to taste and pour over the mushrooms. Sprinkle with the chopped herbs.

2 kg (4 lb) mussels
1 small onion
250 g (8 oz) mushrooms
100 ml (3½ fl oz) (½ cup) dry white wine
300 ml (½ pt) (1¼ cup) Sauce Béchamel (page 214)
50 g (2 oz) (¼ cup) butter
4 tbsp double (heavy) cream
salt and pepper
1 tbsp chopped herbs (parsley, chervil, fennel/tarragon)

Mulet aux Poireaux

GREY MULLET WITH LEEKS

1 grey mullet, approx. 750 g (1½ lb)
    gutted
500 g (1 lb) small leeks
150 ml (¼ pt) (⅔ cup) dry white wine
salt
pepper
300 ml (½ pt) (1¼ cups) Sauce Tomate
    (page 218)

Wash the fish well and remove all the scales (this is best done under a running tap, scraping the fish with a small sharp knife towards the head). Season well inside and out. Trim and wash the leeks and cut into 2.5-cm (1-in) lengths. Cook in boiling salted water for 7–10 minutes until almost tender. Lay the fish in a buttered heatproof dish, pour on the wine and place the leeks round the fish. Cover with greaseproof paper/alumnium foil and cook in a preheated oven 200°C (400°F) (Gas Mark 6) for 20–25 minutes or until the fish and leeks are cooked. Meanwhile, make the *Sauce Tomate*. When the fish is cooked, place on a hot dish with the leeks round. Pour the cooking liquor into a pan and boil until reduced by half. Add to the *Sauce Tomate*, check the seasoning and pour over the fish.

Truites Farcies aux Épinards

TROUT STUFFED WITH SPINACH

4 trout approx. 250 g (8 oz) each, gutted
3 shallots
1 medium onion
500 g (1 lb) spinach
50 g (2 oz) (¼ cup) butter
salt
black pepper
450 ml (¾ pt) (2 cups) dry cider
1 tbsp chopped tarragon
150 ml (¼ pt) (⅔ cup) double (heavy)
    cream
few tarragon leaves

Scale the fish, remove the backbone but leave the heads on. Wash well. Peel and finely chop the shallots and onion. Wash the spinach well and remove any coarse stalks and ribs. Cook in boiling salted water for 10–12 minutes until tender. Drain well and press with a saucer to expel as much water as possible. Heat half the butter in a pan and cook the shallots and onions until tender and a light golden brown. Add the spinach and cook until dry. Season to taste. Place a portion of the spinach mixture inside each fish and tie string lightly around each.

In a frying pan large enough to hold the fish, melt the remaining butter and pour in the cider. Bring to the boil and then reduce the heat so the liquid simmers gently. Cook the trout for 2 minutes on each side, just long enough to loosen the skin. Remove the fish from the pan and place on a board. Remove the string and skin and place the fish in a heatproof dish. Add the tarragon to the frying pan, season with salt and pepper and boil for 8–10 minutes until approx. 150 ml (¼ pint) (⅔ cup) remains. Add the cream and cook for about 15 minutes over medium heat until the sauce thickens. Taste and season. In the meantime, cook the fish in a preheated oven 180°C (350°F) (Gas Mark 4) for about 10–15 minutes so it is ready at the same time as the sauce. Pour the sauce over the fish.

VEGETABLES WITH MEAT

Brochettes de Rognons aux Artichauts

LAMBS' KIDNEYS AND ARTICHOKE KEBABS

Serves 4
8 lambs' kidneys
8 small tomatoes
8 small artichoke hearts
1 tbsp lemon juice
2–3 tbsp oil
salt
pepper

Remove the skin and core from the kidneys and quarter and soak in cold water for 20 minutes. Quarter the tomatoes. Prepare the artichoke hearts (page 10) and cook in boiling salted water with the lemon juice until tender. Drain well and quarter. Dry the kidneys and place pieces of kidney, tomatoes and artichokes alternately on skewers. Brush well with oil and season with pepper. Place under a hot grill and cook for about 10 minutes, turning frequently. Season with salt just before serving.

Choucroute à l'Alsacienne

ALSATIAN SAUERKRAUT

Choucroute, or sauerkraut, is a way of preserving cabbage by fermenting it in brine and flavouring it with juniper berries. Prepared sauerkraut can be bought raw by weight. Sauerkraut is also available in cans and bottles. The instructions on some cans and bottles suggest a short cooking time, but I prefer long cooking to mellow the flavour.

Soak the smoked bacon for 6–8 hours and the unsmoked bacon for 1–2 hours in a large pan of cold water to remove excess salt. Peel the onions and apples. Slice the onions into rings, core and slice the apples. Press the sauerkraut to expel as much water as possible. Loosen the shreds with a fork. Heat the lard/pork fat in a large, heavy-based pan. Add the onion and cook until golden brown. Add the bay leaves, juniper berries and cloves and 150 ml (¼ pint) (⅔ cup) of wine. Cook for 3–4 minutes then add both pieces of bacon and the apple. Pour on the water, cover and cook over gentle heat for 30 minutes. Add the pork and apples. Cook for 1½ hours.

About 30 minutes before the end of the cooking time, add enough chicken stock to moisten the sauerkraut or, for even better flavour, use the remaining wine and make up the rest of the required liquid with stock. Scrub the potatoes and boil/steam in their skins. When cooked, remove the skins and keep hot. Ten minutes before the end of the cooking time, add the sausages. When the sauerkraut is cooked, boil rapidly to reduce the liquid until it has nearly all evaporated. Discard the bay leaves, cut the bacon into pieces and slice the pork. Pile the sauerkraut on to a large serving dish, arrange the meat and sausages on top and the potatoes round the edge. Serve hot.

350 g (12 oz) piece smoked, streaky bacon
350 g (12 oz) piece unsmoked, streaky bacon
3 large onions
2 medium cooking apples
1 kg (2 lb) sauerkraut
50 g (2 oz) (¼ cup) lard/pork fat
2 bay leaves
6–8 juniper berries
2 cloves
300 ml (½ pt) (1¼ cups) dry white wine
450 ml (¾ pt) (2 cups) water
1 kg (2 lb) boned blade bone of pork
450 ml (¾ pt) (2 cups) chicken stock
1 kg (2 lb) small potatoes
6–8 Strasbourg/Frankfurt sausages

Endives Farcies

STUFFED CHICORY

Trim the chicory and wash quickly. Pull back the tips of the leaves and with a potato-peeler or small sharp knife, hollow out the heads of chicory. Finely chop the leaves which were removed. Peel and finely chop the onions. Heat 40 g (1½ oz) (3 tbsp) butter in a pan and cook the onions and chopped chicory until soft but without colour. Meanwhile, soak the breadcrumbs in the milk. When the onions and chicory are soft, add the sausage and pork and cook for 5–6 minutes. Squeeze the excess milk from the breadcrumbs, add the breadcrumbs and parsley to the pan and mix well. Season to taste and fill the centre of each head of chicory.

Remove the rinds from the bacon and stretch each slice with the back of a knife. Wrap one slice around each head of chicory and tie in place with thread or thin string. Place in a casserole and pour on the stock. Melt the remaining butter and pour over the chicory. Cover with greaseproof paper and a lid and cook in a preheated oven 200°C (400°F) (Gas Mark 6) for 40–50 minutes or until tender. Remove the lid and paper for the last 15 minutes. Remove the string and serve in the casserole with the cooking liquor or arrange on a hot dish and pour the liquor over. To thicken the liquor, mix the arrowroot in a little water. Pour the liquor into a pan, add the arrowroot, bring to the boil, stirring all the time, and boil for 2–3 minutes. Pour over the chicory.

4 large heads Belgian chicory
2 medium onions
65 g (2½ oz) (⅓ cup) butter
3–4 tbsp breadcrumbs
2–3 tbsp milk
100 g (4 oz) sausage meat
50 g (2 oz) minced pork
1 tbsp chopped parsley
salt
pepper
4 slices streaky bacon
300 ml (½ pt) (1¼ cups) stock
1 scant tsp arrowroot (optional)

Cassoulet

Cassoulet is a regional dish from Languedoc. There are several variations but all consist of haricot beans with a mixture of meats — pork, bacon, mutton or lamb, sausage and confit d'oie (preserved goose). Occasionally duck is used. I have included it in this recipe instead of goose because it is obtained more easily. When the dish is completed it is covered with breadcrumbs and moistened with the fat. Cut up any fat from the duck. Place in a pan and cook at the same time as the meat until the fat seeps from it. Use this to moisten the breadcrumbs when completing the dish.

Cassoulet is an ideal party dish because the ingredients can be prepared well in advance and assembled for final cooking. Most of the recipes I have read use 1 kilo (2 lb) beans for 8 people. I find 250 g (8 oz) are enough for 5–6 people but you could add another 100–250 g (4–8 oz) and have enough meat to serve 8.

Cassoulet Toulousain

TOULOUSE BEAN AND MEAT CASSEROLE

250 g (8 oz) (1¼ cups) haricot (navy) beans, soaked overnight

4 carrots

3 medium onions

4 cloves garlic

bouquet garni

350 g (12 oz) piece streaky bacon

2 duck portions (quarters)

500 g (1 lb) boned shoulder/neck fillet of lamb

500 g (1 lb) lean pork

50 g (2 oz) (¼ cup) lard/pork/duck fat

40 g (1½ oz) (6 tbsp) flour

300 ml (½ pt) (1¼ cups) dry white wine

300 ml (½ pt) (1¼ cups) chicken stock

4 tbsp tomato purée

250 g (8 oz) garlic cooking sausage

1 large piece bacon rind/pork skin

100 g (4 oz) (2 cups) white breadcrumbs

4–6 tbsp pork/duck/goose dripping

salt and pepper

Soak the beans overnight or for at least 6–8 hours. Drain, rinse and place in a large pan of cold water. Peel the carrots, onions and garlic. Slice the carrots, stick the cloves into 1 onion and slice the rest. Crush 2 cloves of garlic. Add 2 sliced carrots, the onion stuck with cloves, 2 whole cloves of garlic and bouquet garni to the beans. Bring to the boil and simmer gently for 50–60 minutes. Add the bacon and cook for 40–60 minutes until the beans and bacon are tender. Add salt to taste about 15 minutes before the end of the cooking time but do not oversalt.

Cut the lamb and pork into even-sized pieces. Remove excess fat from the pieces of duck and place in a pan. Remove the breast from the ribcage, cut off the wing with a little of the flesh from the breast and discard the first 2 joints. Cut the breast into 3–4 pieces. Cut the drumstick and thigh from the carcase on the other portion. Cut through the joint between the drumstick and the thigh and remove the thigh bone. Cut this piece of flesh into 3–4 pieces. Remove any other flesh from the carcase.

Heat 50 g (2 oz) (¼ cup) lard in a heatproof casserole and cook the lamb, pork and duck a little at a time until golden brown. Remove the pieces of meat from the pan as they brown. Add the bones and when brown, remove. Add the remaining sliced carrots and onions with the crushed garlic and cook until they start to colour. Add the flour, cook for 3–4 minutes and then stir in the wine, stock and tomato purée.

Replace the meat in the pan with the bones on top. Bring to the boil, cover and cook in a preheated oven 170°C (325°F) (Gas Mark 3) for 1 hour. Discard the bones. When the beans are tender, drain them, reserving the cooking liquor. Discard the onion stuck with cloves. Dice the bacon into 2.5-cm (1-in) pieces (there is no need to remove the rind). Slice the sausage thickly. Place the bacon rind/pork skin in the base of a large casserole (earthenware is traditional). The bacon rind will keep the beans moist on the bottom of the dish. Cover the bacon rind with alternating layers of beans and meat, finishing with the sausage.

Mix the liquor from the meat with enough bean liquor to make a thin consistency. Pour in enough to barely cover the sausage. (I like to serve extra in a sauce-boat.) Cover with the breadcrumbs. Melt the pork/ duck/goose fat and pour over the breadcrumbs. Return the casserole to the oven 170°C (325°F) (Gas Mark 3) for an hour until the topping is golden brown and crunchy. Serve in the casserole. If you wish you can garnish with small, grilled chipolata sausages, but I think the dish is substantial enough without them.

Sauté de Mouton aux Haricots Rouges

LAMB AND RED (KIDNEY) BEAN CASSEROLE

If dried red (kidney) beans are used they **must** *be soaked in cold water for at least 18 hours and then boiled rapidly for 15 minutes.*

Cook fresh beans in unsalted water for about an hour. Add salt about 10–15 minutes before the end of the cooking time. If using dried beans which have been soaked, rinse and cook in rapidly boiling water for 15 minutes, then reduce the heat and continue cooking for 1½–2 hours. Add salt just before the end of the cooking time. Meanwhile, remove the rind from the bacon and dice into 1-cm (½-in) pieces. Peel and slice the onions. Cut the lamb into cutlets. Remove excess fat and the spinal cord.

Heat the butter in a heatproof casserole and cook the bacon until golden brown. Remove from the pan, add the onion and cook until golden brown. Remove from the pan. Add the lamb a little at a time and cook until browned on all sides. Sprinkle in the flour and cook for a few minutes until it begins to colour then add the stock and red wine. Mix well and bring to the boil, stirring constantly. Return the bacon and onions to the pan and add the cooked, strained beans. Season to taste and add the bouquet garni. Cover and cook in a preheated oven 180°C (350°F) (Gas Mark 4) for 1¼–1½ hours. When the meat is tender remove from the oven. Check the seasoning and discard the bouquet garni.

250 g (8 oz) (1¼ cups) shelled fresh/dried red (kidney) beans, soaked for 18 hours
175 g (6 oz) streaky bacon
2 medium onions
1 kg (2 lb) middle neck of lamb
40 g (1½ oz) (3 tbsp) butter
1 tbsp flour
200 ml (7 fl oz) (1 cup) white stock
200 ml (7 fl oz) (1 cup) red wine
salt
pepper
bouquet garni

Foie de Volaille à l'Oseille

CHICKEN LIVERS WITH SORREL

This dish can be served as a light lunch or supper, or as an hors d'oeuvre.

Wash the chicken livers and sorrel. Remove any sinews from the livers and cut out any yellow parts stained by the gall bladder. Remove the coarse stalks from the sorrel. Wrap each liver in a sorrel leaf and place in a buttered heatproof dish. Sprinkle the paprika over and season lightly with salt and pepper. Pour the cream over and bake in a preheated oven 200°C (400°F) (Gas Mark 6) for 10–15 minutes.

Serves 4
500 g (1 lb) chicken livers
250 g (8 oz) sorrel
200 ml (7 fl oz) (1 cup) double (heavy) cream
½ tsp paprika
salt and pepper

Pie aux Poireaux et au Lard

LEEK AND BACON PIE

Make the *Pâte à Foncer*. Remove the rind and cut the bacon into strips. Trim, wash and chop the leeks. Heat the butter in a pan, add the bacon and cook for 3–4 minutes. Add the leeks, mix well, cover and cook for 10–15 minutes until almost tender but without colour. Beat the egg with the cream and season well with salt and pepper. Mix the cream and egg with the leeks and bacon and pour into a 17-cm (7-in) pie plate.

Roll out the pastry on to a lightly floured board. Line the rim of the dish with a strip of pastry, brush with cold water and cover the dish with the rest. Seal well and trim any surplus pastry. Flute the edges. Cut 5 'leaves' from the trimmings. Beat the egg yolk with 1–2 teaspoons of water and brush over the top of the pie. Place the leaves in a circle in the centre of the pie and brush with egg. Bake in a preheated oven 200°C (400°F) (Gas Mark 6) for 30 minutes. Serve hot.

Pâte à Foncer made with 175 g (6 oz) (1½ cups) flour (page 219)
250 g (8 oz) smoked streaky bacon
1 kg (2 lb) leeks
50 g (2 oz) (¼ cup) butter
150 ml (¼ pt) (⅔ cup) double (heavy) cream
1 egg
1 egg yolk
salt
pepper

Paupiettes de Boeuf aux Carottes

BEEF ROLLS WITH CARROTS

Quatre-épices, which is used in this recipe, is a mixture of not four but five spices: white pepper, cloves, nutmeg, ginger and cinnamon. If you cannot obtain quatre épices, *used mixed spice with white pepper.*

Serves 4

*4 thin slices of topside/buttock or rump
   steak approx. 100 g (4 oz) each*
1 slice white bread approx. 40 g (1½ oz)
2–3 tbsp milk
2 medium onions
500 g (1 lb) carrots
1–2 cloves garlic
2½ tbsp olive oil
175 g (6 oz) sausage meat
2½ tbsp chopped parsley
salt and pepper
200 ml (7 fl oz) (1 cup) dry white wine
200 ml (7 fl oz) (1 cup) beef stock
2 tbsp tomato purée
pinch quatre épices
pinch nutmeg
25 g (1 oz) bacon rinds/scraps

Remove the crust and break the bread into pieces. Place in a bowl and soak in the milk. Peel the onions, carrots and garlic. Finely chop 1 onion, slice the others with the carrots and crush the garlic. Heat ½ tablespoon oil in a pan and cook the chopped onion until soft and beginning to colour. Add the garlic and cook for a minute or two. Squeeze the excess milk from the bread and mix with the onion, garlic, bread, sausage meat and 1 tablespoon chopped parsley. Season lightly. Divide the mixture in four and place one portion on each slice of beef. Fold the sides in over the edge of the mixture and roll up. Tie with thin string.

Heat the remaining oil in a heatproof casserole and fry the meat rolls until brown all over. Remove from the pan, add the sliced onions and carrots, lower the heat and cook gently until they begin to colour. Pour on the wine and stock, stir in the tomato purée, quatre-épices and nutmeg. Add the bacon rinds and season to taste. Cover and cook in a preheated oven 180°C (350°F) (Gas Mark 4) for 1¾–2 hours until tender. When the meat is tender, take off the rolls from the pan and remove the string. Discard the bacon rinds. Arrange the rolls down the centre of a serving dish with the carrots on each side. If necessary boil the sauce to reduce it to a coating consistency. Pour over the meat and sprinkle with chopped parsley just before serving.

Perdreaux aux Choux

PARTRIDGES WITH CABBAGE

Serves 4

4 partridges
4 thin slices fat bacon
750 g (1½ lb) white cabbage
2 carrots
1 onion
1 × 250 g (8 oz) smoked streaky bacon
75 g (3 oz) (6 tbsp) butter/dripping
bouquet garni
250 g (8 oz) Continental cooking sausage
200 ml (7 fl oz) (1 cup) dry white wine
100 ml (3½ fl oz) chicken stock
salt
pepper

Singe the birds with a candle to remove small feathers or hairs. Stretch the slices of fat bacon with the back of a knife. Wrap a slice round each bird and tie in place with thin string. Trim the cabbage and quarter. Blanch in boiling salted water for 5 minutes, then drain, refresh under cold water and drain well again. Cut out most of the thick centre core leaving the leaves joined. Cut each piece in half. Peel and slice the carrots and onion. Cut the piece of bacon and the sausage in half.

Heat the butter/dripping in a large heatproof casserole and brown the birds on all sides. Remove the pan from the heat and take out the birds. Place half the cabbage in the bottom of the pan. Replace the birds and fill the pan with the bacon, sausage, carrots, onion and remaining cabbage. Pour on the wine and stock. Add the bouquet garni and season well with pepper but only a little salt. Cover with greaseproof paper and a lid and cook in a preheated oven 170°C (325°F) (Gas Mark 3) for 2–2½ hours.

Remove the bouquet garni and take the string off each bird. Slice the bacon and sausage. Arrange the partridges down the centre of a large serving dish, place the cabbage with the carrots and onion round the dish and garnish with the sliced sausage and bacon. Pour the cooking liquor over or, if you wish, just moisten the dish with the liquor and serve the rest in a gravy boat.

Poivrons Farcis

STUFFED PEPPERS

Soak the raisins in warm water for 20–30 minutes. Wash the rice and cook in boiling salted water with the saffron for 12–15 minutes until tender. Drain well. Peel the onion and garlic. Finely chop the onions and crush the garlic. Cut a thin slice from the stalk-end of each pepper and remove the core, seeds and white pith. Drain the raisins. Heat 2 tablespoons of oil in a pan and cook the chopped onion until soft but without colour. Add the garlic and cook for a moment or two, then add the rice, lamb, raisins and parsley. Season to taste.

Fill each pepper with the mixture and place in an oiled dish (choose a fairly small one so the peppers support each other while cooking). Sprinkle the remaining oil over the peppers and bake in a preheated oven 200°C (400°F) (Gas Mark 6) for 40–45 minutes until tender.

Serves 4
40 g (1½ oz) (3 tbsp) raisins
100 g (4 oz) (⅔ cup) rice
pinch saffron
2 medium onions
1 clove garlic
4 red/green peppers
5–6 tbsp oil
175 g (6 oz) cooked minced lamb
1 tbsp chopped parsley
salt and pepper

Saucisses à la Campagnarde

COUNTRY-STYLE SAUSAGES

Scrub the potatoes and, if they are small enough, boil or steam them in their skins, otherwise peel first. When cooked, drain well and if necessary remove the skins. Purée the potatoes through a vegetable mill or mash until smooth. Return to the pan and add the butter, egg yolk and enough warm milk to give a creamy texture. Beat over gentle heat until heated through, then season to taste with salt, pepper and a pinch of nutmeg. Beat in the cheese. Keep hot.

Meanwhile, trim and wash the cauliflower and cook whole in boiling salted water for 18–20 minutes until tender (1–2 tablespoons of milk added to the water will keep it a good colour). Take care not to overcook or it will fall apart. While the cauliflower is cooking, grill the sausages or fry in the lard. Pile the potatoes into the centre of a dish and make a well in the centre. Sprinkle with chopped parsley and place the cauliflower in the centre. Arrange the sausages round the edge of the dish.

750 g (1½ lb) old potatoes
50 g (2 oz) (¼ cup) butter
1 egg yolk
2–3 tbsp milk
salt and pepper
pinch nutmeg
175 g (6 oz) (1½ cups) grated Gruyère
  cheese
1 small cauliflower
500–750 g (1–1½ lb) sausages
25 g (1 oz) (2 tbsp) lard (optional)
1 tbsp chopped parsley

Sauté de Veau Printanier

VEAL STEW WITH SPRING VEGETABLES

Trim the veal and cut into cubes. Peel and chop the shallots/onions and wash and scrape the carrots. Peel and crush the garlic. Heat the butter and oil in a heatproof casserole. Cook the meat a little at a time until brown on all sides. Remove from the pan and add the shallots/onions and carrots. Cook until golden brown. Return the meat to the pan, add the flour and cook for 2–3 minutes. Then add the garlic, Madeira, wine and stock. Stir in the tomato purée. Season lightly and cook in a preheated oven 180°C (350°F) (Gas Mark 4) for 50–60 minutes.

In the meantime, scrub the potatoes and shell the peas. Cook separately in boiling salted water until tender. Drain well. Skin the potatoes. Fifteen minutes before the end of the cooking time, add the peas and potatoes to the veal. When the veal is cooked, taste and adjust the seasoning. Pile the veal into the centre of a hot dish. Arrange the potatoes and carrots in piles round the edges and pour the sauce and peas over the meat. Sprinkle with chopped herbs just before serving.

1 kg (2 lb) stewing veal
3–4 shallots/small onions
350 g (12 oz) small new carrots
1 clove garlic
50 g (2 oz) (¼ cup) butter
2 tbsp oil
2 tsp flour
2 tbsp Madeira
200 ml (7 fl oz) (1 cup) dry white wine
200 ml (7 fl oz) (1 cup) chicken stock
1 tbsp tomato purée
175 g (6 oz) shelled/frozen peas
500 g (1 lb) small new potatoes
1 tbsp chopped parsley, chervil, tarragon

Sou-Fassam

TRADITIONAL STUFFED CABBAGE FROM NICE

1 medium Savoy cabbage
500 g (1 lb) sausage meat
250 g (8 oz) onions
175 g (6 oz) lean bacon
2 tomatoes
1 clove garlic
50 g (2 oz) (¼ cup) butter
75 g (3 oz) cooked peas
100 g (4 oz) cooked rice
salt
pepper
1.5 litres (2½ pt) (6 cups) stock
  (traditionally mutton stock)
2 carrots
2 extra onions
300 ml (½ pt) (1¼ cups) Sauce Tomate
  (page 218)

Remove any damaged or coarse outer leaves from the cabbage but retain as many large ones as possible. Trim the stalk, wash the cabbage and blanch in boiling salted water for 10–12 minutes. Drain well, refresh under cold water and drain well again. Remove the large leaves, cut out the thick ribs and arrange the leaves, overlapping, on a large piece of wet muslin. Chop the inside cabbage leaves and place in a bowl with the sausage meat. Peel and finely chop the onions, remove the rind and cut the bacon into small strips or dice. Peel, seed and chop the tomatoes. Peel and crush the garlic.

Melt the butter in a pan and cook the bacon until lightly coloured. Remove from the pan, add the onion and cook until golden brown. Mix the onions, bacon, tomatoes, garlic, peas and rice with the cabbage and sausage. Season to taste. Place the mixture in the centre of the cabbage leaves. Wrap the leaves well around the mixture so it is totally covered and forms a ball. Gather up the edges of the muslin and tie firmly in place. Peel and slice the carrots and extra onions. Place the cabbage in a large pan, cover with stock and add the carrots, onions and bouquet garni. Cover the pan and simmer gently for 2½–3½ hours, depending on the size of the cabbage. To serve, unmould the cabbage carefully on to a round plate. Pour over a little of the cooking liquor. Slice at table and serve with the Sauce Tomate.

Poulet aux Champignons

CHICKEN WITH MUSHROOMS

For this recipe the chicken needs to be cut into eight pieces, but if you prefer you can buy four drumsticks and two breasts and cut the breasts in half.

1.75 kg (3½ lb) chicken
8 lean slices back bacon
500 g (1 lb) small button mushrooms
2 medium onions
1 tbsp oil
65 g (2½ oz) (⅓ cup) butter
200 ml (7 fl oz) (1 cup) dry white wine
25 g (1 oz) (¼ cup) flour
200 ml (7 fl oz) (1 cup) milk
100 ml (3½ fl oz) (½ cup) double
  (heavy) cream
1 egg yolk
salt
pepper
1 tbsp chopped tarragon

Wrap each piece of chicken in a slice of bacon and tie with string. Trim and clean the mushrooms and halve or quarter. Peel and finely chop the onions. Heat the oil with 25 g (1 oz) (2 tbsp) butter in a heatproof casserole and brown the chicken pieces on all sides. Remove from the pan, add the onions and cook for 4–5 minutes, then add the mushrooms and cook for 4–5 minutes. Return the chicken to the pan, pour on the wine and season lightly. Bring to the boil. Cover with greaseproof paper and a lid and cook in a preheated oven, 180°C (350°F) (Gas Mark 4) for 40–50 minutes. Arrange the chicken pieces on a hot serving dish and keep hot. Strain the cooking liquor into a pan and boil rapidly until reduced by half.

Melt the remaining butter in a pan, add the flour, mix well and cook for 2–3 minutes. Add the milk and most of the cream a little at a time, bring to the boil, stirring constantly, and add the liquor from the chicken. Bring to the boil again and cook for 3–4 minutes. Add the mushrooms and onions and season to taste. Beat the egg yolk with the remaining cream, pour in a little hot sauce and return to the pan. Heat through without boiling. Check the seasoning and pour over the chicken. Sprinkle with chopped tarragon just before serving.

7 PURELY VEGETARIAN

It goes without saying that nearly all of the recipes in this book are well suited for vegetarians. Besides those included in this chapter, you might wish to consider the following: *Bettes au Gratin, Choufleur aux Croûtons, Courgettes aux Yaourts, Ragoût de Courgettes, Épinards et Navet au Gratin, Galette de Panais, Poireaux Gratinés à la Savoyarde, Aligot, Farcement, Pommes de Terres Normandes, Gratinés de Tomates, Courgettes Farcies Froides, Endives et Fenouil au Bleu, Haricot Verts au Fromage Blanc, Terrine de Légumes, Tomates au Fromage Blanc*, as well as 'Vegetables with Eggs' and vegetable tarts.

Nouilles aux Aubergines

NOODLES WITH AUBERGINES (EGGPLANT)

Wash the aubergine (eggplant), remove the stalk and cut into 1-cm (1-in) dice. Sprinkle with a little salt, leave for 30 minutes then wash and dry well. Trim, clean and slice the mushrooms. Peel, and seed the tomatoes and cut into strips. Peel and finely chop the onions/shallots. Heat 2 tablespoons of oil in a pan and cook the onions/shallots until soft. Remove from the pan. Add the aubergine and more oil if necessary. Cook for 4–5 minutes, then add the tomatoes and onions. Season lightly and cover and cook over gentle heat for another 15–20 minutes until the aubergines are tender. Stir occasionally and if necessary add 1–2 tablespoons water to prevent the vegetables sticking.

In another pan heat a tablespoon of oil and cook the mushrooms for 5–7 minutes. Add the olives and almonds and heat through thoroughly. Add to the aubergine mixture and mix well. Check the seasoning. In the meantime, cook the noodles in a pan of boiling salted water with 1 tablespoon of oil for about 10–12 minutes or until tender but still slightly firm in the centre. Drain well. Heat the butter in the pan, add the noodles and stir well. Season to taste with a little salt and plenty of black pepper. Pile the noodles on to a hot dish. Make a well in the centre and pour in the aubergine mixture. Serve with grated Parmesan cheese.

1 large aubergine (eggplant)
100 g (4 oz) small button mushrooms
250 g (8 oz) tomatoes
100 g (4 oz) shallots or onions
4–5 tbsp oil
10–12 stuffed green olives
10–12 blanched almonds
350 g (12 oz) noodles
25 g (1 oz) (2 tbsp) butter
salt
black pepper
2–3 tbsp grated Parmesan cheese

Beignets de Légumes et Sauce Aigre-Douce

VEGETABLE FRITTERS WITH SWEET-AND-SOUR SAUCE

175 g (6 oz) small carrots
250 g (8 oz) cauliflower
175 g (6 oz) small button mushrooms
175 g (6 oz) small onions
Pâte à Frire (page 220)
1 tbsp grated Parmesan cheese
2 tsp sesame seeds
fat/oil for deep-frying
Sauce Aigre-Douce (page 213)

Scrape the carrots and cut into 5-cm (2-in) sticks. Divide the cauliflower into small florets. Trim and clean the mushrooms. Blanch the carrots and cauliflower in boiling salted water for 5 minutes and the onions for 7–10 minutes. Drain well and refresh under cold water. Drain again until completely dry. Make the *Pâte à Frire* and fold in the Parmesan cheese and sesame seeds. Heat a pan of oil/fat to 180°C (350°F), or until a small square of bread browns in 30 seconds. Dip the vegetables into the batter and carefully drop into the pan. Cook for 7–10 minutes until golden brown (take care not to cook too many at once). Drain well on kitchen paper towel and keep hot until all the vegetables are cooked. Pile on to a hot dish and pour the sauce over just before serving.

Navettes aux Légumes

VEGETABLE PASTIES (TURNOVERS)

Navette *means 'incense boat' or 'shuttle', their shape having given a name to these vegetable pasties (turnovers). Smaller pasties can be served with stews.*

Serves 4
Pâte Brisée (page 219) made with 175 g (6 oz) (1½ cups) flour
175 g (6 oz) turnips
175 g (6 oz) carrots
75 g (3 oz) small broad (lima) beans or peas
25 g (1 oz) (2 tbsp) butter
2 tbsp chopped chives
1 egg
Sauce Tomate (page 218)/Sauce Mornay (page 217) (optional)

Make the pastry and refrigerate for 30 minutes. Peel the turnips and cut into small dice. Scrape/peel the carrots and grate moderately finely. Cook the turnips and beans/peas in boiling salted water until almost tender. Drain well and mix with the grated carrots. Stir in the butter and chives and season with salt and pepper. Beat the egg.

Roll the pastry out on to a lightly floured board and cut out 4 circles about 12 cm (5 in) in diameter. Brush a border of egg round the edge of each. Divide the vegetable mixture in 4 and place a portion in the centre of each pastry circle. Bring the edges of the pastry together over the vegetables, seal well and flute the top. Place on a baking sheet and cook in a preheated oven 200°C (400°F) (Gas Mark 6) for 20–30 minutes until golden brown. Serve alone or with a *Sauce Tomate* or *Sauce Mornay* .

Pâté Bourbonnaise

BOURBON PIE

Pâte Brisée made with 350 g (12 oz) (3 cups) flour (page 219)
750 g (1½ lb) medium sized potatoes
1 tbsp chopped parsley
2 medium onions
1–2 cloves garlic
25 g (1 oz) (2 tbsp) butter
salt
pepper
1 egg
150 ml (¼ pt) (⅔ cup) double (heavy) cream

Make the pastry and refrigerate for 30 minutes. Peel and thinly slice the potatoes (the attachment on a food mixer or processor is ideal). Mix with the chopped parsley. Peel and finely chop the onion and garlic. Mix with the potatoes and season well.

Roll out two-thirds of the pastry and line a deep pie plate. Place the potato mixture in the case. Cut the butter into small pieces and dot over the surface. Beat the egg and brush over the edge of the pastry. Roll the remaining pastry into a circle and place on top. Seal well and flute the edges. Brush with beaten egg. Make a hole in the centre of the pie. Roll a small piece of greaseproof paper and insert in the hole. Bake in a preheated oven 190°C (375°F) (Gas Mark 5) for 1½–1¾ hours until the potatoes are tender. If the pastry begins to brown too much cover with greaseproof paper or reduce the heat to 180°C (350°F) (Gas Mark 4). When the pie is cooked, boil the cream. Remove the paper and pour the cream through the hole. Serve hot or cold.

Pain de Légumes

VEGETABLE LOAF

This vegetable loaf can be served as an hors d'oeuvre or as a light meal. It is also very good for picnics.

Wash the spinach, sorrel and Swiss chard and remove any coarse stalks. Blanch the spinach and Swiss chard in boiling salted water for 7–10 minutes. Drain well and press out all the excess water. Chop coarsely with the raw sorrel. Peel and chop the onions and shallots. Melt the butter in a pan and cook the onions and shallots until soft. Add the chopped vegetables and cook for a few more minutes. Remove from the heat and season to taste. Stir in the breadcrumbs. Beat the eggs and mix in well.

Butter the inside of a 500-g (1-lb) terrine or loaf pan and line the base with greaseproof paper. Pour the mixture into the pan and place in a bain-marie or roasting pan of hot water and bake in a preheated oven 180°C (350°F) (Gas Mark 4) for 50–60 minutes until brown on top and shrinking slightly from the sides of the pan. Leave until cold then turn out of the pan. Keep refrigerated until about an hour before needed (if it is too cold, the delicate flavour cannot be appreciated). Slice and garnish with tomatoes and gherkins if you wish. Serve with mayonnaise.

1 kg (2 lb) spinach
175 g (6 oz) sorrel
500 g (1 lb) Swiss chard leaves
3 medium onions
2 shallots
40 g (1½ oz) (3 tbsp) butter
salt
pepper
50 g (2 oz) (1 cup) breadcrumbs
3 eggs
*300 ml (½ pt) (1¼ cups) mayonnaise
  (page 216)*

Tourte de Riz aux Légumes

RICE AND VEGETABLE MOULD

Wash the rice and cook in boiling salted water for 12–15 minutes or until the rice is tender but still slightly firm in the centre. Drain well. Quarter the tomatoes and peel the garlic. Place the tomatoes in a pan with 2–3 tablespoons of water and cook until soft. Purée through a vegetable mill or liquidizer or press through a sieve (if a liquidizer is used, strain the purée). Return to the pan, add the garlic, bouquet garni and 2 tablespoons of oil. Season lightly with salt and pepper and simmer for 15 minutes. Discard the bouquet garni and garlic and check the seasoning. Mix 2–3 tablespoons of the sauce with the rice and grated cheese. Beat the eggs and stir into the mixture and adjust the seasoning.

Meanwhile, wash and shred the lettuces and endive. Heat 2–3 tablespoons of oil in a pan, add the lettuce and endive and cover and cook gently until tender. stirring occasionally. When the vegetables are cooked, chop finely. Season to taste and add a little nutmeg. Butter an 18-cm (7-in) tart ring or loose-bottomed cake pan. Spread half the rice mixture on the bottom. Cover with the cooked salad vegetables and remaining rice. Press down lightly. Cook in a preheated oven 190°C (375°F) (Gas Mark 5) for about 35 minutes until set. Turn out when cold and serve with the remaining tomato sauce, which has been well chilled, and the mayonnaise.

*175 g (6 oz) (¾ cup) long-grain/ risotto
  rice*
500 g (1 lb) tomatoes
3 cloves garlic
bouquet garni
salt
pepper
2–3 tbsp olive oil
75 g (3 oz) (¾ cup) grated Gruyère cheese
2 eggs
2 lettuce
½ curly endive
pinch nutmeg
*300 ml (½ pt) (1¼ cups) mayonnaise
  (page 216)*

Gougère Garnie à la Ratatouille

CHEESE RING WITH RATATOUILLE

A crisp salad goes very well with this dish.

350 g (12 oz) courgettes (zucchini)
250 g (8 oz) tomatoes
2 medium onions
1 large green pepper
Pâte à Choux (page 220) made with
    65 g (2½ oz) (¾ cup) flour
75 g (3 oz) Gruyère cheese
1 egg
1 tsp powdered oregano
3 tbsp oil
salt
pepper

Wash, trim and slice the courgettes (zucchini). Peel and quarter the tomatoes and remove the seeds. Peel and chop the onions. Remove the stalk, core and seeds from the pepper and cut into strips. Cut half the cheese into small dice and grate the rest. Make the *choux* pastry and fold in the cheese. Place in a piping bag with a large, plain nozzle and pipe a ring round the inside of a buttered 18–20-cm (7–8-in) gratin dish. Beat the egg, brush over the surface and sprinkle with most of the cheese.

In the meantime, heat the oil in a pan and cook the onions until soft. Add the courgettes and pepper and cook for 10–12 minutes, stirring occasionally. Add the tomatoes and oregano and season to taste. Pour the mixture into the centre of the *choux* pastry ring and sprinkle with the remaining cheese. Bake in a preheated oven 220°C (425°F) (Gas Mark 7) for 10 minutes, then reduce the heat to 190°C (375°F) (Gas Mark 5) and cook for 25–30 minutes until the pastry is golden brown. Serve hot.

8 SWEET POSTSCRIPT

Cheveux d'Ange

ANGEL'S HAIR

Cheveux d'Ange is a sweet made with carrots and is rather like a very stiff marmalade. It was very popular in southwest France in the latter half of the nineteenth century. The carrots must be a good orange colour. If necessary trim and weigh the orange-coloured flesh and use the paler inside pieces for soup. Tarts or tartlets can also be filled with the marmalade and decorated with cream.

Grate the carrots finely or cut into very thin strips. Grate the lemon rind (if used) and squeeze the juice. Dissolve the sugar in the water and add the rind and 3 tablespoons of lemon juice/vanilla pod and the carrots. Boil until the carrots are tender and the liquid is reduced by two-thirds. Pour the mixture into a wet dish, small ring mould or tarts. Leave until cold then turn out on to a plate or leave in the dish if preferred. Whip the cream until stiff and place in a piping bag with a small star pipe. Decorate round the edge of the mould/dish. Pile the rest of the cream into the centre of the ring or serve separately.

    *After using a vanilla pod, wash and dry it well and it can be used many times again. When the flavour begins to fade, break it into pieces and liquidize with 100 g (4 oz) (½ cup) caster (superfine) sugar. Sieve to remove any pieces of the pod and store in an airtight jar. One to two teaspoons of this vanilla sugar can be used for flavouring custards, cakes and fruit syrups.

500 g (1 lb) dark orange part of carrots
500 g (1 lb) sugar
600 ml (1 pt) (2½ cups) water
1 lemon (optional)
vanilla pod*
200 ml (7 fl oz) (1 cup) double (heavy) cream

Flan de Potiron

PUMPKIN CUSTARD

A recipe from Franche-Comté.

Butter the inside of an 18-cm (7-in) deep sandwich tin or cake pan. Line the base with greaseproof paper. Peel the pumpkin and remove the seeds. Cut into small pieces, place in a pan with the water and bring to the boil and cook for 30–40 minutes until almost tender. Drain the pumpkin then return to the pan with the milk. Simmer gently for 5–10 minutes until the pumpkin is very soft. Mash into the milk with a fork or potato-masher until smooth. Sieve the flour and sugar into a bowl and beat in the eggs, salt, lemon rind and pumpkin mixture. Pour into the prepared pan and cook in a preheated oven 190°C (375°F) (Gas Mark 5) for 30–40 minutes until set and lightly coloured on the surface. Turn out on to a hot plate and serve warm.

500 g (1 lb) pumpkin
300 ml (½ pt) (1¼ cups) water
250 ml (scant ½ pt) (1 cup) milk
65 g (2½ oz) (⅔ cup) flour
50 g (2 oz) (¼ cup) sugar
3 eggs
pinch salt
grated rind of 1 lemon

Flan de Carottes à la Flamande

FLEMISH CARROT FLAN

Pâte Sucrée made with 125 g (5 oz)
(1¼ cups) flour (page 219)
150 ml (¼ pt) (⅔ cup) milk
1 vanilla pod
500 g (1 lb) carrots
25 g (1 oz) (2 tbsp) butter
2–3 tsp caster (superfine) sugar (to taste)
2 egg yolks
½ tsp arrowroot
1–2 tbsp icing (confectioner's) sugar

Make the pastry and refrigerate for 30 minutes. Roll out on to a lightly floured board and line an 17-cm (7-in) flan tin. Refrigerate until required. In the meantime, heat the milk in a pan with the vanilla pod. When it boils, remove from the heat and leave for 20–30 minutes. Peel the carrots and slice thinly. Place in a pan with the butter and 1 teaspoon of caster (superfine) sugar. Pour in only enough water to barely cover the carrots and cook until tender and the water has completely evaporated.

Beat the egg yolks with a teaspoon of sugar and the arrowroot. Reheat the milk and remove the vanilla pod. Pour the milk on to the egg yolks and mix well. Return to the pan and cook gently, stirring continuously, until the custard coats the back of a spoon (do not boil or it will curdle). Stir in the carrots, taste and add more sugar if necessary. Pour into the pastry case and bake in a preheated oven 190°C (375°F) (Gas Mark 5) for 20–25 minutes until the pastry is a light golden brown and the custard has set. Sprinkle the icing (confectioner's) sugar on top and return to the oven for 5–10 minutes until the top is glazed. Serve hot or cold.

Gâteau de Châtaignes

CARAMELIZED CHESTNUT DESSERT

My original recipe from Limousin used fresh chestnuts, but at the time I tested this recipe I was unable to obtain any, so I used canned natural (unsweetened) purée and found it very successful. If you prefer to use fresh chestnuts, prepare 500 g (1 lb) (page 75) and simmer in 600 ml (1 pint) (2½ cups) milk until tender. Purée with a little of the milk and use the remainder for the recipe. In France Crème Chantilly is usually served with the dessert. This is lightly whipped, slightly sweetened cream. I prefer cream without sugar and simply whip the cream until it stands in soft peaks.

350 g (12 oz) (1½ cups) caster
(superfine) sugar
6 tbsp water
450 g (1 lb) canned natural chestnut purée
3 eggs
225 ml (7½ fl oz) (1 cup) milk
150–300 ml (¼–1 pt) (⅔–1¼ cups)
double/whipping (heavy) cream

Crème Chantilly:
2–3 tbsp milk
1–2 tsp vanilla sugar
150 ml (¼ pt) (⅔ cup) double (heavy)
cream

Prepare a 20-cm (8-in) deep sandwich tin or cake pan. Boiling sugar is extremely hot, so for protection fold a dish towel diagonally into 3 or 4 and wrap it round the tin. Tie the corners tightly to keep it in place. Stand the pan on a wooden board as the heat can damage work surfaces.

Place half the sugar in a pan with the water. Stir over gentle heat until the sugar has completely dissolved then stop stirring, bring to the boil and cook until golden chestnut colour. Pour into the prepared pan and twist it round to coat the base and sides. Mix the remaining sugar with the chestnut purée. Separate the eggs and add the yolks to the mixture. Beat well until smooth. Heat the milk until it is almost boiling and beat into the chestnut mixture. Whisk the egg whites until dry and stiff and fold in carefully. Pour into the caramel-lined mould. Place the tin in a bain-marie or roasting pan of boiling water and cook in a preheated oven 180°C (350°F) (Gas Mark 4) for 50–60 minutes. Press the top lightly; if it springs back like a sponge, it is cooked. Turn out on to a hot serving dish and serve warm.

To make *Crème Chantilly*, add the milk and vanilla sugar to the double cream and beat until it stands in soft peaks.

Gâteau de Courgettes

COURGETTE (ZUCCHINI) PUDDING

This pudding can either be turned out immediately and served hot, or left in the pan and, when cool, refrigerated until the next day. In this way, more caramel dissolves to make the sauce.

Trim and slice the courgettes (zucchini) and place in a pan with 150 ml (¼ pint) (⅔ cup) milk and most of the water. Bring to the boil and cook for 5 minutes. Drain (reserve the cooking liquor for soup). Meanwhile, prepare a 20-cm (8-in) deep sandwich tin or cake pan.

Place the caster (superfine) sugar in a small pan with the remaining water (about 4 tablespoons). Heat gently, stirring occasionally, until the sugar has dissolved. Bring to the boil without stirring and boil rapidly until chestnut brown. Pour into the prepared pan and twist from side to side to coat the base and sides with caramel.

Mash or purée the courgettes, separate the eggs and melt the butter. Sieve the flour and icing (confectioner's) sugar into a bowl. Make a well in the centre and add the remaining milk, melted butter, egg yolks and orange rind. Beat in the flour and sugar from the sides of the bowl to form a smooth batter. Whisk the egg white until smooth and dry and carefully fold into the mixture. Turn into the prepared mould and bake in a preheated oven 180°C (350°F) (Gas Mark 4) for 40–45 minutes or until set and golden brown on top.

750 g (1½ lb) courgettes (zucchini)
300 ml (½ pt) (1¼ cups) milk
150 ml (¼ pt) (⅔ cup) water
4 tbsp caster (superfine) sugar
3 eggs
50 g (2 oz) (½ cup) flour
125 g (5 oz) (1 cup) icing (confectioner's) sugar
grated rind of 1 orange

Gâteau de Potiron

PUMPKIN PIE

Make the pastry and refrigerate for 30 minutes. Peel the pumpkin, remove the seeds and cut into even-sized pieces. Cook in boiling salted water for 40–45 minutes or until tender. Drain well and return to the pan. Beat the butter and 50 g (2 oz) (¼ cup) sugar into the pumpkin until smooth. Leave to cool for a moment or two. Beat 2 eggs and the milk together and stir into the pumpkin mixture with the lemon rind. Roll out two thirds of the pastry on to a lightly floured board and line the inside of a 20 × 4-cm (8 × 1½-in) deep loose-bottomed pan. Leave the edge untrimmed. Prick the base lightly, taking care not to prick right through the pastry, and pour in the filling. Roll out the remaining pastry into a circle large enough to cover the tin. Dampen the pastry on the edge of the tin, place the pastry circle on top and seal well. Trim the edge, leaving a slight border to prevent the filling running out. With the back of a small knife flute the edge of the pastry. Beat the remaining egg well and brush over the top of the pie. Place on a hot baking sheet and cook in a preheated oven 200°C (425°F) (Gas Mark 7) for 45 minutes. To prevent the top of the pastry from overbrowning, cover with a piece of greaseproof paper after the first 15 minutes and remove 5 minutes before the end of the baking time. Sprinkle with the remaining caster (superfine) sugar and serve hot or cold.

Pâte Demi-feuilletée made with 225 g (8 oz) (2 cups) flour (page 220)
750 g (1½ lb) pumpkin (to give 500 g (1 lb) prepared pumpkin)
25 g (1 oz) (2 tbsp) butter
65 g (2½ oz) (⅓ cup) caster (superfine) sugar
3 eggs
150 ml (¼ pt) (⅔ cup) milk
grated rind of 1 lemon

Soufflé Glacé aux Avocats

AVOCADO ICE CREAM SOUFFLÉ

This recipe uses a syrup that is boiled to a 'thread' stage (103–104°C [215–220°F]). Not everyone has a sugar thermometer, however, it is possible to test the syrup without one: dip the thumb and first finger into cold water, shake off any excess water and then quickly dip into the hot syrup. It has reached the right temperature when a small thread is formed when the fingers are drawn apart no more than 5 mm–1 cm (¼–½ in). It is essential that the fingers are dipped in cold water each time you test, and that you dip just the tips very quickly in and out of the syrup. The water acts as an insulator making it possible to test the boiling syrup without burning your fingers.

Other fruits can be used for decoration to contrast colourfully with the pale green of the soufflé. Those with a slightly sharp flavour, such as strawberries or canned mandarin orange segments, are best. The sweet will taste better if its taken from the freezer and refrigerated for 30 minutes before serving. This is an asset because it can be decorated with the nuts and cream earlier in the day and returned to the freezer. It can then be decorated with the fruit (so this is not frozen) just before refrigerating.

225 ml (7½ fl oz) (1 cup) double (heavy) cream
200 g (7 oz) (1 scant cup) caster (superfine) sugar
150 ml (¼ pt) (⅔ cup) water
3 egg yolks
2 ripe medium-sized avocados
4–6 tbsp lemon juice
50 g (2 oz) (⅔ cup) browned, flaked almonds
6 tbsp double (heavy) cream
1 kiwi fruit

Tie a strip of unbuttered paper around an 11-cm (4½-in) soufflé dish (page 168). Place the dish in the deep-freeze or refrigerator ice box to chill. Beat the cream until it forms soft peaks and refrigerate until needed (take care not to overbeat — it will stiffen in the refrigerator). Place the sugar and water in a small pan. Stir over gentle heat until the sugar is completely dissolved, then stop stirring, raise the heat and boil until the 'thread' stage is reached. Meanwhile, beat the egg yolks together and immediately the syrup is ready, pour it on to the yolks. Beat well until the mixture is cool and fluffy.

Peel the avocados and remove the stones. Purée or mash with a fork or mash until smooth. Blend in 4 tbsp of lemon juice. Check the consistency of the cream — it should be the same as the egg mixture — and if necessary beat a little more. Fold into the egg mixture with the avocados. Keep the remaining cream for decoration. Taste and add a little more lemon juice if desired but take care not to overfold. Pour the mixture into the soufflé dish and freeze.

To decorate, chop/crush the nuts coarsely. Peel off the paper band and coat the sides of the soufflé with the nuts. Whip the remaining cream until stiff and place in a piping bag with a small star nozzle. Decorate the edges of the soufflé with small stars of cream. Peel the kiwi fruit and slice thinly. Cut each slice in half and arrange round the edge of the soufflé inside the piped border.

Confiture de Potiron

PUMPKIN JAM

(makes 4–5 × 450-g [1-lb] jars)
4 lemons
1.25 litres (2 pt) (5 cups) water
2 kg (4 lb) pumpkin
1 kg (2 lb) (4 cups) granulated sugar

Wash the lemons, slice very thinly and remove any seeds. Place in a bowl. Boil the water and pour over the lemon slices. Leave overnight. Peel the pumpkin, remove the seeds and slice thinly. Place in a pan with the lemon slices and water and simmer gently for 30–40 minutes until tender. Add the sugar and dissolve, stirring occasionally. Bring to the boil and boil rapidly without stirring until setting point is reached. Leave the jam to settle for 5 minutes, then pour into hot jars and seal.

Confiture de Tomates Rouges

RED TOMATO JAM

I have given two methods for this jam. The second produces a larger amount, but I prefer the smoother texture of the first.

Quarter the tomatoes and apples. Remove the stalks and cores but do not peel the apples. Place the tomatoes and apples in a pan with the water and cook gently until both are tender. Rub through a sieve to remove seeds and skins (if you prefer, purée quickly in a food processor and then sieve). Return the purée to the pan and add the sugar, cinnamon cloves and lemon rind and juice, if used. Dissolve the sugar over gentle heat and then bring to the boil and cook rapidly until setting point is reached. Remove the cloves. Allow the jam to settle for about 5 minutes then pour into hot jars and seal.

Peel the tomatoes and apples. Remove the cores and seeds from the apples and cut the apples and tomatoes into small, even-sized pieces. Cook in the water until tender. Do not purée but add the other ingredients and continue as for Method 1.

Method 1 *(makes 2–3 × 450-g [1-lb] jars)*
1 kg (2 lb) ripe tomatoes
350 g (12 oz) cooking apples
150 ml (¼ pt) (⅔ cup) water
750 g (1½ lb) (3 cups) granulated sugar
¼ tsp cinnamon
2 cloves
grated rind and juice of 2 lemons

Method 2 *(makes 3–4 × 450-g [1-lb] jars)*

Confiture de Tomates Vertes

GREEN TOMATO JAM

I have never considered making jam with tomatoes, but it appears in many French cookery books. Again, I tried two methods. They gave quite different results, so I am including both.

Wash and slice the tomatoes and place in a pan with the water. Bring to the boil and simmer gently for 50–60 minutes until tender. Add the sugar, grated rind and lemon juice. Dissolve over gentle heat, stirring occasionally. When the sugar has dissolved, stop stirring, bring to the boil and boil rapidly until setting point is reached. Remove from the heat. To test if setting point is reached, pour a little on to a saucer and leave to cool. If the jam wrinkles when the edge is lightly pressed with a finger it is ready for potting. Otherwise, return to the heat and boil for a few more minutes and test again. Allow to stand for 4–5 minutes. If the scum remains, remove it or stir in a small knob of butter. Pour the jam into a hot jar, cover with waxed paper and seal.

In this method the slices of tomato are macerated in sugar for 24 hours. This keeps the slices firm and, when the jam is cooked, they have a texture similar to crystallized fruit. The long cooking time is essential to tenderize the skins, which never become as soft as the previous recipe. Greater care is needed with this method: the liquid must not be allowed to reduce too quickly or the skins of the tomatoes will be tough, and the jam must be watched carefully during the last 15 minutes because it caramelizes very easily. Remove from the heat before it begins to colour.

Slice the tomatoes and layer with the sugar in a bowl. Cover and leave for 24 hours. Place the tomatoes and sugar (which will have turned to a syrup) into a pan with the water and lemon juice and rind. Bring to the boil and simmer very gently for 2–2½ hours until the skins are soft. If necessary add a little more water to prevent the mixture reducing too rapidly. Test and bottle as for Method 1.

Method 1 *(makes 450-g [1-lb] jar)*
500 g (1 lb) green tomatoes
450 ml (1 pt) (2 cups) water
300 g (10 oz) (1¼ cups) granulated sugar
grated rind and juice of 1 lemon

Method 2 *(makes 450-g [1 lb] jar)*
500 g (1 lb) green tomatoes
300 g (10 oz) (1¼ cups) sugar
1.25 litres (2 pt) (1 quart) water
grated rind and juice of 1 lemon

Tourte de Blea

APPLE AND SWISS CHARD PIE

This is a Provence speciality. If pine kernels are not available, I find sliced almonds are an acceptable substitute. The thick pastry is a feature of this pie.

300 g (10 oz) (2½ cups) flour
2 tsp baking powder
pinch salt
25 g (1 oz) (2 tbsp) sugar
5 tbsp oil
8 tbsp water
50 g (2 oz) (⅓ cup) sultanas (golden raisins)
2–3 tbsp brandy
300 g (10 oz) Swiss chard leaves
1 large cooking apple
1 dried fig
15 g (½ oz) (1 tbsp) pine kernels
1 macaroon
grated rind ½ lemon
1 egg
1–2 tbsp strawberry/gooseberry jam
1–2 tbsp icing (confectioner's) sugar

To make the pastry, sieve the flour, baking powder, salt and sugar into a bowl. Stir in the oil and enough water to form a moderately firm scone (biscuit)-like dough (a round-ended knife is best for this). Wrap in cling-film and refrigerate for about 30 minutes.

Meanwhile, macerate the sultanas (raisins) in the brandy. Wash the chard leaves well and cook in boiling salted water for 10–12 minutes. Drain well, chop coarsely and separate the chopped leaves with a fork. Peel and core the apple and slice very thinly. Chop the fig. Mix the Swiss chard with the apple, sultanas and brandy, fig and pine kernels. Crumble the macaroon and stir into the mixture with the lemon rind. Beat the egg and mix in well.

Brush a baking tray and the inside of an 18-cm (7-in) flan ring with oil. Roll out two-thirds of the pastry into a circle large enough to line the flan ring. Fill the centre of the pastry case with the mixture and spread a little jam over the surface. Roll out the remaining pastry into a circle large enough to cover the top. Dampen the edge of the pastry case with water, cover with the pastry circle and pinch the edges together to form a tight seal. Make a small hole in the centre of the pie. Roll up a narrow piece of greaseproof paper and insert in the hole to form a funnel. Ease the pastry slightly away from the edge of the pan to make it easier to remove the pie once it is cooked. Cook in a preheated oven 180°C (350°F) (Gas Mark 4) for 30–40 minutes until light golden brown. When the pie is cooked, remove the paper funnel and sieve icing (confectioner's) sugar over the top. Serve warm or cold.

9 SAUCES

Sauce Aigre-Douce

SWEET-SOUR SAUCE

Serve with vegetable fritters, kebabs, grilled lamb and pork, and so on.

Peel and finely chop the onion. Heat the butter in a pan and cook the onion until soft and golden brown. Add the flour and cook for 2–3 minutes. Stir in the mustard and add the stock a little at a time and bring to the boil, stirring constantly. Stir in the tomato purée, brown sugar and vinegar. Mix well. Add the bay leaf, partly cover the pan and simmer gently for 20 minutes. Remove the bay leave and serve unstrained.

1 medium onion
20 g (¾ oz) (1½ tbsp) butter
20 g (¾ oz) (3 tbsp) flour
1 tsp Dijon mustard
300 ml (½ pt) (1¼ cups) chicken stock
2 tbsp tomato purée
1 tbsp brown sugar
1 tbsp cider vinegar
1 bay leaf

Aïoli

GARLIC MAYONNAISE

Serve Aïoli with a selection of raw and cooked vegetables; I love to eat it with cold, new potatoes. It is also used in a bourride — *a fish stew from Provence.*

Peel and crush the garlic until smooth and creamy. Beat in the egg yolks. Add the oil as for mayonnaise. A food processor or liquidizer may be used if you wish. Taste and add lemon juice and seasoning as required.

5–6 cloves garlic
2 egg yolks
300 ml (½ pt) (1¼ cups) olive oil
2–3 tbsp lemon juice
salt
pepper

Anchoïade

ANCHOVY AND GARLIC SAUCE

Beside being served with Crudités Anchoïade, *this is also served as an hors d'oeuvre eaten with toasted bread.*

Remove any bones from the anchovies, peel the onion and garlic and chop finely. Place the anchovies in a liquidizer with the onion, garlic and basil leaves. Add 1 tablespoon of oil and blend at fast speed. Slowly add half the oil. Add 1 tablespoon of vinegar and slowly add more oil until a soft paste is formed that is the consistency of a firm mayonnaise. Season to taste with vinegar and pepper.

125 g (5 oz) anchovies in oil
1 small onion
2–3 cloves garlic
few basil leaves
150 ml (¼ pt) (⅔ cup) olive oil
1–2 tbsp wine vinegar
black pepper

Sauce Andalouse

ANDALUSIAN SAUCE

Serve with avocados, salads and fondues.

350 g (12 oz) ripe tomatoes/2–3 tsp
  tomato purée
25 g (1 oz) canned/fresh red pepper
300 ml (½ pt) (1¼ cups) mayonnaise
  (page 000)
salt
white pepper

If using fresh tomatoes, peel and chop and place in a pan over gentle heat until soft, then purée through a vegetable mill or sieve. Return to the pan and continue to cook until a thick purée is formed. Allow to cool. Remove the skin of the fresh pepper, if used. Dice finely. Blend enough prepared/concentrated tomato purée into the mayonnaise to give good flavour and colour. Stir in the chopped pepper and season to taste.

Bagna Cauda

HOT GARLIC SAUCE

This sauce originally came from the Piedmont region in Italy but it is widely used in France. It is served with raw vegetables and is sometimes called a Fondue de Légumes. The sauce can be made at the table or, if you prefer, make it in the kitchen and keep it hot over a fondue stove at the table.

2 cloves garlic
8 anchovy fillets
25 g 1 oz (2 tbsp) butter
300 ml (½ pt) (1¼ cups) double (heavy)
  cream

Peel and crush the garlic and finely chop/crush the anchovy fillets. Melt the butter in a fondue pot, add the garlic and anchovy fillets and cook gently for 3–4 minutes. Stir in the cream a little at a time. Bring to the boil, stirring continuously, and then simmer gently for 8–10 minutes.

Sauce Béchamel

BÉCHAMEL SAUCE

25 g (1 oz) (2 tbsp) butter
25 g (1 oz) (¼ cup) flour
300 ml (½ pt) (1¼ cups) milk
salt
white pepper

Melt the butter in a pan, add the flour and cook for 2–3 minutes. Remove from the heat and stir in the milk a little at a time. If the sauce becomes lumpy, return to the heat and beat vigorously until smooth, then continue adding the milk. Bring to the boil, stirring all the time, and simmer for 5–6 minutes. Season to taste.

Sauce aux Champignons

MUSHROOM SAUCE

Serve with veal, chicken and eggs.

175 g (6 oz) mushrooms
50 g (2 oz) (1 tbsp) butter
2 tsp lemon juice
salt
pepper
300 ml (½ pt) (1¼ cups) Sauce Béchamel
2–3 tbsp Madeira
2 egg yolks (optional)
4 tbsp double (heavy) cream (optional)

Trim, clean and chop the mushrooms. Melt the butter in a pan and cook the mushrooms with the lemon juice until tender but without colour. Season to taste. Stir into the *Sauce Béchamel* with the Madeira and heat through. If a richer sauce is required, beat the cream with the egg yolks, pour on a little of the hot sauce, mix well and return to the pan. Heat through without boiling. Taste and adjust the seasoning.

Crème au Citron

ACIDULATED CREAM DRESSING

Although this dressing is used in many salads, it is never given a name in French cookery books even though the ingredients and method are always included. The nearest term I found was Crème Aigre, but this is soured cream, which is quite different from acidulated cream. After questioning many of my chef friends, one told me that when he worked in Switzerland they called it Crème au Citron. Because I have used it in several recipes, I have taken an author's licence to call it that. The dressing must be used as soon as it starts to thicken otherwise it will become too thick to pour or coat. Serve with cauliflower or turnips, as an hors d'oeuvre, or with vegetable, chicken, meat or fish salads.

150 ml (¼ pt) (⅔ cup) double (heavy) cream
150 ml (¼ pt) (⅔ cup) single (light) cream
3–4 tbsp lemon juice
pinch sugar (optional)
salt
white pepper

Mix the creams together and stir in the lemon juice and sugar. Season to taste.

Sauce à la Crème

CREAM SAUCE

Make as for *Sauce Béchamel* (page 214), but use single (light) cream instead of milk.

Sauce Demi-glace

RICH BROWN SAUCE

Cut the bacon into thin strips (leave the rind on). Peel and finely chop the onion, shallots and carrot. Trim, clean and finely chop the mushrooms. Heat the dripping/lard in a pan and fry the bacon until golden brown. Remove from the pan and reserve. Add the onion, shallots and carrot and cook over very gentle heat, stirring occasionally, until they start to colour (do this very slowly; if the vegetables overbrown the sauce may taste bitter). Stir in the flour and continue to cook very slowly until the flour is chestnut brown. Stir occasionally — this will take 15–20 minutes. Stir in the stock and add the bacon and mushrooms. Bring to the boil, stirring all the time. Lower the heat and simmer for 20–25 minutes. Add the tomato purée and sherry and simmer for 15 minutes. Strain through a conical strainer and discard the vegetables. Season to taste and if necessary add more stock or a little water to adjust the sauce to a coating consistency.

50 g (2 oz) bacon
1 medium onion
2 shallots
1 carrot
100 g (4 oz) mushrooms/mushroom trimmings
50 g (2 oz) (¼ cup) dripping/lard
25 g (1 oz) (¼ cup) flour
450 g (¾ pt) (2 cups) brown stock
2 tsp tomato purée
3–4 tbsp sherry
salt
pepper

Fondue de Trois Légumes

THREE VEGETABLE SAUCE

Cut the tomatoes and pepper into pieces. Peel and coarsely chop the onion and garlic. Place the vegetables in a liquidizer with the oil and purée at high speed for a minute or two. Strain the sauce and season to taste. Cover and chill well until required.

250 g (8 oz) ripe tomatoes
50 g (2 oz) red pepper
25 g (1 oz) onion
2 small cloves garlic
3–4 tbsp olive oil
salt
pepper

Sauce Hollandaise

HOLLANDAISE SAUCE

Use with boiled vegetables, such as asparagus, cauliflower, leeks, celery, etc.

100 g (4 oz) (½ cup) unsalted butter
2 egg yolks
2–3 tbsp lemon juice
salt
white pepper

Melt the butter and allow to cool. Beat the egg yolks and 1 tablespoon lemon juice in a pan over a bowl of hot water, making certain the water does not touch the bottom of the bowl. When the eggs are thick and creamy, add the melted, cooled butter a little at a time, whisking continuously. Season to taste with salt and pepper and more lemon juice. Keep hot over a pan of hot, gently simmering water, taking care that the base of the bowl does not touch the water. If the sauce starts to oil, remove from the heat and whisk in a little more soft butter, or place in a bowl of cold water and when the sauce sets, beat until smooth.

La Mayonnaise

MAYONNAISE

The flavour of the mayonnaise will depend on the quality of the oil used. Olive oil is excellent but expensive. More frequently an arachide (groundnut oil) is used in France. Other vegetable oils can be used instead, although I find the flavour of maize oil too dominant. Always use the oil at room temperature (it is difficult to get an emulsion to form if the oil is too cold — one of the reasons why a mayonnaise separates). If it is taken straight from the larder on a cold day, stand the jug of oil in warm water for a short time. If the mayonnaise is needed for coating, adjust the consistency with hot water.

1 whole egg/2 egg yolks
¼ tsp salt
½ tsp caster (superfine) sugar
white pepper
¼ tsp made mustard
300 ml (½ pt) (1¼ cups) oil
2–3 tbsp wine vinegar

With a food processor: This is the simplest way to make mayonnaise. Simply break an egg into the bowl and add the seasonings. Switch on to fast speed and pour in the oil in a slow but steady stream. When all the oil has been added and the mayonnaise has thickened, add vinegar to taste.

With a liquidizer: Break the egg into the goblet and add the seasonings. Partly cover the blades with oil, cover with the lid and switch on to fast speed. When the mixture has thickened, you will usually hear a change in the sound. Pour in half the oil very slowly, then add half the vinegar. Add the remaining oil in the same way. Switch off the machine, taste and add more vinegar and seasoning if required.

By hand: Beat 2 egg yolks in a bowl with the seasonings. Using a balloon whisk or electric hand-mixer, add the oil very slowly (an easy way is to dip the blade of a knife into the oil and allow it to drip off the end while you are beating). When the mixture thickens, add half the vinegar. Beat well and add the remaining oil a little more quickly from a spoon.

Add more vinegar and seasoning to taste.

Sauce Maltaise Froide

COLD MALTESE SAUCE

If available, use blood oranges for this sauce. Serve with cold asparagus, cauliflower, etc.

300 ml (½ pt) (1¼ cups) mayonnaise
1 orange

Make the mayonnaise and flavour it with the finely grated rind and juice of an orange.

Sauce Maltaise

MALTESE SAUCE

Use with boiled vegetables as for Sauce Hollandaise.

Make in the same way as *Sauce Hollandaise* (page 216) but use orange juice instead of lemon juice and add the finely grated rind of one orange. Blood oranges are considered best for this recipe.

Sauce Mornay

CHEESE SAUCE

Make a *Sauce Béchamel* (page 214). When it is cooked, add 50–75 g (2–3 oz) (½–¾ cups) grated cheese. Heat through without boiling.

Sauce Piquante

PIQUANT SAUCE

Serve with aubergines (eggplant), other well-flavoured vegetables and grilled meats.

Peel and finely chop the shallots. Cut the gherkins into thin strips/slices. Melt the butter in a pan, add the shallots and cook for 3–4 minutes. Then add the vinegar and boil until reduced to 2 tablespoons. Add the *Sauce Demi-glace* and cook gently for 15 minutes. Add the gherkins and parsley but do not boil again.

2 shallots
50 g (2 oz) gherkins
15 g (½ oz) (1 tbsp) butter
6–8 tbsp wine vinegar
300 ml (½ pt) (1¼ cups) Sauce
    Demi-glace (page 215)
1 tbsp chopped parsley

Sauce Portugaise

PORTUGUESE SAUCE

Serve with chicken, eggs, vegetable moulds, and so on.

Peel, seed and chop the fresh tomatoes. Peel the onion and garlic. Finely chop the onion and crush the garlic. Heat the oil in a pan and cook the onion and garlic until soft but without colour. Add the tomatoes, sugar and tomato purée. Season lightly with salt and pepper. Simmer gently for 20–30 minutes. Taste and adjust the seasoning and stir in the chopped parsley. Serve unstrained.

500 g (1 lb) ripe tomatoes/400 g
    (14 oz) can
1 medium onion
2 cloves garlic
2 tbsp olive oil
1 tsp sugar
1 tsp tomato purée
salt
black pepper
1 tbsp chopped parsley

Sauce Ravigote

RAVIGOTE SAUCE

Serve with salads.

Mix the oil, vinegar and mustard. Season lightly with salt and pepper. Finely chop the capers. Peel and finely chop the onion and shallot. Add to the sauce and check the seasoning.

150 ml (¼ pt) (⅔ cup) oil
3–4 tbsp wine vinegar
½ tsp made mustard
salt and pepper
1 tbsp capers
½ small onion
1 shallot

Sauce Soubise

ONION SAUCE

Serve with artichokes, cauliflower, eggs, fish and roast lamb or mutton.

500 g (1 lb) onions
75 g (3 oz) (6 tbsp) butter
300 ml (½ pt) (1¼ cups) Sauce Béchamel (page 214)
6 tbsp double (heavy) cream
salt and white pepper

Peel and finely slice the onions. Blanch in a pan of boiling salted water for 7–8 minutes. Drain well. Melt 50 g (2 oz) (¼ cup) butter in a pan, add the onions and cook over gentle heat until completely soft but without colour. In the meantime, make the *Sauce Béchamel*. Purée the onions through a vegetable mill or food processor and mix with the sauce. Stir in the cream, season to taste and bring to the boil. Cut the remaining butter into small pieces and whisk into the sauce a little at a time.

Sauce Tomate

TOMATO SAUCE

Serve with vegetables, ham, grilled meats, etc.

500 g (1 lb) fresh tomatoes/400 g (14 oz) can
1 medium onion
75 g (3 oz) bacon/bacon trimmings
1–2 cloves garlic
1 tbsp oil
½–1 tsp sugar
bouquet garni
salt and black pepper
little lemon juice

Chop the tomatoes roughly. Peel and chop the onion. Cut the bacon into small strips (leave the rinds on). Peel and crush the garlic. Heat the oil in a pan and cook the onion and garlic until soft but without colour. Add the bacon and cook for 2–3 minutes. Add the tomatoes (if canned tomatoes are used, use the juice as well). Season with ½ teaspoon sugar and a little salt and pepper. Add the bouquet garni and cook over gentle heat for about 20 minutes. Remove the bouquet garni and sieve or purée through a vegetable mill (a food processor or liquidizer can be used but take care not to over-purée or the seeds will make the sauce bitter). Taste and adjust the seasoning, adding a little more sugar and a few drops of lemon juice if required. Sieve the sauce again.

Sauce Tomate Crue

RAW TOMATO SAUCE

Serve with cold meats.

500 g (1 lb) ripe tomatoes
3 cloves garlic
1 tbsp chopped basil
4 tbsp olive oil
salt
black pepper

Peel, seed and finely chop the tomatoes. Peel the cloves of garlic and cut in half. Mix the tomatoes and basil in a bowl and break down the tomato to a pulp with a wooden spoon. Stir in the oil a little at a time. Add the garlic and season to taste. Cover and refrigerate for at least 1 hour. Remove the garlic and check the seasoning.

Sauce Vinaigrette

FRENCH DRESSING

Use olive oil if possible or a good vegetable oil. Wine or cider vinegar is best (malt vinegar is too sharp). For extra flavour add chopped herbs or crushed garlic.

3 parts oil to 1 part vinegar
salt
pepper
pinch of sugar
little mustard

Whisk the ingredients together in a bowl or shake in a screw-top jar. If you wish, you can also make it in a liquidizer.

10 BASIC RECIPES

Pâte à Foncer, Pâte Brisée *and* Pâte Sucrée *can all be made in a food processor. Place the ingredients in a bowl and switch on the machine until all are mixed. The first two pastries will form a ball but it will be necessary to knead* Pâte Sucrée *lightly by hand to mix the ingredients.*

Pâte à Foncer

SHORTCRUST PASTRY

The secret of a really short pastry is to use as little water as possible and to avoid overhandling.

Sift the flour and salt on to a board or into a bowl. Cut the butter into small pieces and rub into the flour using the fingertips. When the mixture resembles fine breadcrumbs, shake the bowl once or twice to bring any large lumps to the surface and rub in. Sprinkle the cold water on to the flour and work in, first with a palette knife or round-bladed knife and then with the fingers, until it forms a ball. Add a little more water if necessary. Knead the pastry lightly until smooth and use as required. If you need to keep it refrigerated before rolling out, wrap in cling-film or place in a plastic box.

175 g (6 oz) (1½ cups) plain flour
pinch of salt
90 g (3½ oz) (6 tbsp) butter/hard margarine
6–7 tsp water

Pâte Brisée

RICH SHORTCRUST PASTRY

Make as for *Pâte à Foncer* and refrigerate for 30 minutes before use. Note: If making 100 g (4 oz) (1 cup) of pastry, use 1 egg yolk and 2 teaspoons of egg white. For 225 g (8 oz) (2 cups) of pastry, use 1 whole egg. For 350 g (12 oz) (3 cups), use 1 whole egg and 1 egg yolk.

175 g (6 oz) (1½ cups) plain flour
pinch of salt
90 g (3½ oz) (6 tbsp) butter/hard margarine
1 egg yolk
4 tsp egg white

Pâte Sucrée

SWEET PASTRY

Sift the flour on to a board or into a bowl. Make a well in the centre and add the egg yolks, sugar and butter. Work together with the fingertips of one hand and gradually work in the flour from the sides with both hands. Blend well together until a ball is formed and knead lightly until smooth. Wrap in cling-film or place in a plastic box. Refrigerate for 30 minutes.

150 g (5 oz) (1½ cups) plain flour
2 egg yolks
50 g (2 oz) (¼ cup) caster (superfine) sugar
90 g (3½ oz) (6 tbsp) butter

Pâte Demi-feuilletée

FLAKY PASTRY

Strong flour — that used for making bread — is best for this pastry.

175 g (6 oz) (1½ cups) plain flour
pinch of salt
50 g (2 oz) (¼ cup) butter/hard margarine
50 g (2 oz) (¼ cup) lard/white fat
6–7 tbsp water

Sift the flour and salt on to a board or into a bowl. Add half the butter and rub in with the fingertips. Using a palette knife or round-bladed knife, work in sufficient water to give a soft, but not sticky, dough. Knead lightly until smooth. Roll the pastry out on a lightly floured board into a long oblong. Ease out the corners so they are square. Mark the pastry into thirds. Cut the lard/white fat in half. Cut one portion into small pieces and dot them evenly over the top of two-thirds of the dough. Fold the lower third over the middle section and fold the top third down over this. Seal the edges with a rolling pin and give the pastry a half turn (it doesn't matter whether you turn to the right or left, but always turn in the same direction). Roll the pastry out to a long oblong again and repeat the process twice, using first the butter and then the remaining lard. Finally, roll and fold the pastry once more without adding any fat. (In very hot weather it may be advisable to chill the pastry between each or every two rollings.) Wrap the pastry in cling-film or place in a plastic box. Refrigerate for 30 minutes before using.

Pâte à Choux

CHOUX PASTRY

Strong (bread) flour is best for this pastry.

65 g (2½ oz) (⅔ cup) strong flour
150 ml (¼ pt) (⅔ cup) water
50 g (2 oz) (¼ cup) butter
2 eggs

Sift the flour. Heat the butter and water in a pan over gentle heat until the butter melts. Raise the heat and when the water boils and rises in the pan, add the flour immediately. Beat well over the heat until the mixture leaves the side of the pan and forms a ball. Remove from the heat and leave to cool for a moment or two. Beat the eggs well and add a little at a time so that with each addition of egg the dough regains its original consistency. If you wish, you can use an electric mixer for this stage but it is best to transfer the dough to a bowl before adding the eggs. The beaters can scratch the pan and in an aluminium pan can discolour the dough.

Pâte à Frire

FRITTER BATTER

50 g (2 oz) (½ cup) plain flour
pinch salt
5 tbsp tepid water
2 tsp olive oil
1 egg white

Sift the flour and salt into a bowl. Make a well in the centre and pour in the water and oil. Stir the flour in gradually from the sides and beat well until smooth. Leave in a cool place for 30 minutes. Just before the batter is needed, beat the egg white until stiff and fold into the batter.

Pâte à Crêpes

PANCAKE BATTER

Sift the flour and salt into a bowl. Melt the butter and allow to cool. Make a well in the centre of the flour and break in the eggs. Add about half the milk and beat in the flour from the sides until the mixture is smooth. Gradually add more milk until creamy. (It may not be necessary to add the last tablespoon or two of milk because the absorption of liquid by the flour can vary.) Lastly, beat in the cool, melted butter.

Heat a crêpe pan and pour in enough oil to cover the base. As soon as the oil is hot, pour it off so there is only a very thin coating left on the base of the pan. Pour in a little batter, tipping the pan from side to side so it thinly coats the base. Cook over good heat. When the batter has set and bubbles appear, turn it over and cook for a moment or two. Add a little more oil to the pan and continue until all the batter has been used. To keep the pancakes hot, place a saucer, rim-side down, on a plate over a pan of simmering water. As they are made, turn them out on to the saucer. If they are to be kept or reheated cover with a large bowl.

(makes 12–16 × 15-cm (6-in) or 8 × 23-cm (9-in) pancakes)
125 g (5 oz) (1¼ cups) plain flour
¼ tsp salt
25 g (1 oz) (2 tbsp) butter
2 eggs
300 ml (½ pt) (1¼ cups) milk
2–3 tbsp oil

Croûtons

Please note: Although 1 cm has been equated with ½ inch throughout this book, this is too thick for croûtons, which should be no more than ⅜ inch thick.

Fried: Cut the stale bread into slices about 5 mm–1 cm (¼–⅜ in) thick. Remove the crusts and cut into even-sized dice. Heat the butter in a frying pan with enough oil to give a depth of approximately 1 cm (½ in). Test the temperature of the oil by dropping a croûton into the pan. It should start to brown immediately. Remove the test croûton and add enough croûtons to give an even layer in the pan. Try to avoid cooking too many at once and keep turning them with a spatula while they are cooking so they all brown evenly. When they are golden brown, remove quickly and drain on kitchen paper towel. Croûtons do not need to be kept hot because they pick up the heat of the soup or sauce and can therefore be made an hour or two in advance.

stale white bread
25–50 g (1–2 oz) (2–3 tbsp) butter
oil

Triangular: Cut the stale bread into 5-mm (¼-in) slices. Remove the crusts and trim to a square. Cut each square into quarters diagonally and fry in hot butter and oil until golden brown on both sides. Drain.

Garlic: Cut a clove of garlic in two and rub over the bread before cutting into croûtons. Fry as before.

Toasted: If preferred, the bread can be lightly toasted on both sides and then cut into dice.

INDEX